Charles King

**Fort Frayne**

Charles King

**Fort Frayne**

ISBN/EAN: 9783337267162

Printed in Europe, USA, Canada, Australia, Japan

Cover: Foto ©ninafisch / pixelio.de

More available books at **www.hansebooks.com**

# Fort Frayne

### BY
### CAPTAIN CHARLES KING
#### U. S. ARMY

**Author of**
"A Garrison Tangle," "An Army Wife,"
"Trumpeter Fred,"
["Noble Blood and a West Point Parallel,"
Associated with Ernest Von Wildenbruch,
of the German Army.]

F. TENNYSON NEELY
PUBLISHER
96 QUEEN STREET    114 FIFTH AVENUE
LONDON              NEW YORK

# Captain Charles King's Works

Captain King is acknowleged to be without a peer in his chosen field, which he industriously cultivates. There has for some years been a steadily increasing demand for his army stories, and if it were put to a vote to-day, as to the most popular American novelist, the name of Captain King would undoubtedly be found among the leaders.

"TRUMPETER FRED,"
Cloth, 75c.

"AN ARMY WIFE,"
Cloth, $1.25

"FORT FRAYNE,"
Cloth, $1.25; Paper, 50c.

"A GARRISON TANGLE,"
Cloth, $1.25

"NOBLE BLOOD and A WEST POINT PARALLEL"
Cloth, 75c.

*For sale by all Booksellers, or sent on receipt of Price by the Publisher,*

**F. TENNYSON NEELY,**
114 Fifth Avenue,          New York

---

Copyrighted, 1895
by
F. TENNYSON NEELY
In the United States and Great Britain
(All rights reserved)

## PREFACE.

There is a story within a story which should perhaps be told in presenting to the indulgent reader this tale of army life. Three years ago I was surprised and pleased by an invitation to collaborate in the preparation of an army play, for the invitation came from those who had won high honors in their chosen field. The months spent in the gradual development of our drama were full of pleasure, yet great was our rejoicing when the work was done. But then came blighting illness to her who was its inspiration and long, long months of utter seclusion. Then followed the mysterious disappearance of the manuscript story of the play—a manuscript of which there was no copy, for it had not even been typed. Finally came the suggestion that the story be promptly rewritten and published, not in the original four parts corresponding to the four acts, but in twenty chapters wherein the entire tale might be told, and this was the work assigned to me.

Reading over now the completed pages, I realize how very much I have missed the guiding hand of one,—the valued suggestions of the other,—of my gifted and gracious collaborators, and how many apologies I owe to both.   C. K.

# FORT FRAYNE.

## CHAPTER I.

THE snow was mantling the wild waste of barren prairie stretching toward the white peaks of the Big Horn, shrouding its desolation, hiding its accustomed ugliness, and warning scout, soldier or cowboy to look well to his landmarks before venturing forth upon its trackless sea, for even the cattle trails were hidden, and the stage road lost to view. Between its banks of glistening white the Platte rolled black and swollen, for a rare thing had happened— one so rare that old trappers and traders said they never knew the like before since first they sighted "Larmie" peak or forced the passes of the Medicine Bow—there had been three days of softly-falling snow, and not a whisper of a Wyoming gale. There had been a thaw in the Laramie plains, preceded by a soft south wind in the Park country of Colorado, and whole fleecy hillsides, said the natives, were "slumping off" in the upper waters of the river, and that was how the Platte came to be tossing high its wintry wave under the old stockade at the ferry and sweeping in power, instead of sleeping in peace, beneath its icy blanket, around the huge bluff where waved the colors of old Fort Frayne.

The roadway winding from the river-side up to the adjutant's office at the southern end of the garrison, was still unbroken. The guard at the ferryhouse had been withdrawn, and as for the veteran stockade, sole relic of the early days of the overland stage route, it looked now in its silence and desolation, heavily capped as it was with its weight of snow, like some huge, flattened-out Charlotte de Russe, at least that was what Ellis Farrar, daughter of the post commander, likened it to as she peered from the north window of their cosy quarters on the crest of the bluff. "And to think of Christmas being almost here, and not a chance of getting a wagon through from the railway," she mumured, "and I so longed to make it bright and joyous for mother. It is always her saddest season."

These low-toned words were addressed to Captain Leale of her father's regiment, a strong, soldierly-looking man of nearly forty years, who, with field glass in hand, had been studying the wintry landscape to the north and east. He turned as the young girl spoke, and, lowering his glasses, followed her eyes and looked anxiously across the bright army parlor to where the fire-light from the blazing logs upon the hearth fell full upon a matronly woman whose luxuriant hair was already turning gray and whose sweet, patient face bore the unmistakable trace of deep sorrow. She was seated at a desk, an unfinished letter before her, and had paused in the midst of her writing and dropped off into the dreamland of far-away scenes and memories. From a drawer in the desk she had taken what was evidently a portrait, a small photograph, and had been intently studying it while the only other occupants of the room were busy at the window.

"It is—you know—Royle's, my brother's picture." whispered Ellis. "I know it, though I haven't seen it in ever so long—five years I think."

Again the captain bowed, inclining his head in the slow, grave way, that was habitual with him. "I know," he said, briefly, and the gaze he fixed upon his colonel's wife was full of anxiety and sympathy. "I have often wished that your father's promotion had brought him to any other garrison in the army. You remember he was stationed here when lieutenant-colonel, and it was from here that Royle went to West Point."

"I remember it but vaguely. That was nine years ago, captain, and I was but seven. We saw him during his cadet furlough two years later—in 1883—and that was the last. Mother only rarely speaks of him, and father, never, unless—unless," she added, with timid appeal, "he does to you. Does he?"

Captain Leale paused a moment before replying. Only that very morning had his colonel talked with him, the most trusted of his troop commanders, of Ellis's long-missing brother. Only within an hour had Farrar sought again his advice as to one whom he could not bring himself to name, and referred to in shame and sorrow as "my eldest," and only rarely as "my son." First born of the little flock, the boy had been given his father's name. The only child for several years, petted, spoiled, over-indulged by a fond, pure-hearted mother, then reared among the isolated army garrisons of the far West, the handsome, headstrong, daring youth but all too early had shown a tendency to wild companionship and reckless living. Few men in the cavalry arm of the service were held in higher esteem than Colonel Royle Farrar, who, entering the service with the first regiment to be sent to the front from New York City in the spring of 1861, had fought his way to the command of a brigade in the last campaign, and then been commissioned as a junior major of cavalry at the reorganization of the regular army. The president himself had tendered Farrar, long afterwards, a cadetship for his son, and it was gratefully yet almost fearfully accepted. The mother could not be brought to believe her boy would not strive to do honor to his name at the Point. The father dreaded that the wayward, reckless fellow, intolerant of restraint or discipline, would merit punishment, and, being punished, would resent. Royle stood the ordeal only fairly well at first. Demerits in profusion and "light prison" twice had clouded his record before the furlough year, but the mother's eyes rejoiced in the sight of the handsome, stalwart young soldier after his two years of rigorous training, even though the mother heart grieved over the evidences of dissipation and vice which speedily marred the long-looked-for days of his vacation. Between him and his father had been more than one stormy scene before Royle returned to the academy—interviews from which the senior issued pale, stern, sorrowful; the young man gloomy, sullen, and more than half defiant. In his second class year came tidings of misdemeanor that almost broke the mother's heart. Farrar hastened from the distant frontier to the banks of the Hudson expecting nothing short of dismissal for the boy, and promising the mother to fetch him at once to her, but the court, even in sentencing, had signed a plea for mercy for the cadet who bore so honored a name, a plea that his classmates would never have indorsed, and the president remitted the punishment to a term of confinement to barracks and camp. The father wasted no words in reproach. He pointed out to the son that this was his last chance. Royle, Jr., had sullenly responded that his disgrace was due entirely to spies and tale bearers and showed neither contrition nor promise of amend. A year later came the last straw. Reported for a violation of regulations in having liquor in his possession, Cadet Farrar wrote a lying explanation to the effect that it was placed in his room by parties unknown to him, and for the purpose of bringing him into trouble, but he had been seen "off limits" at a questionable resort in the neighboring village the previous night, had been drinking and card playing there, had lost money and refused to pay, had been seen returning by two lower classmen to whom he offered liquor, then staggered to his quarters only an hour or so before reveille roll call. He was placed in close arrest after being confronted with the array of evidence, and that night deserted and was seen no more. Again the colonel made his mournful pilgrimage to the Point, and old comrades pityingly, sorrowfully told him the whole story. He went back to his regiment looking ten years older, took his wife and two younger children, Will and Ellis, to his heart, and from that day never spoke again his firstborn's name. It had been for years his custom to sign all official papers in full—Royle Farrar—but the very sound of the Christian name seemed from that time on to give him distress, and R. Farrar became his signature personal or official.

The young man was heard of occasionally, however, borrowing money from officers and friends and relatives on his father's account. Then he went to sea, then returned to New York and wrote a long letter to his mother, telling how he mourned the old days, and was going to lead a new life, and she too gladly sent him all the money she had. Then there was another interval, and, after a year, he again appeared as a suppliant for aid. He had been desperately ill, he said, and kind, but poor, humble people had cared for him, and they ought to be rewarded. The mother would have sent again her last cent to him direct, but Farrar interposed. His check went to a trusted friend, with instructions to investigate, and that friend was his old comrade, Major Fenton, and, as he expected, it proved only another lie.

Then there came an era of apparent prosperity, and now the poor mother in joy besought her husband to recognize the son, for he reported himself in good employ, with a fair salary and brilliant prospects. He even sent a draft to repay a small portion of what he termed his father's loan, but this was soon followed by a draft on his father for double the amount, and later another, and then letters of inquiry came from his employer, and then rueful complaint of how that trusting person had been swindled. In her agony of grief and disappointment the mother's health was giving away, and Farrar concealed from her particulars even worse—that their wretched son had won the love of his employer's only daughter, and that she had followed him from her father's house. There had been a secret marriage. There was another Royle. This news had come to the colonel but a day or two before. It was this that had unsealed his lips and turned him to Captain Leale for counsel and support.

"My daughter," wrote the bereaved father, "was the idol of my heart, the image of the mother who was taken from her long years ago. Yet she turned from me in the passion of her love for him, and they have gone God alone knows where. If you can find him, say that though he has robbed me poor, I can forgive him all if he will but be good and kind to her. She was delicately nurtured, as carefully educated as your own daughter could be, sir, and she was more to me, for she was my all. I own that, having married him, her duty was with her husband, but why should she have hidden that marriage from her father? My own fortune is well-nigh wrecked, but she has her mother's little portion—enough, if he can resist his craving for drink and gambling, to support them in comfort. I pray you help me save my child."

All this sad history was now well known to Malcolm Leale, and his eyes were full of sorrow as he bent them upon the gentle, yearning woman at the desk, lost in her study of her first-born's face. Ellis in turn stood watching him. She was a girl of sixteen, yet seemed older far, because of the years in which she had been her mother's companion and closest friend. Then as he made no answer to her query and seemed plunged in thought, she turned and stepped lightly over to the mother's side.

"Day dreaming again, Queen Mother?" she asked, in the half-playful way that was habitual with her. "If you don't go on with your letter to Will, it won't be ready for the courier. Captain Leale tells me they are to send one out at noon."

"Will they really?" asked Mrs. Farrar, rousing suddenly. "Why, I had given up all hopes of hearing from him this week, or of getting a letter to him. Who is to go, captain? The pass must be breast deep in snow."

"I think not, Mrs. Farrar. There was very little wind, you know, and the fall seems to have been very uniform. Corporal Rorke and a couple of my men are getting ready now. The colonel was only waiting, hoping that there might be still some news from Red Cloud."

"Why, how can it come? The wires are down, the road hidden, and the river unfordable," said

Ellis, eagerly. "The last news was bad enough. I own I don't want to hear further."

Over Leale's face a graver shadow fell. "There are Indian riders who could easily make the journey," he said. "Crow Knife, for instance, whom the colonel sent over with the scouts five days ago. The fact that he hasn't returned makes me hopeful that matters are quieting down," but here he turned again to the window to level his glass upon the broad rolling expanse of white, stretching in wave after wave to the bleak horizon.

"God forbid there should be further trouble," said Mrs. Farrar, slowly, lingeringly replacing the portrait in its drawer. "Surely the general has force enough there now to keep those Indians in check," she ventured, appealingly.

Leale lowered his binocular again. "He has, provided the renegades captured on the Cheyenne are not sent back there. Those people should not be taken to the agency. They are Minneconjous, Uncapapas, Brulés, a turbulent, ill-conditioned lot, who make trouble wherever the others are peaceably disposed. They should have been disarmed and dismounted and put under guard at Fort Robinson until this question is settled. What I fear is that Red Wolf's band is still out and is defying the agent, and that the revolt will spread to Kill Eagle's village. If they go on the warpath, some of our best scouts will be involved. That boy, Crow Knife, is worth his weight in gold, but his father and mother would follow Kill Eagle."

"Do you think—do you think that if they should revolt, we—our command—would have to be ordered out?" asked Ellis, anxiously.

"It might be," he replied, cautiously, "but I am hoping that no winter campaign is in store for us. Think of a march over such a waste as that," and he pointed to the snow-clad scene before them. "We couldn't cross the Platte this side of Laramie, either, even if the stream were fordable. The running ice would cut the horses from under us."

Out across the parade, clear, yet soft, as though muffled by the snow, the cavalry trumpet began sounding orderly call.

"Rorke and his men will start as soon as they have had dinner, Mrs. Farrar," said Leale, "and I must see the colonel before they go. I will send for your letters." He took up the glasses again for one last survey, Ellis narrowly watching him, while her mother went on with her writing. For a moment the search seemed barren of result, as before, but suddenly Leale started, stepped nearer the window, and riveted his attention on one spot. Ellis quickly noted it.

"You see some one?" she asked.

A brief nod was the only answer. Then, glass in hand, the captain suddenly turned to a side door, let himself out into another room, and thence to the outer gallery surrounding the house. Here his view was unobstructed. Two gentlemen were coming up the pathway from the adjutant's office, and a soldier in immaculate uniform and side arms following a short distance behind, indicated that the one in uniform was the post commander—the elder one, a distinguished-looking man of nearly sixty, whose pointed mustache and imperial were well-nigh as white as the new-fallen snow about him, whose complexion, bronzed by years of exposure to prairie sun and wind, was ruddy brown, almost like Russian leather.

Over Leale's face fell the same shadow of anxiety that was noted when he stood gazing in silence upon the sorrowing mother at the desk within. The colonel was talking in an earnest manner to the man at his side, a civilian, so far as his dress would indicate, yet a civilian with the erect carriage and brisk step of a soldier—a handsome fellow, too, of perhaps seven and twenty years. Leale turned from them with some impatience.

"I'd bet a month's pay, if I ever bet a cent in the world," he muttered to himself, "that old Fenton's nephew had no thought whatever of hunting when he came here in midwinter. The question is, What else has brought him besides what I have already learned, and why he haunts Farrar from morning till night?"

At the window the fair, girlish face brightened an instant at sight of the coming soldier, then clouded as quickly as the civilian came in view. "Mr. Ormsby again!" murmured Ellis below her breath, and the bow of recognition which she gave him in answer to the quick uplifting of his sealskin cap lacked all of the warmth and interest that beamed in Ormsby's face at sight of her. Seeing Leale, the colonel pressed on to join him on the northward porch. Catching sight of Ellis, the civilian fell back, entered the gateway, and came briskly to the door. An instant later and his step was heard in the hallway. Ellis turned to the window in something not unlike aversion. The mother it was who rose eagerly to welcome the coming guest.

"Prompt as ever, Mr. Ormsby," she cried as he entered the parlor, fresh and rosy from the keen air. "I wish you might teach my husband to be more punctual at luncheon."

"Indeed, I feared I was detaining him, Mrs. Farrar. He's merely stopped one moment to speak with Captain Leale. He was showing me over the barracks. You have no idea how vividly interesting all this is to me. I have shouldered the musket with the Seventh for eight years, and have never visited an army post before."

"Oh, didn't you see your uncle when he was at Riley? He used to write to my husband of you time and again, and of your pride in your regiment."

"No, he was in New York on recruiting service then, a few years ago, you remember, and we used to get him up to the armory or to our camp occasionally."

"And he was very, very kind to my poor boy, my Royle," said Mrs. Farrar, wistfully, searching the face of her guest, "and when you came to us with letters from our old friend, for we had known him before our marriage," she continued, a faint color rising to her cheek, "it seemed almost like welcoming him. There was nothing too good for Major Fenton that our home afforded after all he *tried* to do, at least for—him." The sigh with which she spoke seemed to well up from the depths of the mother's heart. Ellis, with light footsteps, had left the room to greet her father on the piazza without, and for the first time since his coming, three days previous, just in time to be hemmed in and held at Frayne by the great snowfall, Mrs. Farrar was alone with her guest. "There is something I have longed to ask you Mr. Ormsby," she went on, "something I must ask you, for a mother's intuition is keen, and I feel sure you have seen or known my poor boy in the past. Have you heard—do you know anything of him now?"

"Mrs. Farrar, I give you my word I have not the faintest idea of his whereabouts."

"Forgive me if I am intrusive—importunate," she persisted. But—Major Fenton—he was Major Fenton then, you know, and I think of him with the title he bore when he was so good—so friendly—when my unhappy boy most needed friends. You were with your uncle often then. Did you not meet —did you not know my Royle?"

Ormsby's honest eyes betrayed the deep embarrassment under which he labored, and she, watching every sign with painful intensity, read the truth, despite his faltering reply.

"Once or twice, Mrs. Farrar, but I knew him only very slightly."

"Tell me still more, Mr. Ormsby. You have been most considerate to me. You have sought to spare me, but in my husband's sad face and abstracted manner I have read the truth. He has heard news—worse news of Royle, and so you have been the bearer. Is it not so?"

But Ormsby pulled himself together this time, at least, like a man and braved her.

"I assure you it is not so, Mrs. Farrar. From me, at least, the colonel has heard nothing new,—nothing worse. I beg you to dismiss the thought."

But he did not say that he had come prepared to tell, aye, instructed to tell, of crowning disgrace—come with the written proposition of his employers to relinquish pursuit of Royle Farrar, provided the father would make good the sum they had lost through the son's forgery.

"God bless you, Mr. Ormsby, for the load you have lifted from my heart," she cried. "Ever since you came I have dreaded more and more each day that you were the bearer of evil tidings of him who has almost broken his father's heart, and yet cannot, must not, shall not be beyond redemption, if a mother's love and prayers are of any avail. Even Ellis has seemed to share my dread. I have read it in her manner, as, perhaps, you have, too. She did not mean to be unkind—inhospitable to our guest, but that sorrow has overshadowed us all. Even my bright, brave Will, who is doing all a boy can do to redeem the name at the Point—even Will, I say, is sometimes confronted by the record that his erring brother left."

The tears were starting from her eyes now, and in uncontrollable emotion she turned away. Then came a loud rap at the front door, and a servant hastened to open it. A loud, cheery Irish voice resounded through the hallway an instant later. "Corporal Rorke to report to the colonel for dispatches," and glancing thither, Ormsby saw a stout trooper, with broad, jovial, ruddy face, his burly form clad in winter service dress. Mrs. Farrar, striving to hide and to check her tears, had turned into the dining room. Ormsby stepped to the north window and glanced out upon the little group upon the porch,—Ellis half shiveringly clinging to her father's arm, he intently eying Leale, Leale, with leveled glasses, steadily at gaze at some dim, black object far, far across the turbid Platte, far out to the eastward, across those snow-clad slopes.

"Can you make out what's coming, Leale?"

"I think so, Colonel."

"What is it?"

Leale slowly lowered the glass, and, never turning, answered in low but positive tone:

"Our marching orders—for the agency."

## CHAPTER II.

At noon that bright December day the barracks and quarters of Fort Frayne were resounding with song and laughter, and all "the good-natured, soldierly noise" with which the garrison was busily preparing for the blithe festivities of Christmas. Two hours later, though the scene was unchanged, the preparations were for war.

"Leave the band to guard the post, but take every available trooper," were the injunctions that accompanied the General's brief orders to Colonel Farrar. "Strike when you find—and wherever you find—Kill Eagle's Band."

Tearful eyes along officers' row, watching the silent group at headquarters, told all too plainly with what dread the tidings had been received. With the wires down, the railway blockaded, the stage road deep in snow, there was only one means of communication left, and two Indian scouts on their hardy ponies, leaving the field column at dawn the previous day, had made their unerring way through the trackless maze of snow-clad ridge, ravine, divide and coulée, through a labyrinth of Bad Lands, bad enough in midsummer, and across many a frozen creek, until at last they struck the northern shore of the swollen Platte, and followed on up stream until opposite old Fort Frayne.

And now, indeed, was the road to the ferry broken and plowed and speedily trodden hard, for hosts of stalwart men had rushed to the river side, and out from its winter hiding place they dragged one of the huge pontoon boats and launched it in the ice-whirling flood, and the sweeps were manned by brawny arms in blue, and with boat hooks driving at the ice cakes and the foam flying from the oar blades and from under the blunt and sloping prow, cheered from the southern shore, they fought their way to where, like black, silent statues, the riders waited at the brink and then Indians and ponies both were bundled aboard and ferried back again, landing two hundred yards down stream; but even before they could breast the bluffs and carry their dispatches to the cavalry chief, the news they bore was shouted up the heights: "Red Wolf escaped—Kill Eagle's whole village has jumped for the Bad Lands."

And that meant that the Twelfth must drop its Christmasing and fetch the wanderers home. The old, old story told again, and just as it had been time and time before. Absurdity in the Indian policy; mismanagement in the Indian bureau; starvation in the Indian villages; murmurings of discontent among the old warriors; talk of summary action among the young braves; emissaries from disaffected bands; midnight councils, harangues, dances, threats, an arrest or two, escape, and then a general rush to join the hostiles in the field.

Prompt to act on this occasion, as ever before, the moment he was enabled to learn, through the chagrined officials of the Indian bureau, of the escape of this turbulent leader, and the flight of Kill Eagle's people from the agency, the general commanding in the field dispatched a small force of cavalry to interpose between the latter and the large bands of hostiles already lurking in the Bad Lands, and, giving the commander of this force instructions to turn Kill Eagle westward, and by steady pursuit keep him "on the jump" toward his old hunting grounds behind the Black Hills, he sent couriers across country post haste to Frayne, with orders for Colonel Farrar to start at once with his entire force—four fine troops of the Twelfth Cavalry—to cross the Platte at the first possible point, and by forced marches throw himself across the Indians' front and strive to hem them in. With the Platte sweeping along as it was, bank full, a crossing might be impossible nearer than the rocky shallows at the Fetterman Bend, but that made no difference; prompt action was the thing.

More than half expecting just such a contingency, Farrar had long since completed his preparations. His packers and their lively mules had been kept in trim. Ten days' rations were always set aside in readiness to be packed on the aparejos the moment word should come. Boxes of extra ammunition for carbine and revolver were stacked up in the ordnance storeroom, ready to be lashed, two to each, on the sturdy little burden-bearers' backs. Double sacks of grain, precious as powder on a winter campaign, were banked at the quartermaster's corral.

Every trooper's winter kit of fur cap, gloves, fur-lined canvas coat, boots, blankets and reinforced breeches had been carefully inspected only a day or two before. Every horse had been as carefully shod. Extra shoes and shoe nails had been stored in each pair of saddle bags. The horses themselves in their warm, thick winter coats and uncropped manes and tails, looked shaggy and far from "swell" from the point of view of the eastern avenues, but were eminently fit for campaigning among the blizzards of the plains; and as for the men, they were serving under a soldier who didn't believe in letting troopers grow "soft" and out of condition even in midwinter, and so, no matter what the weather, Farrar had had his people out for exercise every weekday of the year, and the exercise during the snowstorm had consisted in breaking roads in long compact column of fours all around the plateau on which stood the great spreading garrison, and the men liked it, and throve under it, and came in each day glowing with health, to the enjoyment of their substantial dinner, vowing the colonel knew no end of tricks worth their studying, even if he wasn't a West Pointer, even if he had gone into the army "from the militia" in the old days of the war.

And now that all their Christmas fun seemed summarily ended and they themselves were to be hurried forth upon a sharp and sudden campaign, they sprang to their preparations with cheery vim, almost with eager rejoicing. For three weeks they had been excitedly reading and discussing the reports of the doings of their comrade regiment, the Eleventh, around the agency far to the east, and coveting their prominence and distinction. Already they had enviously heard of one or two sharp affairs in which the Eleventh had rounded up a party of young warriors breaking for the Cheyenne country, or had surrounded and disarmed Tall Bull's little band of ugly "bluffers." Even at the expense of Christmas trees, Christmas dance, Christmas dinner, they didn't want to loaf in garrison when other regiments were having stirring service in the field. And so, while women wept, the barracks rang with shout and song and cheery whistle, and the laugh and joke went around as the troopers stowed their treasures in the home chest and packed their bulging saddlebags. Few of their number had wives or children to leave behind. It was over among the officers' quarters that no laughter rang, and the only smiles were piteous through their mist of tears.

"I could bear it better at any other season, Royle," said the colonel's wife, as she clung, sobbing, to his neck after he had donned his rough field dress. "It seems as though the worst blow of my life had come to me at Christmas just this time." He bowed in silence, tenderly kissing her, yet even then checking further reference to that crowning sorrow. He could not shut out the recollection of how the news of their boy's disgrace had been received on Christmas morning, and now with another Christmas so close at hand, he was keeping from her tidings that still more had bowed his head in sorrow uncontrollable

—that his wretched son had robbed, deceived and deserted the sweet woman who had trusted him, leaving her penniless to struggle unaided and unknown. Who can say what would have been his shame had he dreamed that this genial, kindly young New Yorker, this stranger within his gates, was the bearer of evidence that still further was the son a felon in the eyes of the law, and that to all his other crimes Royle Farrar had added that of forgery? At noon this very day Jack Ormsby was striving to nerve himself to carry out his employer's orders and break the tidings, but those few words of the gentle mother, and the sight of her pathetic face again unmanned him, and in the midst of his irresolution came these sudden orders to the field, and that put an end to all thought of anything else.

"I cannot help it," he was saying to Ellis, as the girl, pale and sad, but uncomplaining, was busily packing her father's mess chest. "It would be ridiculous to say I could be of any use, but all the same I want to go. It's the chance of a lifetime. I have never seen an Indian campaign. I haven't an idea what an Indian fight is like; but, do you know, I could'nt go back and face our fellows of the Seventh and tell them I saw the Twelfth Cavalry start on its rush to head off Kill Eagle's band, and that I didn't go, too."

"I should want to go if I were in your place," said she. "I understand it fully. No doubt Captain Leale can fit you out with campaign clothing,—everything you need—."

"Then I certainly shall go," said Ormsby. "It'll be something to tell about in 'I' company for the next ten years."

And that was how it happened that five days later, in a blinding snowstorm, there rode with the advance of the Twelfth Cavalry a sergeant of the famous New York Seventh at the very moment when the word came from the scouts that Kill Eagle's village was not two miles ahead.

Left to his own devices in the matter of carrying out his orders, Farrar had made a close and careful calculation. With the Laramie road out of sight in snow it might take three days of hard marching to reach the ford, with the prospect then of finding themselves almost as far from the Indians as before, for the fords lay some ninety miles off to the southeast, while, when last heard from, Kill Eagle was striking across the country south of the Cheyenne between the Upper Niobrara and the Mini Pusa. In the deep valleys were scattered ranches and countless herds of horned cattle, so he was living high on the country as he fled, his rear well guarded by three score young braves, who hovered just ahead of the pursuing column, peppering its advance guard with long-range shots from every ridge, and so retarding its movement as to enable their old war chief to move his whole village, tepees, lodge poles, women and children, pony herd, dog herd, and all, with calm deliberation. By going southeast Farrar would have taken the flooded Platte alongside on his left hand, only to have to turn an acute angle to the north again, march them over rough and broken country, with old Rawhide Butte, perhaps, as his guide, with every probability of finding himself far behind the chase after reaching the broad, deep-lying valley of the Niobrara. Wiser by far, he sent back brief word by courier to Laramie, ordering it forwarded by wire from that point.

"We go westward up the Platte, confident of lower water and a crossing this side of the big bend. Thence we will swing around northeastward, and, covering a broad stretch of country, keep sharp lookout for Kill Eagle's band. We should meet him somewhere among the breaks of the Mini Pusa, southeast of old Cantonment Reno, and, unless they will surrender, I shall strike at once and strike hard."

And here among the breaks of the Mini Pusa, after four days of severe winter marching, Farrar had thrown his little command just as he had planned, square across the path of the foe. Direful were the tales that had reached him from ranchmen and settlers, who, having abandoned their homes, were fleeing for the protection of the frontier forts, far back at the base of the Big Horn. Day after day had the young warriors swooped from the traveling village down upon the valleys on either side, murdering men, women and little children, burning the ranches, driving off such cattle as they fancied, and ruthlessly butchering all the rest. And still, one or two days' march behind, the pursuing column plunged heavily through the snow.

Farrar was an expert, however, and had shrewdly judged their route. Farrar was merciful, and even in the face of the atrocities that had been committed and under the warrant of his orders and in the belief that the band was few in numbers, he would not strike when the blow might fall on women and children, too, until he had given the red chief a chance of surrender.

He had been marching since dawn and it was now 11 o'clock. An hour earlier, far out at the front along a low, snow-covered ridge that stood out sharply against the black bank of cloud that spread from horizon almost to zenith, the scouts began that fierce sudden circling of their ponies that denoted "enemy in sight." With their field glasses the officers at the head of the column could see that one of the number, dismounted, was lying close to the crest, peering cautiously over and signaling excitedly to his fellows who kept well behind him down the slope. They, in turn, were signaling to the column, and, leaving Leale in command with orders to move steadily on, the colonel put spurs to his horse—old Roderick—and followed by his adjutant and an orderly or two, cantered on out to the front. Ormsby, riding at the moment with Leale at the head of the first troop, felt a thrill of excitement as the captain coolly interpreted the meaning of the rapid movements of the scouts. Eagerly, too, the men seemed to rouse from the almost slumberous condition of the command after its hours of plodding, and a murmur ran back from troop to troop: "Indians ahead!

Now for it, fellows!" And then all eyes were strained on that low ridge against the sky line, and unconsciously the horses seemed to close up toward the head of the column, answering, perhaps, some involuntary pressure of the knees, for suddenly, while the leading troop continued its placid gait—the swift, steady, four-mile walk—those in the rear of the column broke into a jog trot and never resumed the walk again until the cautioning voice and hand of the captain seemed to restrain them. And then they could see that Colonel Farrar, reaching the ridge, had himself dismounted, and was lying on the snow and peering over as Little Bat had done before him. Still no word came to accelerate the march, and, at the same steady walk the long column, moving by fours here, for the prairie was wide and open and comparatively level, pushed on for the distant ridge, and when at last they came within hailing distance of the group at the front the adjutant slowly raised his hand and gave the signal, "Halt!" and in an instant the snake-like column stood in its tracks and the men swung out of saddle and began dancing and thrashing their arms in the effort to start the sluggish blood.

All the morning it had been threatening snow, and now it was sifting slowly down, but presently the flakes fell thicker and thicker, and then in a dense cloud that soon shut out even the crest ahead of them. Captain Leale, a calm, thoughtful battalion commander, picked out certain level-headed sergeants, and sent them, with a few men each, out to the right and left front and flank, so as to guard against surprise, and then as the men danced about in the snow and sparred or wrestled laughingly, many and many were the conjectures as to the cause of the halt and delay. "What are we waiting for? Why don't we pitch in?" were the queries that passed from lip to lip, and many were the inquiring glances toward the little group of officers smoking and talking, and chaffing Ormsby at the head of the column. With an Indian village barely a mile away, an Indian fight probably not an hour ahead, the Twelfth was taking things as coolly as befitted the season, and Ormsby, after looking once more to the chamber of his revolver and trying the breech block of his Springfield carbine, joined in the chat with all the coolness he could command, and strove to appear more interested in what was being said than in the immediate business at hand.

And yet when the adjutant came riding rapidly back from the ridge, there was instant movement to meet him.

"What's the trouble, Jimmy?" was the query on many a tongue. "What are we waiting for?"

"They're going regularly into camp—putting up their tepees," was the answer. "It looks as though they were waiting to palaver with the pursuit. The colonel thinks they're willing to come to terms rather than march further in such weather. I suppose the Eleventh can't be very far behind them, and as yet they don't suspect we're over here at all.

Luckily for us, too," said he, gravely, "for it's two to one in their favor, if I'm any judge at all."

"The devil you say! How many lodges are there?"

"Bat says nigh onto seventy, though they're not all up yet, and you can't see a thing now for the snow. The old rip must have been reinforced heavily. There seem to be two or three bands rolled into one. What I can't understand is how the Eleventh happens to be so far behind. We thought they were right at their heels. I hate to think how the settlers down the Dry Fork must have suffered."

"Seen or heard anything of them—or of any refugees?"

"Yes; two outfits passed up the valley going for all they were worth this morning. Bat and Chaska saw them from the ridge yonder to the south. The scouts say they abandoned their wagons and took to their horses."

Even as they were speaking there came indications of some unusual object off to the right rear of the column. One or two officers and men were seen to ride out in that direction, and were quickly swallowed up in the snow-cloud. A sergeant coming up from the rear saluted Captain Leale, and said: "Captain Amory's compliments, sir, and there are some mounted men coming in who seem about played out. He thinks they're settlers seeking protection."

And presently this proved to be the case. Out from the fleecy clouds there soon came in sight four or five horseman slowly escorting one or two riders on broken down and exhausted quadrupeds, and there was a general movement on the part of half the men of the Twelfth to leave their linked horses and gather about these new arrivals. There were two men, rough bearded, typical frontiersmen, garbed in the roughest of plain's wear—men with faces so drawn and haggard with terror and suffering that they did not brighten even with the joy of reaching the protection of a strong force of cavalry. There was a third, a man heavily bearded like his associates, but with dress of costlier make, with features that told of gentler birth than theirs, but whose eyes, shifting, restless, filled with a dread as great as theirs, gave no symptom of reassurance. Like shipwrecked mariners on the broad ocean, they had sought the succor of the first craft that came in sight, but even now seemed to dread the storm and to doubt the stability, the safety of the rescuing ship. "How many men have you?" they had eagerly asked, and when told two hundred and twenty had wrung their hands and implored their first rescuers not to dare confront the Indians, who were at least a thousand strong. "They have wiped out everything in the valleys below, fired every ranch, murdered every man. They've got a dozen of our women prisoners now in that very camp, and the first thing they'll do will be to butcher them if you attack. For the love of God come away," they implored, "and let them by. The troops in pursuit must be fifty miles behind."

Thus eagerly, incoherently, the two ranchmen said their say. The third was strangely silent, yet seemed to be full as eager to get away.

"What say you to this story?" asked the young lieutenant, who had ridden out to bring them in.

"It's all God's truth!" was the answer. "You'll be wiped off the face of the earth if you attack. Give us some provisions—hardtack, bacon—anything, and some grain for our horses, and let us go."

"Well, you'll have to come in and see the commanding officer first," was the short reply. "He'll decide after hearing your story."

"What's his name?" asked the stranger.

"Colonel Farrar."

"Farrar! Is this the Twelfth Cavalry? I thought they were ordered to Arizona."

"We were, but the devil's work of the ghost dance keeps us here. Now follow, and we'll get you something to eat."

But the stranger said that he would go no further to the front. "I'm too near that cursed band now," he protested, shaking his fist through the wintry air. "Go, you, Mullen, and see the colonel. Get what help you can. I'm too weak to ride until I can have something to eat."

Even then it was noticed that Mullen and his friend seemed anything but cordial to their companion. "Damn him!" they growled, as, sullenly, they left him dismounting at the pack train. "His saddlebags are crammed with meat. He hasn't suffered. Other men stayed and fought and tried to defend Crawford's ranch and Morgan's. They are dead, poor devils, but that sneak who calls himself Graice, he only came among us six weeks ago, and if he ain't a jailbird I'm no judge. He's afraid to see your colonel, lieutenant. That's what I believe." And when Captain Leale heard their story at the head of the column he called to his orderly, mounted and rode back through the falling snow.

"Where is that third refugee?" he asked of the pack master, "that man they call Graice."

"He was here just this minute, sir. He's worse scared than the others. He wants to go on. There he goes now, by God! He's lighting out by himself."

Just then there came a movement along the column. Every trooper was springing to his horse. "They're mounting, sir," said the orderly. But the captain was staring fixedly after the disappearing rider, who clapping spurs to his jaded bronco was hurrying away. "Where on earth have I seen that form before?" said Leale to himself. "Orderly, ride after that lunatic and bring him in here. What?" he asked, turning quickly about in his saddle as a trumpeter came trotting to his side. "Move where?"

"Off to the right, sir. The adjutant is leading the way," and peering through the fast falling flakes, the battalion commander saw the dim figures of the horsemen already in motion.

"Come on with your packs, Harry," he called to the chief packer, "and when that fellow returns, send him to the front."

Five minutes more and they were stumbling down into the depths of one of the deep ravines which opened out from the valley of the frozen stream to the eastward. Then, and without a word of command or trumpet call—only the uplifted hand of the troop leaders and observant sergeants,—the column halted. "Dismount!" was passed in low tone from front to rear. "Silence now! No noise, men. Stand to horse!" were the muttered cautions, and then once again the foremost officers gathered in a little group about the two refugees.

"We'll fight with you gladly. Count us in," said one of them, refreshed by a long pull at Ormsby's flask. "But that sneak that slipped away would see you all in hell first. He's a fugitive in more senses than one. That man's fleeing from the law."

"How do you know? Have you any idea who he is and where he came from?" asked Captain Leale. "I didn't see his face, but somewhere before this day I've seen his back."

"I don't know him from Adam. He was on his way to the Black Hills when the Indians jumped the reservation and cut us off. He's been afraid to go ahead and afraid to go back, and he's just been staying there with us—seemed to have plenty of money, but there ain't a white man left alive from here to the South Cheyenne now."

And then in silent respect the group opened and made way for the gray-mustached soldier who rode slowly into their midst and addressed them in low, quiet tones:

"Look to your men and horses, gentlemen. Big as that village is, I think that all the warriors are not there, and our best plan will be to attack before they can send and call in those who are watching the pursuing column. We will attack at once."

## CHAPTER III.

The snow was falling now in a dense white mist, powdering beards and broad-brimmed campaign hats and silvering the dusty black of the fur caps of the men. Objects fifty feet away were invisible, and all sounds muffled by the soft, fleecy blanket that everywhere covered the earth. Silently, yet with soldierly alertness, the officers hastened to look quickly over their troops. Silently the veteran colonel turned once more to the front and rode a few yards out beyond the head of the column and sat there on his horse, a white mantled statue, peering intently through the slowly falling flakes.

"We move the moment Bat gets back," murmured the adjutant to Captain Leale. "He crawled out to locate the herds and pick our way. There are some cross gullies beyond that ridge and down near the village. Bat says he feels sure most of the warriors are miles away to the east, but—there are enough and to spare right here."

"Is Kill Eagle still to be given a chance to surrender?" asked Leale. "That was the understanding at one time, wasn't it?"

"That was it—yes, and Bat was to hail as soon as we deployed within striking distance. Unless some scouts or the ponies find us out, we can creep up under this snow cloud to within a few yards, and they'll be none the wiser. The colonel hoped that the show of force would be ample and that the old scoundrel would throw up the sponge right here, but —I don't know," he added, doubtfully. "If only the women and children weren't in that village, it would be simple enough. We could pitch in and double them up before they knew what struck them. As it is—" and here the young officer broke off with a wave of the hand that meant volumes of doubt. Then he turned and looked eastward again to where, silent and stauesque still, Colonel Farrar was seated on old Roderick.

The same thought seemed to occur to both officers at the same instant. Ormsby, once more testing the lock of his revolver and narrowly observing his new comrades, remarked it at the time and spoke of it often thereafter.

"Can't you make him keep well back?" asked Leale.

"Won't you remind the chief he oughtn't to be in the front?" asked the adjutant.

And then each shook his head, as though realizing the impossibility of getting their old war horse of a colonel to take a position where he would be less exposed to the fire of the Indian marksmen.

"*You* might give him a tip, Ormsby," said the adjutant, in the cheery confidence the comradeship a few days' campaigning engenders. "You are his guest, not his subordinate. Tell him what the Seventh thinks the colonel should do," he added, with an attempt at jocularity that somehow failed to provoke a smile.

But Ormsby in turn shook his head. "I haven't known your colonel a week," said he, "but I've learned to know him well, and when he means to go in, all you've got to do is to go, too. That's what I've mapped out for myself, and doubtless so, too, have these gentlemen," he continued, indicating the two ranchmen, now eagerly fingering their Winchesters and getting ready for business. The elder of the two it was who answered:

"No man who has been through what we have, and seen the sights and heard the sounds of their raids on the ranches down the Fork, would do less than thank God for a chance of meeting those brutes on anything like equal terms. My poor brother lies there, hacked and scalped and mutilated; his wife and daughter, I believe, are somewhere among those foul tepees now, unless God has been merciful and let them die day before yesterday. We fought as long as there was a show, and we got away in the dark. These poor women wouldn't leave their dead."

A tear was tickling down his cheek as he finished speaking, but his lips and jaws were firm set. "You gentlemen," he continued, "are going into this thing just from sense of duty, but think what it is to me and to young Crawford here. His old father and mother were just butchered, by God!—butchered —and the worst of it is that if that damned hound Graice had stood by him ten minutes he might have got them safely away. They were too old to make any time, and it was no use. That fellow's a white-livered pup, and if I ever come upon him again I'll tell him what I think of him."

"I wish you had seen that fellow, Ormsby," said Leale, in a low tone "The more I think of it, the more I feel sure he had some reason for fearing to meet our party here. They tell me he seemed excited and worried the moment he heard we were the Twelfth Cavalry. I only saw his back as he rode away, but I've seen that man before somewhere. He rode like a trooper, and it's ten to one ho's a deserter."

"He's a deserter this day if he never was before," said Ormsby in reply. "I judge we need every man, do we not?"

"Looks like it," was the brief reply. "All right, gentlemen?" he continued, turning with courteous manner to the two younger officers, his first and second lieutenants, who came striding up through the snow. Leale was famous in the cavalry for his subalterns. He had the reputation of never speaking hastily or harshly, and of getting more out of his men than any other captain in the regiment.

"All right, sir!" was the prompt reply. "Every man in my platoon boiling over with ginger," added the younger, his blue eyes flashing, though his cheeks were pale and his lips twitching with pent-up excitement.

"I see the guidon is being unfurled, Cramer," said the captain, quietly. "Perhaps Sergeant West wants to land it first in the village, but tell him to handle his revolver instead, if we charge," and touching his fur cap, the officer turned back. "The colonel has said nothing about the plan of attack. We may be going to charge right in, for all I know. Ha! Ormsby, there comes the word!"

Looming up through the snow a young German trooper rode rapidly back toward the little group, and, reining in his horse a few yards away, true to the etiquette of the craft, threw his carbine over his shoulder and started to dismount before addressing officers afoot, but Leale checked him. "Never mind dismounting, orderly. What's the message?"

"The colonel's compliments, sir, and he would wish to see Captain Leale a minute, and the command will mount and move slowly forward."

Instantly the group dissolved, each officer turning quickly to his horse and swinging into saddle. No trumpet signal was given. "Mount," said Leale, in the same quiet, conversational tone. "Mount," repeated the first sergeant, halted alongside the leading set of fours, and, all in a few seconds, the burly forms of the riders shot up in the eddying fleece, and every horse, far back as eye could penetrate the mist, was suddenly topped by an armed rider. Then, first thing, the fur-gloved right hands went up to the shoulder and drew over the little brown carbines and drove the muzzle through its socket. Then, in the same soldierly silence the horsemen edged in toward the center of each set, and there sat, boot to to boot, erect and ready. One or two spirited young horses began to paw the snow in their impatience, and to snort excitedly. The adjutant trotted briskly back along the column in order to see that all four troops were similarly ready, cautioned the rearward troop leaders to keep well closed on the head of the column and signaled "Forward," while Leale disappeared in the snow clouds ahead.

Not knowing what else to do, Ormsby ranged alongside the senior lieutenant of Leale's troop, as in perfect silence the column bore steadily on. A few seconds brought them in sight of the colonel's form again, and he waved his hand cheerily, as though to say, "All right, lads, come on." Then, sitting Roderick as squarely as ever, the gray-mustached commander took the lead, a swarthy half-breed Sioux scout riding on one side, the grave, soldierly Leale on the other. The adjutant, the chief trumpeter, sergeant major, and orderlies fell in behind, and the crack battalion of the old Twelfth rode noiselessly in to take position for the attack.

For perhaps a hundred yards they followed the windings of the ravine in which they had been concealed, had concealment been necessary. Then, turning abruptly to his left as he passed a projecting shoulder, Little Bat looked back and motioned to the colonel, "This way." And then the leading horsemen began to ascend a gentle and almost imperceptible slope, for the snow was sifting down so thick and fast that the surface was invisible thirty feet ahead.

"We might ride square in among them at this rate," muttered the sergeant-major to his friend, the chief trumpeter, "and never know it until we stumbled into the tepees."

"How far ahead is it?" asked the latter.

"A mile, they say. We'd be deployed by this time if it were less."

Less than five minutes of gradual ascent, and the crest of the divide was reached, and, one after another, every horseman realized that he was then on the downward slope of the eastern side. Somewhere ahead, somewhere between this ridge and its nearest neighbor, lay the hostile village, all unconscious of foemen's coming, looking for disturbers as yet only from the eastern side. Old cavalrymen used to declare their horses could smell an Indian village before the sharpest eyes could "sight" it, and the packers swore the statement was true, "if it were only made of the mule."

"The colonel knows. He hasn't forgotten, you bet," was the comment, as again the orderly rode swiftly rearward with orders for the pack train to halt just west of the crest, and then every man seemed to know that the village couldn't be far ahead, and some hands went nervously to the holster flaps, others loosened the carbines in their leather sockets, and men took furtive peeps at one another's faces along the shadowy column, and then at their officers riding so confident and erect along the left flank. And still no man could see more than the depth of three sets of fours ahead. "Ain't we going to dismount and go afoot?" muttered a young recruit to his neighbor. "I thought that was the way we always did."

"Of course; when one could see to shoot and would be seen himself anywhere within five miles," was the disdainful answer. "What'd be the good of dismounting here?"

And now in places the horses plunged deeper into the snow and tossed up drifting clouds of feathery spray as the column crossed some shallow ruts in the eastward face, and then once more, snakelike, it began to twist and turn, following the track of those invisible guides, and then it seemed to take to evil courses and go spluttering down into sharp, steep-banked coulées, and scrambling out again on the other side, and still the sure-footed horses tripped nimbly on, and then, presently, his eyes a-twinkle, the adjutant came riding back.

"Just half a mile ahead, Billy," he murmured to the lieutenant riding in Leale's place at the head of the first troop. "Form left front into line and halt. I'll post the other troop."

Quickly the young officer reined out of column to the left about. "Keep straight to your front, leading four," he cautioned. Then barely raising his voice and dropping for the time the conventional commands of the drill book, he rode back along the column, saying "Left front into line," until all the rearward fours were obliquing; then back to the front he trotted, halted the leading set, each of the others in succession reining in and generally aligning itself, all without a sound that could be audible ten yards away. Almost at the same time the second troop headed diagonally off to the left and presently rode up into line with the first, while the third and fourth were halted in similar formation at troop distance in rear. "By all that's glorious, we're going in mounted!" was the word that seemed to thrill down along the line. "Then we're not going to wait—not going to give him a chance to surrender."

Another moment and the word was, "Hush! silence there!" for dimly seen through the drifts, the colonel, with his little party of attendants, came riding to the front of the line. Long, long afterward they remembered that clear-cut, soldierly, highbred face, with its aquiline nose, keen, kindly, deep-set eyes, the gray-white mustache, snow-white now, as was his close-cropped hair.

"Men," said he in the firm tones they had known so long and well, "fully half the band are some miles away, but Kill Eagle, with over a hundred warriors, is right here in our front; so, too, are his women and children; so, too, worse luck, are some of our own unhappy captives. You all know the first thing those Indians would do, were we to attack as usual, would be to murder those poor white women. This snowstorm is in our favor. We can creep right in upon them before we charge. The ponies are down in the valley to the south. Let the first line dash straight through the village and stampede the herd, then rally and return. Let the second follow at a hundred yards and surround the tepees at the eastward end—what white women are with them are there. The Indian men, as a rule, will make a dash in the direction of the ponies. Shoot them down wherever you can, but mark my words now, be careful of the women and children. I had intended summoning Kill Eagle to surrender, but we did not begin to know he had so many warriors close at hand, and did not know about the captives. Bat has seen, and that is enough. There is no other way to settle it. It's the one chance of rescuing those poor creatures. Now keep together. Watch your officers' commands and signals and spare the squaws and papooses. Be ready in two minutes."

And then every man took a long breath, while the colonel rode through to say similar words to the second line. Then, returning, he placed himself just in the rear of the center of the first squadron, the second line noiselessly advancing and closing up on the leaders, and then he seemed to think of another point.

"Ask Mr. Ormsby if he will ride with me," said he to the adjutant. "Now, Leale, forward at a walk. Follow Bat. It's all level ahead of you. You'll sight the village in three or four minutes.

The tall, stalwart captain touched his hat, took off his "broadbrim," shaking away a load of snow, and spurred out a little to the front. There, looking back to both his right and left, he gave the signal forward, and with almost a single impulse, the long dark rank of horsemen, open at the center in an interval of some half a dozen yards, without other sound than the slight rattle of accoutrements and the muffled rumble of five hundred hoofs, moved steadily forward. A moment the colonel sat and watched them, smiled a cordial greeting to Ormsby, who, pistol in hand, came trotting over with the adjutant, then signaling to the second line, he too gave his horse the rein, and at a steady walk followed close to the center of Leale's command. In his hand at the moment he held a little pocket compass, and smiled as he noted the line of direction.

"Almost due southeast at this instant," said he. "We ought to bag our game and be well across the Mini Pusa with them in less than an hour."

Unconsciously the pace was quickening. Foremost of all, well out in front of the center, rode the half-breed Indian guide, bending low over his pony's neck, his black, beady eyes peering ahead. Well out to the right and left were other scouts, eager and alert, like Bat himself. Then, squarely in the center, on his big, powerful bay, rode Leale, commander of the foremost line, and Ormsby's soldierly heart throbbed with admiration as he marked, just before Leale was hidden from view, his spirited, confident bearing, and noted how the eyes of all the line seemed fixed on their gallant leader. And now some of the horses began to dance and tug at the bit and plunge, and others to take a jog trot, for the Indian scouts were at the lope, and their gesticulations became every moment more vehement, and then Bat was seen, though visible only to the first line, to grab his revolver, and Leale's gauntleted hand almost instantly sought the holster, and out came the ready Colt, its muzzle raised in air. Out in quick and ready imitation leaped a hundred more, and instinctively the jog changed to a lively trot, and the dull, thudding hoofs upon the snow-muffled earth rose louder and more insistent, and Ormsby, riding at the colonel's left, gripped tighter his revolver and set his teeth, yet felt his heart was hammering loud, and then dimmer and dimmer grew the first line as it led away, and still the colonel's firm hand kept Roderick dancing impatiently at the slower gait and then, just as it seemed as though the line would be swallowed up in snow and disappear from view, quick and sudden, two muffled shots were heard from somewhere just in front, the first syllable perhaps of some stentorian shout of warning, and then one magnificent burst of cheers and a rush of charging men, and a crash and a crackle and sputter of shots, and then fierce rallying cries and piercing screams of women and of terrified little ones, and like some huge human wave the first line of the Twelfth rode on and over and through the startled camp, and bore like a whirlwind, yelling down upon the pony herds beyond.

And now comes the turn of the second line. Seeking shelter from the snowstorm, warriors, women and children were for the most part within the tepees, as the line crashed in. Some few were with the miserable captives, but at the first sound of danger every warrior had seized his rifle and rushed for the open air. Some few, throwing themselves upon their faces, fired wild shots at the foremost troopers as they came bounding through, but as a rule only a few opposed their passage, so sudden was the shock.

Then came the realization that the herds were being driven, and that not an instant must be lost in mounting such ponies as were still tethered about the villages, and darting away in a wide circle, away from the troops, yet concentrating again beyond them and regaining the lead. And so, where the first line met an apparently sleeping village, the second comes cheering, charging, firing, thundering through a swarming mob of yelling braves and screaming squaws. Farrar, foremost in the charge, with the civilian guardsman close at his side, shouts warning to the women, even as he empties his pistol at the howling men. Close at his back come Amory and his sorrel troop, cheering like mad, battering over Indians too slow to jump aside, and driving their hissing lead at every warrior in their path. And still the colonel shouts, "This way!" and Ormsby, Amory, and the adjutant ride at his heels, and the sorrels especially follow his lead, and dashing through a labyrinth of lodges, they rein up cheering about two grimy tepees at which Bat is excitedly pointing and the ranchmen both are shouting the names of loved relatives and listening eagerly for answer; and thrilling voices within are crying, "Here! Here!" and stalwart men, springing from saddle, are rushing in, pistol in hand, and tearing aside the flimsy barriers that hide the rescued captives from the eyes of their deliverers, and the other troop, reinforced again by strong squads from Leale's rallied line, are dashing to and fro through the village, firing at the Indians who are scurrying away. Just as Amory and the adjutant charge at a little knot of scowling redskins whose rifles are blazing at them at not a dozen yards' distance, just as the good old colonel, afoot now, is clasping the hand of some poor woman whose last hope was gone but a moment before, and even while listening to her frantic blessings, finds time to shout again to his half maddened men, "Don't hurt the women, lads! Look out for the children!" a haglike, blanketed fury of a Brulé squaw springs from behind the shelter of a pile of robes, levels her revolver, and, pulling trigger at the instant, leaps screaming down into the creek bottom, leaving Farrar sinking slowly into the snow.

An hour later, with strong skirmish lines out on every side of the captured village, with a score of Indian warriors sent to their last account and the others scattered over the face of the earth, the little battalion of the Twelfth is wondering if, after all, the fight were worth winning, for here in their midst, his head on Leale's arm, his fading sight fixed on the tear-dimmed eyes of his faithful comrade, here lies their beloved old colonel, his last messages murmured in that listening ear: "Leale—old friend—find—find that poor girl—my—my son robbed and ruined and deserted—and be the friend to her—you've been to me—and mine. God 'bless—"

And this—while the regiment, obeying its stern duty, goes on in pursuit—this is the news Jack Ormsby has to break to the loving, breaking hearts at Frayne.

## CHAPTER IV.

ALL this was but part and parcel of the story of the old Wyoming fort. Long years had it served as refuge and resting place for the emigrants in the days before the Union Pacific was built, when the overland stage route followed the Platte to the Sweetwater, and then past the Devil's Gate and Independence Rock, old land-marks of the Mormons, and on to the back-bone of the continent, where the mountain streams, springing from rocky beds not long pistol shot apart, flowed rippling away, the one to the Missouri and the Gulf of Mexico, the other to the Colorado and that of California. Frayne was but a huge stockade in the early days of the civil war, but the government found it important from a strategical point of view, even after the railway spanned the Rockies, and the emigrant and the settler no longer trudged the weary trail that, bordering the Sioux country, became speedily a road of fire and blood, second only in its terrors to the Smoky Hill route through "bleeding Kansas." Once it was the boast of the Dakotas, as it has been for generations of their enemies, the Absarakas, or Crows, that they had never shed the blood of a white man. Settlers of the old days used to tell how the Sioux had followed them for long, long marches, not to murder and pillage, but to restore to them items lost along the trail or animals strayed from their little herds. But there came an end to all this, when, resisting an unjust demand, the Sioux being fired upon, retaliated. From the day of the Grattan massacre beyond old Laramie, there had been no real peace with the lords of the Northwest. They are quiet only when subdued by force. They have broken the crust of their environment time and again and burst forth in the seething flame of a volcano that is ever bubbling and boiling beneath the feet of the frontiersman to this day.

And so Frayne was maintained as a military post for years, first as a stockade, then as a sub-depot of supplies, garrisoned by four companies of infantry and four of cavalry, the former to hold the fort, the latter to scour the neighboring country. Then as time wore on and other posts were built further up in the Big Horn, Frayne's garrison dwindled, but there stood upon its commanding bluff the low rows of wooden barracks, the parallel rows of double sets of broad-piazzaed quarters where dwelt the officers, the long, low, log-revetted walls of the corrals and cavalry stables on the flat below. Here, oddly enough, the Twelfth had spent a lively year or two before it went to Arizona. Here it learned the Sioux country and the Sioux so well that when, a few years back, the ghost dance craze swept over the plains and mountains like the plague, the old regiment was hurried from its sunshiny stations in the south and mustered once again, four troops at least, within the very walls that long before had echoed to its trumpets. Here we found them in the midst of the Christmas preparations that were turned so suddenly into summons to the field, and here again, three years later still, headquarters and six troops now, the proud old regiment is still at Frayne, and Fenton "vice-Farrar, killed in action with hostile Indians," holds the command.

A good soldier is Fenton; a brave fellow, a trifle rough at times, like the simple plains-bred dragoon he is, but a gentleman with a gentle heart in his breast for all the stern exterior. Women said of him that all he needed to make him perfect was polish, and all he needed to give him polish was a wife, for at fifty-four the grizzled colonel was a bachelor. But Fenton had had his romance in early youth. He had loved with all his big heart, so said tradition, a New York belle and beauty whom he knew in his cadet days, and who, so rumor said, preferred another, whom she married before the war, and many a garrison belle had since set her cap for Fenton, and found him faithful to his early love. But, though the ladies often speculated as to the identity of the woman who had held the colonel's heart in bondage all these years and blocked the way for all successors, no one of their number had ever heard her name or ever knew the truth. One officer there was in the Twelfth who, like Fenton himself, was a confirmed bachelor, and who was said to be possessed of the whole story, but there was no use asking Malcolm Leale to tell anybody's secrets, and when Fenton came to Frayne, promoted to the command so recently held by a man they all loved and honored, it was patent to everybody that he felt sorely, as though he were an usurper. Fenton was many long miles away, with another battalion of the Twelfth, the day of the tragic battle on the Mini Pusa, and it was long months thereafter before he appeared at regimental headquarters, and then he brought with him as his housekeeper his maiden sister, Lucretia, and in Lucretia Fenton—the dreamiest, dowdiest, kindliest, quaintest, middle-aged prattler that ever lived, moved, and had her being in the army—the ladies of the Twelfth found so much to make merry over that they well-nigh forgot and forgave the unflattering indifference to feminine fascinations of her brother, the colonel.

When Fenton came, the Farrars, widowed mother and devoted daughter, had been gone some weeks. The shock of her husband's death had well-nigh shaken Mrs. Farrar's reason, and for months her condition was indeed deplorable. Loving him devotedly, glorying in his soldierly record and reputation, yet ever dreading for him just such an end, she had been so prostrated by her grief that Ellis almost forgot her own bitter sorrow in the contemplation of her mother's woe. For months the daughter was her main prop and comfort and attendant. Will, her bright, brave boy, could not be permitted to leave his studies at the Point. Royle, her first-born, was an outcast and wanderer she knew not where. Ellis, her youngest, her one daughter, proved to be her chief dependence. Loving friends and relatives she had in plenty, to be sure, and, through the providence of her soldier husband, her fortune was unimpaired, and, fortunately, more than sufficient for her needs. And so, for over six months after that fatal Christmastide, the widow lay either apathetic or in the depths of an overwhelming grief, and Ellis never left her side. And then they went for a summer at the seashore, for Ellis herself was drooping, and then while visiting at her own sister's home Mrs. Farrar began to realize how all this time Ellis's education was being neglected, and, despite her protest, the girl was sent back to school in New York, where she could be within call. This was her one stipulation, for Ellis well knew what her mother only faintly suspected— that no more sudden shocks could come into the gentle sufferer's life, without danger of ending it at once.

And all this time Jack Ormsby had been so helpful, thoughtful and attentive. It was he who met them and escorted them, most of that miserable homeward way. For the time being, at least, the honored remains of the grand old colonel had been laid to rest under the shadow of the flag at the post he had so well commanded, but in the course of the second year they were brought East and buried in the beautiful cemetery near his own father's side, and the veterans of a famous regiment bowed their heads beside the helmeted regulars from the forts in the harbor, and Jack's company sent a superb floral emblem to be laid on the flag-draped coffin of the commander by whose side their popular sergeant had won his spurs in Indian battle. A famous fellow, with all his modesty and good sense, was Jack Ormsby in the armory of the Seventh all the year that followed his homecoming from the Sioux campaign, and again and again did his comrades make him tell the story of his sensations and experiences when he followed Farrar into the heart of that fire-spitting village, through that veil of softly falling snow. How red it grew in many a place! What scenes of carnage were there not after the noble colonel fell! Jack's brain used to turn sick at the thought of it sometimes, but still there was the exultation of the rescue of those helpless captives, those poor women, being dragged away to a fate to which torture at the stake were mercy. There was the triumph of the overwhelming defeat and punishment of that great village of hostiles even when it was reinforced, as it soon was, by the return of many of the warriors who had been watching and hindering the pursuit of the Eleventh. Leale had taken command, cool, yet raging over the murder of his beloved chief, and while even then seeking to carry out Farrar's injunctions to protect the women and children, had dealt vengefully with the warriors who had rallied to the attack. Ormsby was through it all, and bore himself like a man and a sergeant, even of the Seventh, and swore that his Creedmoor training had been more than enough to help him empty at least two saddles. If he had "only had my old Remington," said he, "instead of a cavalry carbine, Kill Eagle himself would have bit the dust," for twice he drew bead upon that savage chief when the snow clouds lifted late in the afternoon and let the battle-field be seen. Great work had the little battalion done that day, but all the same were they glad to see the coming column of the Eleventh just before the red, red sun went down.

Once, just once, after they had been home about a month, Ellis made him tell her something of that stirring, fatal day, but soon she shut her ears and fled. Ormsby came again. He began coming often —so often that that became one reason why it was deemed best that Ellis should return to school. Mr. Ormsby was a very fine fellow, and all that, said Mrs. Farrar's many relatives, but, really, "Ellis is still too young, and she might do better," and so poor Jack, who was learning to do nothing less than worship that exquisite face, so pathetic above the deep mourning of her attire, became dismal in his turn and found no comfort in anything outside of the armory or Wall Street.

The next summer the Farrars spent at West Point. It was Will's first class camp, and Will was cadet captain of the color company, and a capital young officer despite a boyish face and manner, and then Jack Ormsby, who never before had "taken much stock in West Point"—the battalion looked so small beside the Seventh, and the band was such a miserable little affair after Cappa and his superb array—Jack not only concluded that he must go up there every few days to pick up points on guard and sentry duty and things of that kind, but Jack decided that Kitty, his precious sister, might as well go, too, and spend a fortnight, and she did, under the wing of a matron from Gotham with daughters of her own, and Kitty Ormsby, only sixteen, and as full of vivacity, grace, sprightliness, and winning ways as girl could be, pretty as a peach, and brimming over with fun, coquetry and sweetness combined, played havoc in the corps of cadets, and —could anything have been more fortunate?—the victim, most helplessly, hopelessly, utterly gone was Cadet Captain Will Farrar. To the contsernation of the widowed mother she saw her handsome soldier boy led day after day more deeply into the meshes, led like a slave, or like the piggy in the nursery rhyme with the ring in the end of his nose, by this bewitching, imperious, fascinating little creature, and there was absolutely no help for it. Anywhere else, almost, she could have whisked her boy under her wing, and borne him away beyond range, but not at West Point. She had to learn the lesson so many mothers learn with such bewilderment, often with such ill grace, that the boy was no longer hers to do with as she would, but Uncle Sam's, and Uncle Sam unfeelingly said stick to your camp duty with its drills and parades, roll calls, practical engineering, pontooning, and spooning in stolen half hours, no matter what the consequence. Mrs. Farrar couldn't carry Will away, and couldn't order Kitty. About all she saw of her boy was drilling with the battalion at a distance or dancing with Miss Ormsby close at hand, and, on the principle that misery loves company, she soon was comforted by a fellow sufferer, for just in proportion as the mother heart was troubled by the sight of her boy's infatuation for this pretty child, so was Jack Ormsby made miserable by seeing the attentions lavished by officers and cadets alike on Ellis Farrar.

And yet the little blind god was doing Jack far better work than he ever dared to dream. The mother longed for Will and no one else could quite take his place. The lover longed for Ellis, and what earthly chance has a "cit" lover at West Point, even though he be a swell and a sergeant in the Seventh? It resulted that in the hours when the mother and Jack had to sit and look on they were brought constantly together, and then in these hours of companionship Mrs. Farrar began to see more and more how manful, honest, self-reliant was the gallant fellow who had fought by her husband's side. Little by little she learned to lean upon him, appeal to him, defer to him, and to see in him, after all, a man in whom she could perhaps confide even so precious a trust as her daughter's heart, and that summer at West Point won the mother even if it did not win the lady of his love.

That winter the boys came down to New York, half a dozen of Will's classmates, for Christmas leave, and such a day and night of adulation as they received! At last did Mrs. Farrar quit her seclusion to give a little dinner in their honor, and consent to attend, as a looker-on, the dance that night at Sherry's, where Ellis gave Ormsby one blessed waltz and Kitty gave Will the mitten. Oh, darts and flames and furies, what a turmoil there was over that Christmas dance! Will had to go back with his classmates in time to report at a certain hour, but he told his mother in tragic tone that all was over between him and Miss Ormsby, forever—forever—and so, perhaps, it might have been had Kitty so minded. She had flirted outrageously with Charley Bates, a fellow Will Farrar simply couldn't bear, and, though neither would admit that a girl had anything to do with it, there was the usual cadet challenge and as spirited a midwinter "mill" as ever was seen in cadet barracks—a "mill" in which Farrar fought like a hero and was only knocked out after having been knocked down time and again, and then Kitty was properly punished, for Will was still in hospital when the New Year's hop came off, battered and bruised and generally miserable, while Bates, though mouse-colored as to his eyes, was able to attend, but Kitty went up to Craney's with Mrs. Farrar, a penitent indeed, and never went near the hop, but had Will in ecstasy and a dark corner of the parlor for a long, long hour, and cried and cooed over and comforted him and surrendered at discretion. Will Farrar was practically an engaged man when he was graduated in June—and only twenty-one.

All that winter Ellis had continued her course at school, but was to come out in May, and during the long months from September she was comforted in the comfort her mother found in the companion that had been chosen for her, a gentle, refined, and evidently well-bred woman, who came upon the recommendation of their rector, and who was introduced as Mrs. Daunton—Helen Daunton, a woman with a sad history, as the grave old pastor frankly told them, but through no fault or foible of her own. She had been married, but her husband was unworthy of her, had deserted her some years before, leaving her to struggle for herself. Dr. Morgan vouched for her integrity and that was enough. By the time Ellis was to return to her mother's roof Helen Daunton was so thoroughly established there, so necessary to her mother, so devoted to her in every way, that for the first time in her life, even while glad to mark the steps of improvement in the beloved invalid's health and appearance, Ellis Farrar felt the pangs of jealousy.

And this was Will's graduation summer, and they had a lovely time at the seashore. Kitty was there, and Kitty was an accepted fact—and more so—now. Will would be content nowhere without her, and would have married her then and there but for his mother's gentle admonition, and Kitty's positive refusal. She had been reared from girlhood by a doting aunt, had been petted and spoiled at home and at school, and yet had not a little fund of shrewd good sense in her bewilderingly pretty head. She wouldn't wear an engagment ring, wouldn't consent to call it an engagement. She owned, under pressure, that she meant to marry Will some day, but not in any hurry, and, therefore, but for one thing, the mother's gentle heart would have been content.

And that one thing was that Will had applied for and would hear of no other regiment in all the army than that at the head of which his father had died— the Twelfth Cavalry, and no one could understand, and Mrs. Farrar couldn't explain, how it was—why it was that that of all others was the one she had vainly hoped he would not choose. He was wild with joy and enthusiasm when at last the order came, and with beaming eyes and ringing voice he read aloud, "'Twelfth regiment of cavalry, Cadet Will Duncan Farrar, to be second lieutenant, vice Watson, promoted, Troop 'C.' Leale's troop, Queen Mother—blessed old Malcolm Leale. What more could I ask or you ask? What captain in all the line can match him? And Kitty's uncle in command of the regiment and post! Just think of it, Madre dear, and you'll all come out and we'll have grand Christmas times at Frayne, and we'll hang father's picture over the mantel and father's sword. I'll wire Leale this very minute, and write my respects to Fenton. What's he like, anyway, mother? I can't remember him at all—nor can Kitty."

But Mrs. Farrar could not tell. It was years, too, since she had seen him, "but he was always a faithful friend of your father, Will, and he wrote me a beautiful, beautiful letter when we came away."

And so, late in September the boy lieutenant left his mother's arms and, followed by her prayers and tears and blessings, was borne away westward to revisit scenes that were once familiar as the old barrack walls at West Point. Then it required long days of travel over rough mountain roads to reach the railway far south of the Medicine Bow. Now the swift express train landed him at the station of the frontier town that had grown up on the site of the prairie dog village he and his pony had often "stampeded" in the old days. Here at the station, come to meet the son of their old commander, ignoring the fact that the newcomer was but the plebe lieutenant of the Twelfth, were the ruddy-faced old colonel and Will's own troop leader, Captain Leale, both heartily, cordially bidding him welcome, and commenting not a little on his stalwart build and trying hard not to refer to the very downy mustache that adorned his boyish lip. And other and younger officers were there to welcome the lad to his new station, and huge was Will's comfort when he caught sight of Sergeant Stein, the veteran standard-bearer of the regiment, and that superbly punctilious old soldier straightened up like a Norway pine and saluted with rigid precision and hoped the lieutenant was well and his lady mother and Miss Farrar. "There's nothing," thought Will, "like the discipline of the old regiment, after all," as the orderly came to ask for the checks for the lieutenant's baggage, and all went well until the luckless moment when the colonel and Leale, with some of the elders, turned aside to look at a batch of recruits sent by the same train, and Farrar, chatting with some of his fellow-youngsters, was stowing his bags in the waiting ambulance, and there in the driver Will recognized Saddler Donovan's freckle-faced Mickey, with whom he had had many a hunt for rabbits in the old, old

. . . .

days, and then an unctuous, caressing Irish voice fairly blubbered out: "Hiven save us if it isn't really Masther Will!" and there, corporal's chevrons on his brawny arms, was old Terry Rorke, looking wild to embrace him, and even as Will, half ashamed of his own shyness, was shaking hands with this faithful old retainer of his father's household in years gone by, the squad of recruits came marching past. The third man from the front, heavily bearded, with a bloated, ill-groomed face and restlessly glancing eyes, gave a quick, furtive look at the new lieutenant as he passed, then stumbled and plunged forward against his file leader. The squad was thrown into momentary disarray. The sergeant, angered at the mishap at such a time, strode quickly up to the offender and savagely muttered: "Keep your eyes to the front, Graice, and you won't be stumbling up decent men's backs," and the little detachment went briskly on.

"I thought I'd seen that man before," said Leale an instant later, "and now I know it—and I know where."

## CHAPTER V.

THE winter came on early at old Fort Frayne. Even as early as mid-October the ice was forming in the shallow pools along the Platte, and that eccentric stream itself had dwindled away in volume until it seemed but the ghost of its former self. Raging and unfordable in June, swollen by the melting snows of the Colorado peaks and the torrents from the Medicine Bow, it spent its strength in the arid heat of a long dry summer, and when autumn came was mild as a mill stream as far as the eye could reach, and fordable in a dozen places within rifle shot of the post. Many a time did old Fenton wish it wasn't. Frayne's reservation was big and generous, but, unluckily, it never extended across the river. Squatters, smugglers and sharpers could not intrude upon its guarded limits along the southern shore, and the nearest groggery—that inevitable accompaniment of the westward march of civilization—was a long two miles away down the right bank, but only a pistol shot across the stream.

In his day Farrar had waged war against the rum-sellers on the north shore and won, because then there were only soldiers and settlers and no lawyers —outside the guardhouse—within ninety miles of the post. But with the tide of civilization came more settlers, and a cattle town, and lawyers in abundance, and with their coming the question at issue became no longer that of abstract right or wrong, but how a jury would decide it; and a frontier jury always decides in favor of the squatter and against the soldier. Fenton strove to take pattern after Farrar and very nearly succeeded in landing himself in jail, as the outraged vendor went down to Laramie, hired lawyers there, swore out warrants of assault and appealed to his countrymen. The fact that no less than four of the Twelfth within six months had died with their boots on, victims of the ready knives or revolvers of the squatters across the stream, had no bearing in the eyes of the law. Fenton had warned the divekeeper a dozen times to no purpose, but when finally Sergeant Hannifin was set upon and murdered there one fine April evening within easy range and almost within hearing of his comrades at Frayne, Fenton broke loose and said impetuous things, which reached the ears of his men, who went and did things equally impetuous, to the demolition of the "shack" and the destruction of its stock of spirits and gambling paraphernalia, and it was proved to the satisfaction of the jury that Fenton did not interpose to stop the row until it had burned itself and the "shack" inside out. The people rallied to the support of the saloonkeeper—he, at least, was a man and a brother, a voter, and, when he couldn't lie out of it, a taxpayer. The officers at Frayne, on the other hand, in the opinion of the citizens of that section of Wyoming, were none of the four, and Bunko Jim's new resort across the Platte was a big improvement in point of size, though not in stock or sanctity, over its predecessor. Jim ran a ferryboat for the benefit of customers from the fort. It was forbidden to land on the reservation, but did so, nevertheless, when the sentry on the bluff couldn't see, and sometimes, it must be owned, when he could. The boat was used when the water was high, the fords when it was low, and the ice when it was frozen, and it was a curious thing in winter to see how quickly the newfallen snow would be seamed with paths leading by devious routes from the barracks to the shore and then across the ice-bound pools straight to Bunko Jim's. Bowing, as became the soldier of the republic, to the supremacy of the civil law, Fenton swallowed the lesson, though he didn't the whiskey, but Jim had his full share of customers from the fort, and the greatest of these, it soon transpired, was the big recruit speedily known throughout the command as "Tough Tom" Graice.

Joining the regiment at the end of September, it was less than a month before he was as well, though not as favorably, known as the sergeant-major. There is more than one way of being conspicuous in the military service, and Graice had chosen the worst. Even the recruits who came with him from the depot, the last lot to be shipped from that once-crowded garner of "food for powder," could tell nothing of his antecedents, though they were full of gruesome details of his doings since enlistment. He was an expert at cards and billiards, said they—for they had found it out to their sorrow—and a demon when aroused by drink. Twice in drunken rage he had assaulted comparatively inoffensive men, and only the prompt and forcible intervention of comrades had prevented murder on the spot, while the traditional habit of the soldier of telling no tales had saved him from richly merited punishment. Within the month of his arrival Graice had made giant strides to notoriety. He was a powerful fellow, with fine command of language and an education far superior to that of the general run of non-commissioned officers, and it was among the younger set of these he first achieved a certain standing. Professing to hold himself above the private soldier, proving himself an excellent rider and an expert in drill with carbine or sabre, he nevertheless declared it was his first enlistment and gave it to be understood that a difficulty with the sheriff, who sought to arrest him, had been the means of bringing him to the temporary refuge of the ranks. For the first few weeks, too, he drank but little, and wearing his uniform with the ease and grace of one long accustomed to the buttons, and being erect and athletic in build, he presented a very creditable appearance. The bloated, bloodshot look he wore on his arrival, the result of much surreptitious whiskey *en route*, passed somewhat away and it was only when one studied his face that the traces of intemperance, added to the sullen brows, and shifting, restless eyes, banished the claim to good looks that were at first accorded him. From the first, however, the old sergeants and such veterans among the corporals as Terry Rorke, looked askance at Trooper Graice. "Another guardhouse lawyer," said the first sergeant of Leale's troop, as he disgustedly received the adjutant's notification of Graice's assignment. "Another wan of thim jail birds like Mr. American Blood, the newspaper pet," said Rorke, in high disdain. "We'll have a circus with him, too, as they had in the Eleventh, or I'm a Jew. Where have I seen that sweet mug of him before?" he added, reflectively, as he watched the new-comer surlily scrubbing at his kit, and the new-comer, glancing sideways at the Irish corporal, seemed to read his thoughts, although too far away to hear his muttered words. It was plain to every man in "C" troop that there was apt to be no love lost between Terence Rorke and "Tommy the Tough."

And there was another still who wore the simple dress of a private soldier, whose eyes, black, piercing and full of expression, were constantly following that new recruit, and that was the Sioux Indian, Crow Knife, a youth barely nineteen years of age. He had been a boy scout before the days of the ghost dance craze. A valued and trusted ally of the white soldiers, he had borne dispatches up to the very moment when Kill Eagle's mad-brained ultimatum drove his band into revolt and launched them on the warpath. With them went Crow Knife's father and mother, and the boy rode wildly in pursuit. He was with them, striving to induce his mother to abandon the village, when the warriors made their descent on the ranches of the Dry Fork, and later, when Farrar's fierce attack burst upon them like a thunderbolt through the snow-clouds. Seizing his mother in his arms, the boy had shielded and saved her when Leale's vengeful men rushed upon the nearest Indians, when unquestionably, yet unavoidably, some squaws received their death wound in the furious fight that followed Farrar's assassination. Recognized and rescued by his former friends, Crow Knife went back to Frayne when the brief but bloody campaign was ended, and then was sent to the Indian school at Carlisle. Returning in the course of three years, he had been enlisted in what was left of the Indian troop of the Twelfth, and was one of the few of his tribe who really made a success of soldiering. By the autumn of this eventful year Crow Knife's comrades were rapidly being discharged and returning to their blankets and lodge life at the reservation, or hanging about the squalid cattle town across the river. Crow Knife, sticking to his cavalry duty and showing unlooked-for devotion to his officers, was regarded by the Twelfth as an exceptional case, and was made much of accordingly.

"What do you think of that fellow, Crow?" asked Corporal Rorke one day as he watched the expression in the Indian's face. "You don't like him any more than I do. What's the reason?"

"There is a saying among my people," was the answer, in the slow, measured tones of one who thought in another tongue, "eyes that cannot meet eyes guide hands that strike foul. He-that-stabs-in-the-dark is the name we give such as that man."

"D'ye know him, Crow? Did ye never see him?" persisted Terry. "Ever since the day he came the captain has had his eye on him, and so have you, and so have I. I can't ask the captain, but I can you. Where have you seen him before?"

But Crow Knife shook his head. "I cannot remember his face. It is his back I seem to know. My people say that way they see their enemies."

And so Rorke could find no satisfactory solution of the ever-vexing question. Twice or thrice he accosted Graice and strove to draw him into talk, but the new-comer seemed to shut up like an oyster in the presence of the Irish corporal, a great contrast to the joviality he displayed when soliciting comrades to take a hand at cards. The recruits had hardly any money left. Graice had won what little there was on the way to Frayne, and now he had wormed his way into the gambling set that is apt to be found in every fort—all comers who have money being welcome—and for a few weeks fortune seemed to smile upon the neophyte. He knew, he protested, very little of any game, but played for fellowship and fun. Then he kept sober when others drank, and so won, and then came accusations of foul play and a row, and the barracks game was broken up, only to be resumed at night in the resort across the Platte, and there whiskey was plenty, and so were the players, and there Graice began to lapse into intemperate ways, and by the time the long, long nights of December came, his reputation as a "tough" was established throughout the garrison. All but three or four of the most dissolute members of the command had cut loose from him entirely, a matter he regretted only because pay day was at hand—the soldiers would then have money in plenty for a few short, feverish hours. The squatters and settlers had none until the soldiers were "strapped" and so Graice and three or four Ishmaelites like unto himself were left to the concentration of brutality to be found in one another's society.

The winter, as has been said, set in early, and when December came duties were few and hours for sleep and recreation were many. Time was hanging heavily on the hands of those whose brains were empty among the households along officers' row and in the quarters of the married soldiers, although Christmas was not far away. Garrison balls were all the go among the rank and file. Hops were frequent among the officers and ladies, and, while other soldier swains found bliss and enjoyment in the society of the half dozen maidens wintering at the fort—guests and relatives of some of the officers' families—one inconsolable fellow watched and waited, watched and waited, with feverish impatience for the coming of a certain train on a certain day, for the coming of mother and sister to his own roof, revisiting as inmates of the quarters of the junior second lieutenant the post where three years gone by they occupied the house of the commanding officer. But boy lieutenants do not consume with feverish longing for the coming of blood relations. Proud and glad as was Will Farrar at the idea of welcoming the "queen mother" and sweet sister Ellis to his roof, it must be owned that the thrill of his impatience was all due to the fact that the same train was to bring Miss Kitty Ormsby to become for the time being an inmate of the army home now presided over by loquacious Aunt Lucretia.

And Will Farrar was not the only man in this big, bustling garrison to look forward to this coming with strange and sweet emotion. There are natures upon which the first strong, fervent love of manhood leaves an impress indelible even when the object of that love has passed out of one's life, possibly into the keeping of another and happier man. Aunt Lucretia couldn't understand why on earth her brother, the colonel, should be so fussy and excited about Kitty Ormsby's coming. Why on earth should he insist on sending away to Cheyenne for new carpets, curtains, furniture, and all manner of contraptions, to say nothing of swell new uniforms from New York, all because that precious little chit of a niece was coming to spend a month or so at Frayne. Lucretia thought it was ridiculous. Of course, it was her brother's own affair. He was a well-to-do bachelor, with no one but her to take care of, and he could do as he pleased, especially when he pleased to insist on surprising her with some charming addition to her maidenly store of gowns and furbelows and kickshaws. Really, the idea of Kitty's coming and turning everything topsyturvy in the household didn't strike her as being so inappropriate now after all, for Aunt Lou, whom Kitty had not seen in years, was still young and volatile enough to feel the influence of dress upon one's

views of life, and from being actually incensed at the
initial excitement and preparation, Lucretia first
grew reconciled, then, as her own remembrances
came with the early installments of goods and
chattels, manifestly interested, and later, infected
with all her brother's marked enthusiasm, for one
wonderful day Lucretia almost fainted with excitement and delight when the colonel came over from
the office wearing a face of unwonted perplexity and
dismay, and, when the maiden asked the cause, her
virgin heart stood still an instant, then fluttered
wildly at his reply.

"That blessed old day-dreamer Wayne is ordered
here for duty. Why! O Lord! yes, I remember."

Nearly twenty years before, when she was but a girl
of nineteen and Wayne a lone subaltern, there had
been a long winter in which life seemed to have no
joy for either Wayne or Miss Fenton save in the
hours spent in each other's society. Every one at
Leavenworth vowed they must be engaged. Indeed,
Lucretia believed it must come any day, but the
days dragged on, Wayne came ever, but the fateful
words were never spoken up to the moment when he
was ruthlessly hurried away to bear his part on a
frontier campaign, and rarely, and then only for a
moment or two, had they ever met again. Wayne
was one of the wonders of the army, the best fellow
that ever lived in almost every way, said almost
everyone who knew him, and yet at once a trial and
a delight. Without exception, he was the most
absent-minded, dreamy man in all the service and

the stories of his absurdities were innumerable. It was Wayne who asked Miss Sanford to the german at Leavenworth and was found playing whist at the general's at ten o'clock. It was Wayne who kept dinner waiting for his arrival at the same general's two evenings later and was found by the orderly on his way to town to call at the rector's. It was Wayne who appeared at a garrison hop one evening in cavalry trousers and a black "claw-hammer." Wayne who implored his brother officers to keep him constantly reminded that it was Mrs. Burton now and not Mrs. Hallet, as he had known her for years, upon whom they were about to call, and who, after infinite mental labor, had well-nigh finished the interview without a break, only to dash it all by precipitating himself upon the new possessor of these charms and covering him with confusion by saying: "Hallet, old boy, hearty congratulations!" It was Wayne who immortalized himself at Royle Farrar's christening when, as was the hospitable way of the army, the officers and ladies were bidden to the ceremony and caudle, by wishing the proud young mother "many happy returns." It was Wayne who hung his *pince-nez* on his finger and was seen vainly struggling to set his seal ring on his aquiline nose, Wayne who gravely took his post as captain commanding battalion parade one evening with his helmet wrong side foremost and without his sabre. It was Wayne who, as senior officer present, had to toast the mother of the bride at a gorgeous wedding breakfast on a famous occasion and plumped down in this sea expectant of joyous applause only to be confounded by an awful silence, followed an instant later by an outburst of irresistible, uncontrollable, almost hysterical laughter, led by that blessed matron herself, for poor Wayne had wound up his halting, stumbling incoherencies with the astounding sentiment, "And I am sure I can wish the lovely bride no future more—more—delightful than that she may grow ever more—more beautiful than her beautiful mother—and—and—and m-more—more—er—virtuous."

No wonder Fenton, with all his liking for the man, felt appalled at the idea of having for second in command an officer just as apt to get things inextricably mixed on drill as he was in daily life. No one could ever count on Wayne's getting a thing straight. He was absurdity itself, as has been said, and yet so penitent, so distressed when any one became involved through his propensities as actually to win the affection of his very victims. He was the soul of truth and honor and knightly bravery. He woke up under fire to an enthusiasm that was grand. He was generous, tolerant, kind as kind could be, and, but for this one trait, as reliable and thorough a friend as man could ask. But what could a woman do with a lover like that? And, all of a sudden, Colonel Fenton had recalled the almost forgotten episode of Lou's early romance, and wondered what new complication might not now arise. Verily, it promised lively developments for old Fort Frayne, did this bright and bracing December, for, full a fortnight before the sacred anniversary, the Farrars were to arrive—the Farrars, with the gentle invalid's now devoted and inseparable companion, Helen Daunton, and bachelor Will had turned his whole little house into a bower for the women folks, while he, as he expressed it, "took a bunk in Billy's camp" next door. And Kitty was to journey with them, and Will was to have leave to go as far east as Omaha to meet them, for they were to travel to that point unescorted, Jack Ormsby, whom Will had looked upon as certain to be on hand, being still abroad, and probably no one but Ellis knew why. At the very time when, no longer an employe now, but his own master and a successful, driving, thriving business man, Jack Ormsby thought he had some chance of being looked upon as a suitable suitor, at least from the point of view of worldly goods, he found the lady of his devoted love nervous, embarrassed, and anything but kind. Ever since her father's death she had seemed to like him well. She had spoken to him of the prospect of his being with them when they went to the seashore the summer of Will's graduation, and he had intended to go and join them when they returned from the mountains, where they spent July, but first there was the week of camp with his beloved Seventh, and then, just as he was hoping to run down the Jersey shore for a lovely Sunday by her side, there came a summons to arms, and every man of Jack's company answered the call, and the Seventh, in fuller ranks even than it appeared in camp, went striding away to face the thugs and toughs and rioters of greater Gotham, and there was a week of trying, exasperating duty, and then a fortnight of invalidism as a result; for Sergeant Ormsby got an ugly gash as his share of the casualties from brickbats, and erysipelas set in. Not until late September did he see Ellis again, just after Will had gone, and then his doctor advised a sea voyage, for he could not understand his patient's unfavorable symptoms, and then followed a short sojourn abroad. Wounded sorely in his honest heart, Ormsby went, and when he returned to Gotham the Farrars were gone to Frayne.

## CHAPTER VI.

FOR several days Trooper Graice had been in the guardhouse. Absent from check roll call, from his quarters over night, and from reveille, he had turned up at sick call with a battered visage and all the ear-marks of a drunken row. He had been hauled up before a summary court, Major Wayne's first duty after reporting at the post, and received sentence of fine with a scowling face and no word of plea for clemency or promise of betterment. What cared he for fines? He could win more in a night than they could stop in a month. He was out again doing penance with the police cart about the post the day the available transportation came driving back from the railway with a load of precious freight, and Trooper Graice, splitting wood in the major's back yard, dropped the axe with a savage oath and turned a sickly yellow for one minute when he heard the busy tongues of the domestics next door proclaiming the arrival of Lieutenant Farrar's mother and sister. The sentry on duty over prisoners bade him stop his swearing and get to work again, for Captain Leale was passing rapidly up the walk in front, and Leale was a man whose eyes were ever about him and whose ears seemed never to lose a sound, but the captain merely glanced keenly at the soldier with his brace of malcontents and hurried on. It was he who opened the door of the stanch Concord and assisted the ladies to alight—Mrs. Farrar, Ellis, and a stranger, a gentlewoman, evidently, yet one who seemed to shrink from accepting aid or attention, and whose beautiful blue eyes ever followed Mrs. Farrar. "My friend, Mrs. Daunton, my older friend, Captain Leale, of whom you have heard so much," were the words in which these two were made known to each other, while Will and the servants were tumbling out bags and rugs and wraps, even as another and similar vehicle was being unloaded in front of the colonel's. Leale dined *en famille* at the Farrar's that evening, Will proudly presiding, as became the head of the house and the foot of the table, and beaming upon his mother, who sat facing him and rejoicing in his happiness. Very bright and cozy were the prettily-furnished quarters, for, with boundless enthusiasm, the ladies of the garrison had aided the young gentleman in making them attractive against the coming of the wife of their honored old colonel and his fair daughter, and right after dinner the visitors began to arrive, welcoming, army fashion, the old friends long endeared to all the other members of the garrison, men and women both; and, while Mrs. Farrar and Ellis had hosts of questions to ask and answer, Captain Leale found himself interested in entertaining the stranger, to whom all this blithe and cheery intercourse, all the cordial, hospitable, homelike army ways, were so odd and new. It was tattoo when he rose to leave, and met poor Will without—Will, who had twice gone up to Fenton's hoping to steal a word or two with Kitty, only to find that such portion of post society as was not gathered about his mother and sister was congregated at the colonel's—and then, fatigued by the journey, and showing plainly the effect of the excitement of her arrival, Mrs. Farrar was induced to seek her room, while Ellis remained in the parlor to chat with others still coming in to bid them welcome home, and not until long after ten were the lights turned down in No. 5, and not until even later did they gleam no longer from the big house on the edge of the bluff.

Whatever trepidation her friend had felt as to the effect of this return upon Mrs. Farrar, it was soon evident that it was groundless. Even the day on which she returned Lucretia's call and was received in the familiar rooms, once her own, she controlled admirably every sign of deep emotion. She seemed happy in being with Will, her idolized boy, and was never tired of watching him as he strode or rode away upon his various duties. An admirable soldier was Will, as all the officers admitted, devoted to his duties, full of snap, spirit, and enthusiasm, a fine drill instructor, and teacher of the non-commissioned officers' school, yet ever handicapped by that exuberant boyishness and by the fact that to save their souls the old soldiers and their families seemed to find it absolutely impossible at first to forget him as "Masther Will." Many of the old sergeants and their wives had come to pay their respects to Mrs. Farrar, and to talk, as she loved to hear them talk, of the colonel they loved so well and mourned so loyally. One and all they rejoiced in saying everything that soldier speech could frame in praise of their new lieutenant, their boy officer, their colonel's soldierly son, even while struggling against the impulse that ever possessed them to refer to him as Masther Will, or, as he hated still more to be called Master Willie. Little by little the army punctilio had prevailed, and most of the men had learned to refer to him respectfully as "the lieutenant," and to brace up and salute him with all the gravity and precision lavished on Fenton or Leale. Even the Irish trumpeter, with whom he had ridden races and played hookey, and gotten into all manner of mischief about the post in by-gone days—McQuirk, at first could not suppress the affable grin that overspread his freckled "mug" at sight of his whilom playmate as a full-fledged officer, bearing the president's commission. But Mac was savagely roasted by Sergeant Stein and other elders, and did his best to amend. It was Terry Rorke that was incorrigible. Time and again he broke the rules he laid down for himself, and, as Terry had been the household "striker" in the days when it was Captain Farrar, and they first lived at Frayne, he found especial favor in the gentle eyes of the widowed mother, and was encouraged to come and see her, for in all that crowded garrison he alone could recall her first-born, her handsome, daring, dashing Royle, when he was a boy of fourteen. To all the world he was an outcast, but the mother's heart had never yet been able to quench the flame of love that, burning like a beacon in her pure and prayerful heart, seemed ever beckoning to him to return. Yes, Terry Rorke had never forgotten "Masther Royle," and he alone could come and talk with her of the son, when all the rest of the world would only too gladly believe him dead and forgotten.

Thrice had Will, bustling into the hallway, as was his custom, without knock or ring, come suddenly upon his mother in conference with his old friend and hers, and Rorke had sprung to attention and stood like a statue and had striven to say "the lieutenant," and not "Masther Will," in his reference to his officer, but Will plainly showed he thought this frequent coming an imposition. "Mother, dear," said he one day, "if old Rorke is annoying you by coming so often, I can give him a gentle hint."

"Annoying? Why, Willy, dear, I love to talk with him. He was the most faithful, devoted creature we ever knew. All through your boyhood he watched over you, and he was almost the only friend your poor brother seemed to have."

"I appreciate all that, mother," said Will, tugging uneasily at his budding mustache, "at least, I try to, but all the same, you know, it isn't the thing. Of course, Rorke never presumes exactly, I understand that, and he only comes because you bid him, and then it is only to the back door and all that, but still it's the effect of the thing on the other men, and it's time he was learning to understand I'm decidedly no longer Master Will."

Ah! there was the rub. Two days before in the presence of Will's fair little lady love, had one of Rorke's lapses occurred, and the lieutenant had been Masther Willed and had reddened to the roots of his hair, seeing which, Kitty Ormsby, as determined a tease as ever lived, had taken to calling him "Masther Will" on her own account, and thunderstorms were imminent. There were other fellows, presentable fellows, in the garrison who were quick to feel the fascination of this charming little niece of Fenton's, and just the moment Will showed a disposition to sulk she showered smiles and sunshine on the first subaltern to appear, and thereby drove Will nearly rabid. Had his comrades ventured to dub him "Masther Will" there would have been a row. Had any of the other belles of the garrison so transgressed he would have turned his back upon her then and there, and so elegant a dancer and reputably wealthy a young officer was not to be offended, even before Kitty came. But Kit could and did torment him without mercy, and without fear of consequences, and, before she had been at Frayne a week, was making life a burden for the fellow who had prayed for her coming as its sweetest blessing.

And so, like the big outside world, the little community of Fort Frayne was living its life of hopes and fears, smiles and tears, love and jealousy and hate, while Kitty had speedily made herself completely at home, and was tyrannizing over everybody at the colonel's as well as over Will, and tormenting Aunt Lucretia by making eyes at Major Wayne, who never saw them, while Wayne had got to drifting over to his new colonel's almost every evening, just as twenty years before he infested the quarters of his old friend at Leavenworth, arousing once more all the fluttering of that maidenly heart, and, while Mrs. Farrar, rejoicing in the evidences of love and reverence in which her husband's name was held on every side, and in the honors Will was winning in his chosen profession, and even while she found comfort in the fact that one faithful old friend could recall her wayward boy as he was before dishonor and disgrace had swamped him, she would have been less than a woman had she been insensible to Fenton's repressed but unvarying devotion. Never intruding, rarely calling, he was gentleness, tenderness personified in every look and word. It was evident that all these years had never served to banish her image from his heart. Mourner though she may be, can woman live and not rejoice in knowing herself the object of so much love on every side? Widowed though even by a few brief months, does she resent it that the man lives who would be glad to teach her to forget? Life was not without romance, then, even to one who had lost her best beloved not three years gone by, and for whose first born she still shed bitter tears.

And to another sorrowing heart, to another gentle and stricken soul this wintry sojourn on the far frontier was bringing strange emotion. Day after day had Malcolm Leale been a visitor at the Farrar's. Time after time had he found himself seated in conversation with the woman whose beauty of face had thrilled him on the day of her coming, and whose sweet, subdued but gracious manner had charmed him more and more. First to notice his marked preference for Helen Daunton's society, was Ellis Farrar, who noted it with mixed emotions, with an interest of which she felt ashamed, and which she strove to repress. For months she had been struggling against herself or rather against some strange distemper that was not herself, for the pang of jealousy with which the girl had marked her mother's dependence upon Mrs. Daunton when Ellis returned from school, had deepened and taken root early that graduation summer. Her jealousy had been doubled by an event that occurred shortly after her brother's last parade. Mrs. Daunton had not gone with them to the Point,—Craney's was crowded in June, and Mrs. Farrar and Ellis would go nowhere else. For the week they would be there the services and administrations of a companion might, perhaps, be dispensed with, and Helen remained at the home. But the evening after graduation, when they were all seated in the parlor of their New York home, and Will was lounging at the window, delighted with the life and bustle of the city streets, and vaguely longing to get out and air his new "cits," yet not quite daring to go to Kitty's in them, because she declared she'd never speak to him except in uniform, and Mrs. Farrar was leaning back in her easy chair, fanning herself slowly, with her eyes and thoughts on her boy, even though Helen Daunton was reading aloud to her a long, interesting letter, there came a shout from Will that brought the blood to Ellis's face and drove it instantly from Helen Daunton's. Confronting each other as they sat, each saw and marked unerringly the effect upon the other of Will's jubilant announcement.

"Here's Jack Ormsby!"

Helen made her escape from the room that night before he entered, had never been in the parlor on the occasion of his brief visits thereafter, yet had seen him. Ellis never forgot how the evening of his last call, when his card came up to her she remembered that Mrs. Daunton was searching at that moment for a book in the library back of the parlor. She noted that Helen did not come at once away, as had been her wont. She lingered a few minutes over the last touches to her toilet, for, even though she was distrustful, jealous of her lover, she was woman enough to loose no chain that bound him. Her heart was fluttering and her face was pale as she stepped into her mother's room and stooped to kiss her forehead, and Mrs. Farrar looked at her wistfully, as though half ready to plead for the honest fellow she had grown to trust and honor. From Mrs. Daunton Ellis had wrung the admission that some years ago she had met and known Mr. Ormsby. From Jack Ormsby she had learned that he had never known a Mrs. Daunton in his life, and her heart was filled with misgivings as she went swiftly down the stairs, turned sharply at the bottom and in an instant stood at the library door. Just as she expected, there, peeping through the heavy meshes of the portiéres, invisible to any one in the parlor, yet able to study its occupants at will; there, clutching the silken folds in her beautiful white hands, with her face pallid and quivering with emotion, with great tears trickling down her cheeks, there, deaf to her coming, stood Helen Daunton, gazing spellbound at the man who had dared to approach her—Ellis Farrar—in the guise of a lover.

And Jack Ormsby had vowed that never until he met her had he known what it was to love a woman, vowed that his heart had been all her own ever since the winter of her father's death, ever since the bitter day he had to break to her the dreadful news, and yet, here before her eyes, was evidence that this woman could look upon him only in uncontrollable emotion. What folly to talk to her of never having seen Helen Daunton before! And even then an idea flashed upon her. Under some other name he must have known her, and, though he might deny the name he could not deny the woman. Jealous, doubly jealous, she sought to bring them face to face, and, entering the library, quickly turned on the electric light, and would have opened the portiére and bade him come to her there, but Helen Daunton turned and fled. All Ellis could afterwards extort from her was that in her unhappy past Jack Ormsby had befriended her—stood by her in the sorest need, and she would be grateful to him to her dying day.

"And yet," said Ellis, ever doubtful and suspicious, "you refused to see him, you shrank from him, and you would not meet him." But to this there was no reply.

That night was Ormsby's last call before he wen; abroad. And now, with Christmas near at hand, and her jealousy ever wrestling with her better nature, and the respect, even the regard she felt growing within her for this lovely woman who was so devoter to her mother, Ellis Farrar knew not what to think or say when she noticed the unerring signs of Malcolm Leale's growing love and of the evident pleasure despite all her gentle reserve, the woman felt in his society.

Even to Helen then the coming Christmastide was bringing that which women prize and welcome. Only Ellis in all the busy garrison found no comfort in the happy season, for the lover she longed and longed to see was by her own act banished from her life.

Day after day, as December wore on, and she noted the faint color that had come back to her mother's face, and even at this altitude, so far up toward the heights of the Rockies, her mother's heart gave no symptoms of distress, Ellis grew thankful for their coming, even when she heard that Ormsby had at last returned and was again in New York. Day by day, as she watched Mrs. Daunton, all her old fears and fancies seemed shamed to silence,—so gentle, so pure hearted, so full of grace and loving kindness she seemed. Sometimes it was even on Ellis's lips to speak an impetuous appeal, to throw herself on Helen's mercy, proclaim the injustice, the cruelty of her jealousy and her suspicions, but to implore her to tell the whole truth. They who watched soon saw that even in proportion as Mrs. Farrar grew in gladness and health and new lease of life from her coming to Frayne, it was Ellis who was drooping day by day. Yet, proud and plucky, and determined, the girl bore up against her sorrow, redoubled her devotion to her mother, strove hard to interest herself in Will's friends, was attention itself to Will's imperious sweetheart, who little dreamed what thought of brother Jack was really in that hidden heart, and was making heroic efforts to believe that all would yet come right, and perhaps Jack, too, when there came an odd adventure and renewed jealousy and dismay.

Only four days more to Christmas eve! All preparations were being made for a genuine old-fashioned Christmas ball for the officers and their families, and a Christmas gathering for the rank and file. The big assembly room of the post, over across the parade, near the old log guardhouse, was to be the scene of both. In loving memory of her husband, Mrs. Farrar had had a large portrait painted in New York which, beautifully framed, was to be hung in the assembly room and presented as a Christmas gift. Already detachments had been out in the Medicine Bow country, bringing in huge loads of evergreens and pines, and the men were hard at work with the decorations. Terry Rorke was in his glory, for, as major domo of the Farrars long years before, he had never let the year go by without rigging up the Christmas trees and the bright festoons of green. Even Crow

Knife, heathen though he was from Terry's Catholic point of view, seemed glad to take a hand, and the sounds of bustle and preparation were so like those that rang throughout the fort three years before that people feared the thoughts inspired by the sounds might only serve to sadden Mrs. Farrar. But, on the contrary, she seemed full of sweet and gracious interest, Ellis, hovering about her constantly, found her own fears allayed. Then came a typical December evening, clear and sharply cold, with abundant snow under foot and a cloudless sky over head. The sun had just gone down, after flinging his royal robes of red and purple about the distant mountains. The gun had answered with its thunderous salute, and the flag had come fluttering down. Far away up the cañon the whistle of the express seemed a farewell to Frayne as the train sped swiftly on its westward way. They had been out for a brisk walk, Will and Kitty, Ellis and Lieutenant Martin, her brother's chum, and several other young people of the post. There was good skating down the Platte, where the snow had been swept away, and many of the little party came back dangling their skates in their hands, and the keen air was joyous with laughter and merriment as they climbed the bluff under the colonel's piazza, and came in sight of Wayne and Miss Lucretia sedately spooning at the gate, and far out on the road to the station they caught sight of the Concord spinning postward with the mail, and Kitty was persuaded to come over a moment to No. 5, before dressing for dinner, and there at the gate the party had dispersed, Ellis and Kitty entering the house, where Will promised to join them in a little while, and there Mrs. Farrar had joyously welcomed them, and there they were seated, the four, while the servant came in to light the lamps and draw the curtains, and Kitty was chatting like a magpie and Ellis, listening with only languid interest, though her mother and Mrs. Daunton were full of smiles and sympathy when the Concord went bustling up the road without, and still the chat went on, for no one there was interested in the Eastern mail just then, and all of a sudden Will's voice was heard without, joyous, hearty, ringing, "By jove, old fellow! This is just too good for anything! No-no, come right in, right in here—mother'll be delighted—Kitty's here and Ellis." And the door opened and two big burly men in furs were ushered in, and Kitty gave a scream and precipitated herself upon the breast of the foremost and hugged and kissed and cried over him a bit, even as he was striving to shake hands with Mrs. Farrar, even as his eyes were searching for Ellis, even as he was brought face to face with a woman who had turned deathly white, who strove vainly to squeeze past him to the doorway, who bowed her head into her very breast as she sought first to avoid, then to hurriedly acknowledge the embarrassed, wondering, troubled salutation of the new arrival, for at the instant his eyes fell upon Helen the voice of Ellis fell upon his ear: "My mother's friend, Mr. Ormsby, Mrs. Daunton."

And all he could find words to say was simply her name, "Mrs.—Daunton?"

## CHAPTER VII.

THAT night Ellis Farrar was as wakeful as the sentries on their snow-bound posts. It was after midnight when she returned from progressive whist at the doctor's, and though luck had befriended her and kept Ormsby from her side, she had been able at times to watch him when chance brought him near Helen Daunton. She noted with jealous misery the appealing look in Helen's eyes when once they were for an instant left to themselves. She could have sworn she saw a little scrap of paper handed Ormsby at that moment and quickly stowed in his waistcoat pocket. But the rest of the evening, it was Leale who devoted himself to Helen, and Leale who escorted her home, and this fact Ellis saw was something that seemed to give Ormsby no concern whatever. Had she not been blinded by her suspicions, she would have seen that poor Jack had only one real source of trouble that night, and that was her own determined avoidance of him.

Wheels within wheels were whirring in the garrison, and Ellis Farrar was perplexed and worried more than she could say. Even placid, garrulous Aunt Lucretia was involved in the recent complications, for, within the past three days Major Wayne had been, on no less than three occasions, in close and confidential talk with Mrs. Farrar—a talk that on one occasion had left the gentle invalid in tears, and from which she had gone to her room, and was found there, on her knees, by Ellis, half an hour later. Explanation was denied her at the time. "Not now, Ellis, dear," was the pleading answer. "I cannot talk to-night. Later—after Christmas—I will tell you all about it," and with this the girl had perforce been content. Yet here again she mourned because, while refusing to tell her own daughter the reason of her tears and agitation, Mrs. Farrar had welcomed Helen to her room and found solace and comfort in her society.

This lovely, placid, moonlit night, as they came away from Dr. Gray's, old Fenton was plainly disappointed and Lucretia as plainly disturbed, when Mrs. Farrar quietly and possessively took the major's arm and led him, rather than leaned upon his strength, on the homeward way. Ellis, escorted by Mr. Martin—anything to get away from Ormsby this night—had hurried homeward and then to her room and out of sight, yet noted how long her mother detained the dreamy major at the gate, while Leale and Helen Daunton conversed in the little parlor. There had been a gathering at the Amorys' that same evening, a little dinner party, as Mrs. Amory expressed it, "in honor of those who are engaged and those who ought to be," and pretty Nell Willetts, a captain's daughter, and young Alton, of "K" troop, were the first named, and bewitching Kitty and Willy Farrar, one couple, at least, included in the second. Mrs. Amory was a charming hostess. She was of an old Kentucky family, had wealth and beauty to add to her charms, and had been wooed and won by her dashing husband long years before, when he was a boy lieutenant doing Ku-Klux duty in the distant South. She declared Will was a dark-eyed edition of just what her Frank was in the early seventies, and that Kitty Ormsby was "too like I was twenty yuhs ago fo' anything," and Mrs. Amory was so loyal a Kentuckian as never to forget even the sweet, soft dialect of the blue-grass country she so fondly loved. Ellis, to Mrs. Amory's relief, had begged off the dinner, saying she felt she ought not to be away from her mother's side just now, and frankly explaining to Mrs. Amory the apprehensions they all felt on that mother's account, especially at this trying time, so near the anniversary of the colonel's death.

With all the worldly goods with which she had endowed her husband twenty years gone by, pretty Mrs. Amory couldn't add to the government allowance of quarters, and her dining-room would only hold ten; so, as Ellis wasn't especially interested in any man at the post, despite the attentions paid her by Martin, Jessup, and other available fellows, Mrs. Amory wisely decided her to be deeply interested in somebody far away, and knew the man the moment Ormsby came. So Ormsby and Ellis, as has been said, went to whist and came away dissatisfied and unhappy, and Will and Kitty went to dinner and a dance at Amory's, and had a thrilling tiff, as a result of which she refused to ask him in when he took her home, even though Aunt Lucretia, hoping it was

Wayne, beamed upon them, though it was after midnight, from the doorway, and the colonel and Brother Jack, looming up through a cloud of cigar smoke, shouted to the suffering subaltern to come in. Wrathful and stung to the quick by Kitty's coquetry, Farrar turned indignantly away and sought his own quarters. The lights were still burning in the parlor, and he felt sure Leale and Mrs. Daunton were there, and he was too "miffed" to care to see them. A dim light was burning in his mother's room, and he believed her to have retired earlier, and so made it an excuse not to go for her good-night kiss and blessing. The door opened just as he was hurrying by, and Wayne came forth into the clear moonlight, and the boy wondered that he should be there, instead of at Fenton's, as usual, but he didn't wish to see or speak with him. He slammed the door of his chum's bachelor den as he bolted in, never noticing the bright light in Ellis's window, or dreaming that his sister sat there alone in her trouble, while he, with a lover's selfishness, saw nothing beyond his own. She heard his quick, impetuous step, however, and peeping through the curtains, saw the light pop up in the window opposite her own, and readily she divined that Kit had been tormenting him again. Verily, the Ormsbys seemed to exercise a baleful influence over the Farrars, and, with all her admiration for Kitty's better qualities and her remembrance of all Jack's goodness in the past, her heart was hardening against them, as it was, in jealous disquiet, against Helen

Daunton. At that moment she seemed to long for the companionship of her brother and wished he had come in. She heard her mother's gentle words mingling with Leale's deep baritone and Helen Daunton's low, soft voice, and again the feeling gained ground within her that she, to whom the mother clung with such love and dependence in the past, was herself in need of advice and sympathy, while that mother was finding other helpers now. Wayne had gone, the servants had retired and still the pleasant, friendly chat went on. It was all well enough so far as Malcolm Leale was concerned, but why should her mother so utterly confide in one of whom she knew so little and of whom Ellis was beginning to suspect so much? Why should Helen Daunton be allowed to accept those unmistakable attentions from Captain Leale even when her actions plainly showed that there had been some mysterious tie between her and Jack Ormsby in the past?

Then, again, came recollections of the note she had seen her slip in Ormsby's hand that night, and, longing for somebody, for something, to distract her thoughts from her own angry self, she tore aside the curtain and peered out on the night. There, not fifty feet away, was Will's window. There, to her right, the snow-covered expanse of the parade, terminated at the far southern side by the black bulk of the one-story barracks and the glistening lights of the guardhouse tower, where, on the lower floor, the sergeant of the guard and his corporals held their sway. Off to the left lay the rolling slopes, all white and peaceful in their fleecy mantles and glistening in the moonlight, save where seamed by pathways leading to the river and disfigured by the wooden fences of the back yards. Far across the Platte the red lights burned at Bunco Jim's and some unhallowed revelry was going on, for even at the distance the black shapes of horses could be seen tethered about the premises, and one or two more dim dots of pedestrians seemed slowly creeping across the stream. The post of the sentry on No. 5, at the north end of the garrison began back of the colonel's quarters on the point of the bluff, and continued on to the rear of the officers' quarters at the eastern front, where it joined that of No. 6, and even as Ellis gazed from her window, she could see that the two sentries, approaching each other, were apparently having some conference about the situation. There was a low fence separating their yard from that next door, and the snow was almost untrodden. There was no pathway around the bachelor den next door, as there was around No. 5. Post servants and orderlies thought nothing of utilizing the hallways of quarters occupied solely by subalterns. The back gate stood open, as she could see, and the board walk leading from it to the rear door was visible for half its length. That had been cleanly swept during the day, and, leading from the gate diagonally across the yard through the snow-drifts was the track of a man, and right at the rear corner of the bachelors' quarters, half concealed from the front and peering eagerly around, evidently studying the windows of the ground floor of the house occupied by the ladies of the Farrar family, was the man himself—a big, burly, heavily-bearded fellow, in the fur cap and rough great-coat of the cavalry.

Even as half alarmed, half annoyed, yet certainly fascinated, Ellis hung at the window, she heard the party breaking up down stairs, heard Leale wishing them a cordial good-night, and closing the door. The silent watcher heard that, too, for at the sound of the slam, without which few frontier-made doors were ever known to shut, the dark figure popped back and remained out of sight until Leale's soldierly form had gone striding away down the row. Then once more, slowly, cautiously, it came partially into view, steadily scrutinizing those lower windows.

Ellis was a soldier's daughter and no coward. She was conscious of an impulse to throw open the window and challenge the skulker, but even then her mother's slow step was heard ascending the stairs, and Helen's sweet voice, as the latter came on to assist her.

"Indeed, you need not, Helen," Ellis heard her say. "I have grown better and stronger with every hour, every hour. Even the sadness has been sweet. Even the old scenes have brought new comforts. Even the new sorrow has brought relief and peace."

"You have not yet told me of that, nor have you told Ellis."

"She shall know, and so shall you, dear friend, to-morrow. To-night I want to kneel—I want to be alone." Then Ellis heard her hand seeking the knob of the door. Hastily she turned to meet her mother at the threshold.

"You *are* better, Queen Mother, God be thanked. You have looked better every day. Will you—not come in, Mrs. Daunton?"

"Thank you, no; not just now. I will go and put out the lights and leave you two together for a while. I know Mrs. Farrar is pining for a peep at her soldier boy's window." Already Mrs. Farrar was moving thither, and Ellis darted eagerly forward.

"One moment, mother dear," she cried. "Let me draw the curtain—it—it doesn't work well."

And with the words she boldly threw aside the heavy curtain, and noisily, ostentatiously raised the sash. Just as she believed would be the case, the skulker, alarmed, sprang back behind the corner of the adjoining house and deep within its shadow. Will's light was still burning brightly, and in her clear, silvery voice his sister called his name. "He'll answer in a minute, mother. Don't come to the window yet," she added. Then again, "Willy, Willy."

And, as though answering her call, as though watchful, ready, eager to serve, even though unsummoned, another form came suddenly into sight on the moonlight walk in front, and a voice she well knew hailed from over the low picket fence: "Will has just gone up our way, Miss Farrar. I brought him a message a moment ago. Can I be of any service?" And there, of course, was Jack Ormsby.

"Thank you, no," was the answer, in cold constraint. "I had no idea he had gone and that you were there. Mother merely wished to speak with him a moment," and with that she meant to dismiss him, but her mother, pained by her tone of constraint and coldness towards one whom she herself so greatly liked, came to the window herself.

"Ellis, you are not even courteous to that honest gentleman," she said, in gentle reproach. "Mr. Ormsby," she added, in cordial tones, "are you going anywhere? Are you busy?"

"Entirely at your service, Mrs. Farrar. I found myself *de trop* at the house after the colonel took his nightcap and his leave, so I came out for a stroll. The major and Aunt Lou are trying to remember where they left off last night, and Kitty, I fancy, is bullying the lieutenant."

"Then would you mind coming in one minute? I have a little packet that I want Willy to find on his dressing table when he comes in."

"Mother," pleaded Ellis—almost breathlessly, "I—I—"

"Hush, dear. Mr. Ormsby will be glad, I know."

And Mr. Ormsby was only too glad. Promptly he came to the door. Promptly he was admitted by Mrs. Daunton, who stood with palpitating heart at the foot of the stairs.

"Thank you so much," was Mrs. Farrar's hail from the landing above. "It is in my room and will be ready in one minute, if you will kindly step into the parlor."

And then, as Mrs. Farrar passed on into her room, and with no audible word, Mrs. Daunton and Jack passed into the parlor, Ellis standing a moment confused, confounded, irresolute—turned back into her own room, and only by a miracle, recovered herself in time to prevent the loud slam of the door. Then, with heavily beating heart, she stood there in the middle of the floor listening for, yet not listening to, the sound of voices from below, the cold night air blowing in from the open casement unnoticed, even the mysterious prowler at the back of the house for the moment utterly forgotten.

And, meantime, turning quickly upon Ormsby, the moment she had led him within the parlor below, Helen Daunton, in low, trembling, yet determined accents, spoke hurriedly: "I had not hoped for this. At best I thought to see you no sooner than to-morrow night. You have read my note?"

Ormsby bowed coldly. "Yes, but no words can tell you my surprise at seeing you here in this household, and as the trusted companion of whom I have heard so much. Do they know you are—"

"They know nothing. They have made me welcome, and made life sweet to me again, after it was wrecked and ruined by their own flesh and blood. I meant—God forgive me—when first I came to them, lonely, destitute, that some time they should know, but from the first I grew to love her; from the day of my reception under her roof my heart went out to her as it has done to no other woman since my own blessed mother died, long years ago; and then, then

I learned of her precarious health, and I temporized, and now I love her as I love no other being on earth, and, knowing that she never heard of her son's marriage—for she has talked of him occasionally to me—I determined never to tell her of that or of the little one murdered by his brutality. I have hid it all—all. I hid from you, for you alone knew me under the name she bears and loves and honors. O, Mr. Ormsby! you were kindness, helpfulness itself to me in those bitter days. Can you not see how impossible it is for me to tell her now? Can you not help me to keep the hateful truth? See, she has been gaining here day after day. Don't let her know—don't make me tell her—perhaps kill her with the telling—that I am Royle Farrar's wife."

"Hush," he whispered, for in her excitement, her voice was rising, and he, listening nervously for a footfall that he knew and loved and thrilled at the sound of, heard Ellis pass rapidly along the narrow hall above, as though in answer to her mother's call. "Hush!" he repeated, "I must think of this. Tell me—has Miss Farrar at any time—in any way—seen that you have known me before?"

"She has, Mr. Ormsby, and I, with all the deep, deep gratitude I feel towards you, I have been unable to tell her the truth and explain what I cannot but know has made her suspicious of me, has hurt you in her estimation. Oh, what shall I do? what shall I do?" she cried, wringing her white hands in grief unutterable. "Keep my secret, I implore you, just twenty-four hours, until this sacred anniversary so fatal to, so dreaded by her, has passed away. Let no shock come to her at Christmas. Then if need be—"

"Hush!" he again warned, for Ellis was almost at the doorway. "I must see you to-morrow. Until then—" And then though the sweat was standing on his forehead, he turned with such composure as he could assume, with yearning and tenderness beaming in his frank, handsome face, to meet the proud girl whom he loved and in whose averted eyes he seemed to read his sentence. Never entering the room, but halting short at the doorway, she gave one quick glance at the woman, who, turning her back upon them, first seemingly busied herself at the curtains, and then moved on into the dining-room, which opened, army fashion, from the little parlor, and then was lost to sight.

"Mother desired me to hand you this, Mr. Ormsby," was all that Ellis said, and then coldly turned away.

"Ellis!" he cried in a low, eager, sorrowing tone, as he sprang after her. "Ellis—Ellis!"

But instantly, with uplifted hand, she turned, first as though to confront and warn him back, then as though commanding silence. "Hush—listen!" she said. "What is that?"

Something like an inarticulate, stifled, moaning cry came from the direction of the dining-room, and rushing thither, swiftly, noiselessly as he could, Ormsby was just in time to see Helen Daunton reeling back from the window and staggering toward the sofa.

## CHAPTER VIII.

'TWAS the day before Christmas, and Frayne was merry with the music of Christmas preparation. Ever since reveille the men had been busily at work, and while most of them were engaged in the decoration of their barracks, messrooms, and the little chapel, Terry Rorke, with a good sized squad, was still putting the finishing touches on the assembly hall. An odd thing had happened that morning. No one had ever known that fellow Graice to offer to do a stroke of work of any kind, especially where Rorke had anything to do with the matter, yet here he came, right after reveille, to tell that very man that if it was all the same to him, he'd take the place of Higgins, who had been put on guard, and would help at the assembly room.

"There's no whiskey to be had there, Graice, if that's what you want—and ye look more'n like it. Answer me this now. Where'd ye been whin ye came running in at wan o'clock this morning?"

"On a still hunt, Corporal," answered Graice, with a leer. "It's to keep away from whiskey this day I'm ready to work with you. I'm supernumerary of the guard."

"You were drinkin' last night, and you've had yer eye opener and brain clouder this morning—bad scran to ye! There's an internal revenue tax on the breath of you that would make an exciseman jealous. But

God be good to us! av it's to kape mischief away from the garrison this day, I'll go you. G'wan now, but whist—you've no liquor about you, Graice?"

"Devil a drop outside of my skin, Corporal."

"Then kape out of reach of it and out of the way of the ladies, lest the sight of yer ugly mug would throw them into fits. Gwan!" and Graice went. "Was it you, you black-throated devil, that gave that sweet lady her fright last night?" he continued reflectively. "There's no provin' it beyond the boot tracks, and they'd fit worse looking feet than yours— it's the wan mark of the gentleman that's left to ye. Yes, Sergeant, I'll kape me eye on him," he continued, in response to a suggestion from the senior non-commissioned officer of the troop, who came forth from the office at the moment. "The captain's hot about that business of last night, an' like as not there's the blackguard. Now, what on earth does he want to be playin' Peeping Tom about the officers' quarters?"

"No good, of course, but we can prove nothing, as you say, except that he was out of quarters and wasn't at Bunko Jim's after eleven o'clock. He was here and in bed when I inspected."

Very little was known about this episode. Mrs. Daunton had quickly revived under the ministration of Ellis and Mr. Ormsby, and, half laughing, half crying, had declared that just as she reached the window, the blind swung slowly back and the moonlight fell full on the head and shoulders of a man with a fur cap, black beard, and soldier's overcoat

She could describe no other features. He saw her at the same instant. Each recoiled, but in her excited, nervous state, it was too much of a shock. Ellis, who, at first, had been prone to attribute Helen's prostration to the interview with Ormsby, recalled the prowler she herself had seen and could not but corroborate Mrs. Daunton's story. Jack had rushed out, only to find boot tracks in the snow and an unfastened blind, but no other sign of a man. Mrs. Farrar was kept in total ignorance of the affair, and only Leale and Will at first were taken into the secret,. though the captain at once went to consult his trusty non-commissioned officers. All the same, though Helen laughed at her weakness when morning came, she and Ellis, parting for the night with but few words, and each feeling conscious of the gulf between them, passed a restless and disquieting night.

Just what mischief that fellow Graice was meditating puzzled not a little the honest pate of Terry Rorke. For a time the man worked busily, silently, lugging bundles of greens into the hall, and bare, stripped branches out. Once or twice in answer to chaffing remarks of the other men, he had retaliated. Once again, colliding with Crow Knife at the door, he had muttered an angry curse and bade the redskin keep out of his way unless he coveted trouble. The Indian's eyes flashed vengefully, but he spoke no word. It was just after guard mounting that Graice had offered his services, when, as supernumerary, he really did not have to work at all, and was not properly detailable for any such fatigue duty. By ten o'clock, however, it was apparent to more than one present that he was drinking more liquor, and had it concealed, probably, somewhere about the premises or in his overcoat. Rorke warned him and got a sullen reply. Not a minute after, although strict orders had been given against smoking, because of the flimsy nature of the structure and the large quantity of inflammable material scattered about, he precipitated an excitement. Right in the entrance of the hall a big square box had just been placed by two of the men, and Crow Knife was carefully removing the lid, when Graice, lurching in from the dressing room with a bundle of greens, stumbled against the edge of the case, and dropping his burden with a savage curse, he drew back his heavily-booted foot as though to let drive a furious kick.

Instantly the Indian interposed. "Don't kick!" he said. "Hold your hoof there!" shouted Rorke, and others of the men joined in their cry of warning. Wonderingly he looked about him on the quickly-gathered group, swaying a bit unsteadily even now.

"Why not?" he scowlingly, sullenly, thickly asked. "What harm's there kicking a rattlebox that's almost broken my shin? What's the matter with you fellows, anyhow?"

"It isn't the box, you goneril, it's what's inside of it! That's Col. Farrar's picture—God's praise to him for the finest soldier that iver rode at the head of the Twelfth."

"That Col. Farrar's picture?" muttered the man, in a strange, half awed, half defiant manner. "Well, I swear, that's—that's queer." And then, in some odd, nervous abstraction, he whipped out a cigar, and the next thing they knew, had lighted it at the stove and tossed the flaming paper among the sweepings on the floor. Instantly, there was a rush, a trampling of feet, and just as Rorke wrathfully had collared the stupefied man, Lieut. Farrar burst in upon the scene, stamping out the few remaining sparks and then turning angrily upon the group.

"Who dropped that fire? Who, I say?" he repeated, for, in soldier silence, the men had stood to attention, but, true to soldier ethics, would tell no tales. "Don't let that happen again, Corporal," he went on sternly. "You know well enough what a fire would mean hereabouts with the cannon powder stored in the tower yonder. Remember the orders —the guardhouse for the first man, fooling with fire. Go on with your work." And then, as the men turned silently away and Terry stood there looking abashed and troubled at the implied rebuke, Will sought to soften the effect. "Why, you're doing great work here, Corporal; the old place is wearing Christmas dress and no mistake."

"It is; Masther Will," said Rorke, delightedly.

"Masther Will!" repeated Farrar, indignantly. "On my soul, Rorke, you—"

"I beg the lieutenant's pardon," said Terry, all contrition and soldierly respect. "But I've known him such a few weeks as lieutenant and so many and many a long year as Masther Will—"

"That'll do, Corporal. Have the picture in its place as soon as you can. Mother will be over here to look at it."

"Yes, Mas—yes, Sor."

And again, as Will turned angrily to rebuke the poor fellow, there was a gathering of the men at the window looking out upon the parade, and something was said about a lady slipping on the ice, which carried Will away like a shot. Two strides took him to the door, and one glance sent him rushing to the rescue. It was Miss Ormsby.

And then, while some of the men went on with their work, others seemed to hang about Graice, who was oddly fascinated by the box and cast furtive glances at it, while Crow Knife, under Rorke's direction, was quietly unpacking it. Again had Graice wandered unsteadily over by the stove, and stood there, sullenly kicking at it until one of the men bade him quit, or he'd start a fire in spite of them. "You'll have us all in blazes before our time," were the soldier's words.

"Not I. Fire's my friend," answered Graice, in a surly tone.

"An' likely to give you a long and warm welcome if you carry to purgatory the spirit you so sweetly manifest here. How yer friend?" retorted Rorke.

"I mean it saved my life a year ago in Mexico. I saw a girl once too often for her lover's good—hot-headed cur! He would have it and got it—in the heart— and I got in quod and our Consul couldn't help me. I am not the kind of citizen the United States hinders a foreign Government from sending to kingdom come, and I was mighty nigh getting there."

"And ye didn't," said Terry highly interested. "The dishpensations of hiven are past findin' out."

"Fire's stood my friend, I say. I had my pipe— greasers ain't the damned martinets you have here— and a spark went into the straw. It blazed in an instant. There was hell to pay, with the guard and greasers and prisoners running every which way. The prison had a little tower like that yonder," said he, pointing to the wooden structure above the old log guardhouse. "I saw my chance in the confusion and ran for it. It was stone and never took fire, and I got safely away at night and vamoosed the country, and read afterward how the flames had devoured the ruffianly murderer Roy—" and here he caught himself, with sudden gulp, seeing Rorke's suspicious eyes upon him."

"Eh, Graice, Roy, you were saying."

"Murderer, roisterer, and rascal, Tom Graice," he went on. "So I've nothing to fear from fire."

Rorke eyed him long and distrustfully, grunting audible comment on the story, to which some of the men had listened in absorbed interest, while others were busily removing the picture and setting it in place upon the wall. Then, as it was fairly hung, Crow Knife stepped back across the room, his eyes reverently fixed upon the fine, soldierly face. Graice, meantime, after a hurried glance about him, had drawn a flask from his vest pocket, and had lifted it to his lips when Rorke grabbed it.

"I thought so, ye mad-brained gabbler! You'll be drunk before the day's half over. Get up and look at the picture, man. It's looking at you straight and stern."

"Who—who's looking at me? What damned rot are you talking?" shuddered Graice.

"The colonel is, and as if he didn't relish the sight—small blame to him."

"It's a saying of my people," said Crow, in his slow solemn tone, "Whom the eyes of the dead call must rise and follow."

"You croaking—" hissed Graice, leaping to his feet and rushing at the Indian, but Rorke threw himself between them.

"Play wid fire when ye may, man, but niver wid a tame tiger. Hush, now. Go out this door and cool that crazy head of yours. Here come the ladies."

Instantly the excited group scattered, the men resuming their work as though at no time thought of crime or quarrel had entered there, but Rorke's heart was thumping hard as he went to his station. First to enter were Captain Leale and Mrs. Daunton, though the blithe voices and cheery laughter of the others could be heard without. Evidently there was fun at Kitty's expense, and Leale had seized the opportunity to draw Helen to one side. They were talking earnestly as they entered.

"It seems providential that Will's first station should bring his mother back to the old home. Here and now at least she should be safe from all shock, especially with your care to guard her, Mrs. Daunton. She said to me only yesterday: 'Helen came to me only a little over a year ago, but I think I have needed her for years. She is dear to me, almost as my own daughter.'"

"God bless her for those words," said Helen, deeply moved. "I came to her as a dependent, but she has taught me a new definition of motherhood."

"Motherhood has its sorrowful meaning for Mrs. Farrar," said Leale, gravely, his handsome, dark eyes fixed upon her face. "Has she never spoken to you about Royle, her eldest son?"

"She has sometimes mentioned him," said Helen, with great constraint. "But she can hardly bear to speak of him, and I know the bitter sorrow he brought to every one who loved him, but," she added, quickly, as though eager to change the subject, "how cozy and warm and Christmasy it looks and smells! I shall have another new definition—what Christmas means. We learn many definitions, do we not, as life goes on, and sometimes fate is good to us and lets us learn the happiest last."

"And you have learned a sad one of Christmas?"

"I? A very sad one. My own baby died in my arms on Christmas Eve."

Leale bent earnestly towards the sad, sweet face, a deep emotion in his own, but at the moment Ellis entered followed closely by Ormsby. She bowed in evident constraint at sight of the couple already there, and looked as though she would gladly have turned about again. After her came Will and Kitty, and other young people of the post, all eager and intent on inspecting the preparations being made, all full of compliment to Rorke for the success attending his labors, all full of admiration of the portrait which they grouped about and admired, while Ellis hung her father's sabre underneath. And then once again the whole party, chatting merrily, went drifting out into the crisp air and glorious sunshine, leaving glowering after them from the doorway of the little room that opened off the main hall the ill-favored, ill-liked soldier Graice.

Two minutes later, and no one could explain how it started, or what was its exciting cause, with hardly a spoken word or premonitory symptom, two men were clinched in furious struggle—one heavy, burly, powerful, and gifted with almost demoniac strength, had hurled the other down. That other, lithe, sinewy, panther-like in every motion, writhed from underneath his huge antagonist, and had sprung to his feet, while the first, more slowly heaved himself upward, and then, like a maddened bull, dashed at his foe. Springing lightly to one side, Crow Knife, for it was he, whipped from its sheath a glittering blade, and poised it high in air, and Graice, even in his blind fury, saw and hesitated. There was a rush of the workmen to the spot, but Captain Leale was first of all. Clear and cold and stern his voice was heard: "Drop that knife! drop that knife, I say!" and slowly, reluctantly, though his eyes were blazing with hate and rage, the Indian turned towards the man he had learned to trust, to honor, and to obey, and the knife fell clattering to the floor. Graice made a lunge as though to grab it, and Rorke's ready foot tripped and felled him. Then, with both hands, the Irishman grabbed him by the collar and dragged him, dazed and scowling, to his feet.

"There are ladies coming, sir," was the low-murmured warning of one of the men.

"Take that man out and cool him off," said Leale, still calmly to the corporal. "I'll hear the story later. Quiet now one and all," he added, as the group dispersed. "It is Mrs. Farrar."

They met at the very doorway, the fair, radiant woman, closely followed by her daughter, the dazed, hulking soldier, led or rather driven forth by Corporal Rorke, and instantly a change, swift and fearsome, shot across the sweet, pathetic face. One glance was all, and then, pale as death, she tottered feebly forward. Ellis sprang to her side in sudden alarm. "Mother, dearest, what is wrong? How you tremble!"

For a moment she could not speak. "It is folly, it is weakness!" she faltered. "But that face—that dreadful face! The look in those eyes--the awful glitter that only liquor kindles. I have not seen that look since—Oh, whenever I see it I say, God pity, pity his mother."

And then Helen Daunton came hastily in and helped to lead the agitated woman to a seat, and there she knelt beside her and soothed and comforted and cooed to her as women croon over a tired child, and Leale hovered helpfully about, grave, strong, and gentle, and it was on his arm she leaned, with Helen at her side, when finally she stood to look at her husband's portrait. And little by little she grew calm and the fluttering at her heart ceased to distress her, and Ellis, turning reluctantly away at the bidding of her garrison friends, left her mother to the ministrations of the woman whom with every hour, more and more, she learned to look upon as a rival; and then, saying that he would call for them in a few minutes with his sleigh, believing that a short drive in the exhilarating air would be of benefit, Leale, too, left them, and Mrs. Farrar and Helen Daunton were practically alone. Mess call sounding cheerily had called the men to their noonday meal.

The eyes of the elder woman had followed the tall, soldierly form of Leale as he left the room, and then, tenderly, questioningly, almost entreatingly, turned upon Helen.

"I love him almost as I do my own son, Helen. My husband died in his arms. Surely you must realize that his great heart has belonged to you ever since he first set eyes on your bonny face."

Mrs. Daunton almost started to her feet.

"Oh, not that! Surely, not that! He is my good, true friend," she cried.

"Not the less your friend because all your lover, Helen."

"Oh, never my lover! I have no right—I am not free!"

"Listen to me, Helen," pleaded her friend. "Shall one mistake blight a lifetime? I know your short marriage experience was a cruel one."

"It was—heaven knows it was," assented Helen, shuddering.

"Then do not make youth's mistake, dear," continued Mrs. Farrar, "and think the story ended because one chapter is closed. I thought my story ended when they brought me home my dead soldier. I've prayed many a time my story might end in the years my first-born was an outcast. Helen, I have hardly spoken to you of my eldest boy, but I can tell you now that, standing here to-night, I realize how out of sorrow peace has come to me. Death, which took away my husband, gave me back my son."

"Death!" cried Helen. "Royle Farrar is not—dead?"

"Helen, how strangely you speak. He has been dead a year, though only recently did they give me all the cruel facts. Major Wayne learned them from the Consul in Mexico."

In uncontrollable agitation Helen Daunton had turned away. "Royle Farrar dead!" she gasped. "Then I—Oh, God be thanked!"

The tears were blinding Mrs. Farrar, and for a moment she saw nothing of Helen's agitation. The bells of Leale's sleigh came trilling merrily up the road without. Hastily she dashed away the pearly drops, and smiling fondly drew her shrinking friend to her embrace. "Helen, dear, there is a new look in your face," she whispered.

"It is because I rejoice in my soul that your heart is at rest. It is because it is Christmas—Christmas, the time of burdens dropped, of old sorrows healed, of new births and sweet beginnings. Dear, the Christmas chimes are pealing in my heart. It is the first real Christmas I have known in years." And so, her arms twining about her friend, she led her forth into the radiant day, with all its sunshine beaming in her face. One minute only had they gone when, crouching from the dressing room at one side, his face bloated and distorted, the soldier Graice sped swiftly across the floor and stopped to peek through the eastern window. Suddenly, back he sprang and stood swaying at the door of the anteroom, as Helen Daunton hurriedly returned. Coming from the dazzling glare of the sun without into the dimly-lighted room, she almost collided with the hulking figure before seeing it at all.

"Mrs. Farrar has left her cloak," she faltered, "will you kindly move from the way?"

"You thought I *had* moved from your way," was the thick, husky answer, "but you're mistaken, my dear."

Back she started as though stung, an awful terror in her staring eyes, her blanching face.

"You—Royle Farrar—and here!" she gasped. "You—Royle Farrar—Oh, my gracious God!"

## CHAPTER IX.

ALARMED at Mrs. Daunton's failure to rejoin them, Leale had tossed the reins to his orderly, and, leaving Mrs. Farrar seated in the sleigh, hurried into the building in search of her. It was a prostrate, senseless form he found close to the inner door, and only after a deal of trouble did she revive. Greatly alarmed, Mrs. Farrar had caused her to be driven straight home, and there the doctor came, and Ellis, and ministering angels without stint, and questioners without number, but meantime, Leale, with wrathful face, had gone to his troop quarters and summoned his first sergeant. Graice had not been with the men at dinner, was that worthy's report. He was at the post exchange eating sandwiches and drinking beer at that moment, and Leale sent for him.

Something had tended to sober the man, for he came into the captain's presence, looking sullen, but self-possessed. "I warned you, after that affray with Crow Knife," said Leale, "that you were to keep out of temptation and mischief until you were sober enough to understand what I had to say to you. Where were you between dinner call and 12:30?"

"Walking off my heat, sir, as the captain directed."

Leale stood closely scanning the swollen face of the soldier. He was always grave and deliberate in dealing with the malcontents of his command, rarely speaking in anger and never in a tone indicative of irritation. Under the captain's calm, steadfast scrutiny Graice plainly winced. His bloodshot eyes wandered restlessly about and his fingers closed and unclosed nervously.

"You have made but an ill name for yourself thus far, my man," said Leale, "and this day's work has not added to your credit. What started the trouble with Crow Knife?"

"He struck me," was the surly answer.

"You have been drinking liquor to-day, Graice, and it is said of you throughout the whole troop that when drinking you are ugly and ill-tempered. I have known Crow Knife a long time and never knew him to be in trouble before. You are the first man of this command to quarrel with him. Let it be the last time. He bears a good name; you have made a bad one. Another thing: you were working there at the hall this morning under Corporal Rorke. What became of you when the other men left and went to dinner?"

"I—was thirsty—and went for a drink," was the shifty answer.

"Went where? You were not then at the post exchange."

The soldier turned redder, if possible, hitched uneasily, the bloodshot eyes still wandering warily about, as though eager for any light other than that which burned in the clear, stern gaze of his captain. "I went for a drink," he repeated, "and I'm not bound to say where, and so get some one else in trouble. I'm not without friends here, even if I haven't them among my officers, and I can be true to those who are true to me."

"Such talk is buncombe, Graice," said Leale, coolly, "and you know it. You will do better to keep clear of friends who give you liquor. You are sober enough to appreciate now what you hear and what you say. Keep clear of it, I warn you, or it will be your undoing. Are you not for guard?"

"I am, sir, and ready to take my turn when needed, but I can take no such affront as that redskin slung in my teeth."

"Enough on that score! I'll hear your story to-morrow, when you're both cooled down. Now, go to your quarters, and for the rest of this day keep away from three things—Crow Knife, liquor, and—understand me—the assembly hall."

The sullen eyes glowed with new anger. The man had been drinking just enough to be reckless. "I'd like to know why I'm not considered fit to work, at least," he muttered.

"You are not fit to be seen by the eyes of gently-nurtured women, Graice. Your face is bloated, your eyes inflamed, your whole carriage tells of the havoc liquor plays. You may as well know that the sight of you was a shock to our guest Mrs. Farrar, and I suspect that you could tell what it was that so startled Mrs. Daunton."

"I don't know any such—" began the soldier in the same surly tone, but Leale uplifted his hand.

"The less you say when you've been drinking, my man, the less you're likely to fall into further trouble. You go no more to the assembly room to-day, because I forbid. Do you understand?

"I've got rights to go there—ay, or, where my betters cannot go—" burst in Graice in sudden fury, but the instant his eyes met those of his captain the words died on his lips, and the red lids drooped.

"You have said more than enough, sir," sternly answered Leale. Then, turning sharply to a little knot of non-commissioned officers who, at the barrack steps, were curiously watching the scene, he called, "Sergeant Roe!" and a young soldier in natty uniform came springing forward, and, halting close at hand, stood at the salute.

"I leave this man in your charge. He is for guard, I believe. Set him to work at his kit, and see that he is in proper trim—in every way—for to-morrow."

"He may be needed to-day, sir. He's supernumerary."

"Indeed! Worse than I thought, Graice," said Leale, calmly. "You will be wise to take a cool bath and a nap then. At all events, see that he does not leave the barracks this afternoon, sergeant."

"I will, sir. Come on, Graice."

And conscious that he had been indeed playing with fire, yet raging over the sense of his en-

forced submission, the half-drunken fellow turned
and followed his young superior.

Meantime there had been anxiety and dismay at
the Farrars'. Helen had speedily been restored to
consciousness, only to be overcome by a fit of hysterical weeping, succeeded by a nervous attack that defied the efforts of her fondest friends. Mrs. Farrar
had, of course, sent for the doctor, but Helen insisted that his presence was utterly unnecessary. She
begged to be left alone. She declared the attack to
be no new thing. She had suffered just in the same
way before, though not for two or three years. She
seemed eager to rid herself of all attendants. In
truth, her one longing was to be allowed to think
uninterruptedly. Even at night this might have been
difficult. By day, with sympathetic inquirers coming every few minutes to her door, and with her
gentle friend sitting at her bedside, she found it impossible. If she closed her eyes, that leering, half-drunken, swollen, triumphant face came to torment
and distract her. If she opened them, it was only to
find sweet, anxious features bending over her, full of
tenderness, sympathy, and unspoken inquiry. Do
what she could to allay it, Helen Daunton saw plainly
that Marjorie Farrar more than suspected that there
was some exciting cause for that sudden prostration.
In utter helplessness she lay striving to plan, striving to see a way out of this new and most appalling
complication. That the man who had wrecked her
life should return, as it were, from the grave was in
itself horrible enough, but that he should reappear

in the flesh here, at Frayne, where his presence was a menace to the peace of so many who were dear to her, and to the very life, perhaps, of the gentle invalid who was nearest of all, was torment indeed. For some hours she lay there facing her fate, shutting out all thought of her newborn hope and joy thus summarily blasted, seeing only—thinking only— of the peril that involved her friend. The short winter day wore on. The spirits of the younger members of the social circle seemed undimmed, for, as stable call was sounding, she could hear merry chat and laughter again in the parlor below stairs. Ellis alone seemed to share with her mother the anxiety or uneasiness which followed the events of the morning. She had refused to join the little party that had gone up, as they expressed it, "to call on Kitty." She had refused partly from a feeling of indisposition to any gayety, partly from a sisterly sympathy for Will, who, she felt well assured, longed for an uninterrupted half hour with his capricious lady love, and partly because he shrank from appearing in the colonel's parlor, thereby possibly giving Ormsby half a reason to think she sought him. Evidently the young people had had small mercy on Will. Evidently Kitty had lent herself not unwillingly to the fun at his expense, for, after biting savagely at his finger nails and tugging furiously at his mustache, the boy had pitched angrily out of the colonel's house and come home for comfort, and thither had they followed him, two or three happier couples, and, catching him in the parlor, all unconscious of Mrs.

Daunton's seclusion aloft, were as bent on coaxing him to return with them as he, with assumption of lordly indifference, was determined to make it appear that he had no such desire or intention. He carried his point, too. He knew well enough that Kit's complicity in the plot was for the express purpose of teasing him. He couldn't afford to let them see he was indignant at her or at them, neither could he afford to let her see that he was not justly offended. And right in the midst of all the babel of protest and appeal and laughter the door bell rang, and at the head of the stairs, just as stable call was sounding, listening ears heard the unctuous, jovial tones of Corporal Rorke inquiring for Capt. Leale.

Then Will's voice responded, and Will was very distant and dignified. "Captain Leale is not here, corporal. Have you been to his quarters?"

"Sure, I went there furst, sorr, an' they told me he was here, if anywhere. Thin, bedad, he's nowhere."

"He's gone down to the stables already, perhaps," said Farrar, "and you'll find him there. Yonder goes the call now."

"I know, mast—I know, sorr, but the throuble's right here, sorr. Higgins has been took ill on guard. He was right out here on No. 5, sorr, back of the quarters, and that spalpeen Graice is supernumerary, an' they've sint for him, and the first sergeant's afraid, sorr."

"What of?"

"Graice had been drinking this morning. He's sober enough now, sorr, but he's nervous, wild-like, excited, tramping up and down the barrack flure like a caged hyena, sorr."

"Then tramping up and down the sentry post will be just the thing for him. It'll cool him off. Put him on."

"Very well, sorr. Just as the loot'nant says. I'll tell the sergeant at once.

Five minutes later the parlor was deserted and all was silence below. Now, at least, Helen Daunton could close her eyes and plan and think. He was to be placed on guard. He would be on post right out here on the bluff. Then what was to prevent her slipping out in the dusk of the evening when all the others had gone over to the assembly hall, speaking with him, pleading with him, imploring him to go away anywhere—anywhere where he would not again in drunken mood endanger that poor mother's life by the sudden shock of his presence. She would agree to anything, she would follow him, slave for him, starve with him, be his wife or his handmaid—anything to get him away—far away from the sunshine, the smiles, the hopes and joys and blessings that had been hers at old Fort Frayne. One other plan. She had but little money, and in their flight much might be needed. She must obtain it, for that drink-sodden wretch would surely have none. Go she must and would. Go he must and should, for any day, before the whole garrison—oh, shame unutterable! he might take the notion boldly to throw off all disguise and claim her as his wife. Possibly with money she might bribe him to take kindly to her proposition and agree. Then before he could spend what she had given him, she could escape, return to the East, and somewhere, anywhere hide her head from him, from friends, from the world, and all. Home she had none. That went when her father died, lonely and heartbroken, two years before.

And in all that garrison to whom could she appeal—upon whom could she call? One man there was who, well she knew, would open his hand as he had his heart, and its uttermost treasure could be hers for the mere asking, and that man of all others, was the one who she prayed might never know the miserable truth that this was Royle Farrar—that she was Royle Farrar's wife.

Another there was, generous, helpful and kind, who, did he but learn the identity of the man slinking here under that disguise given by years of drink and debauchery, would aid her to his uttermost farthing, aid her as he had before out of pity and compassion, aid her now with eager hand through thought of the shame that would come to the girl he loved, the shock that might be in store for her beloved mother. There was the man—Jack Ormsby! But how to see him—and when and where! Not a moment must be lost, because, now that Royle's presence was known to her, his wife, any moment might bring on the further catastrophe. She had never known him to stop until sodden and stupefied.

Drink, drink, drink; in some form he would find the poison and gulp it down, waxing crazed and nervous if it were withheld from him, turning mad and reckless if it were given. Drink he surely would all through this blessed Christmas eve, and at any hour, any moment on the morrow she might expect him to appear before them all, in the midst of their joyous Christmas gathering, in drunken exultation, demanding his seat at his wife's side at his mother's board. What that would mean to that gentle mother whose very life seemed now hanging by a thread, God alone could say.

And here she lay, hesitant, impotent, cowardly—when the lives and happiness of those dearest to her were at stake, shrinking even now from an appeal to Ormsby, who alone in all the garrison, probably, was competent to advise and help, and Ormsby had already suffered and suffered much on her account. In the loyal observance of his promise he had brought himself under the ban of suspicion, and with half an eye Helen could see that Ellis looked upon their relation with utter distrust. Great heaven! was she to be a curse to every one who had been kind to her? The thought was intolerable.

Helen Daunton amazed her friend by springing from her bed and throwing up the window sash. "Air, air!" she moaned. "I feel as though I were suffocating," and leaning far out into the wintry twilight, bathing her aching head in the cold, sparkling air, she gazed wildly northward toward the bluff. Aye, muffled in the heavy canvas overcoat, the fur cap down about the bloated, bearded face, slouching along the sentry post was the form she dreaded—hated to see, yet sought with burning eyes. As she gazed he saw and stood and leering over the intervening drifts of spotless snow, kissed his fur-gloved paw and tossed his hand in half defiant, half derisive, all insulting salutation.

"Mrs. Farrar," she cried, in utter desperation, turning madly away from the hateful sight. "I—I must get into the open air awhile. You won't mind, dear. I must walk—walk, run, rush in the cold. No, don't come, and pray let Ellis keep with you. In ten—twenty minutes at most, I'll return."

"Ah, Helen, wait until Willy—until Malcolm Leale returns from the stables. See, they're coming now. They will walk with you."

"Oh, no, no, no! Do you not see? I must be alone. I cannot talk with any one. Let me go," she cried. Then before either the mother could interpose or Ellis, who came hurrying into the room, could urge one word, she had seized a heavy wrap and gone almost bounding down the stairs.

At the threshold she recoiled, for there, his honest face full of eagerness as the door flew open, stood Jack Ormsby. "I—I was just about to ring," he faltered, "and inquire after you—and for—Miss Farrar. You really startled me."

And up aloft they heard—Ellis heard—the eager, low-toned, almost breathless answer. "Oh, Mr. Ormsby. It was you I sought. Come—right in here."

And drawing him into the parlor she closed the door, reckless now of anything Ellis might suspect, thinking only of the peril that menaced one and all. Perhaps Jack Ormsby's longing eyes caught one fleeting glimpse of feminine drapery at the head of the little staircase. Perhaps his own wrongs and woes had overmastered him. Perhaps he thought that already he had been too heavily involved, all on account of this fair sufferer and suppliant, but certain it is he followed hesitant, and that it was with a far from reassuring face he confronted his captor.

"Mr. Ormsby," she burst forth. "How much money would you give, at once, this day, to rid this post of the greatest shame and misery that could be brought upon Ellis and her mother?"

"I can't imagine what you mean," was the uncertain reply.

"I mean that Royle Farrar is here—in this garrison—a private soldier in Capt. Leale's troop."

"Mrs. Daunton! Are you mad?"

"Mad? My heaven, I well might be! He came before me this noon, with her, with his mother, not twenty steps away, and taunted me and threatened them. Oh, God, he means it—he means to make himself known to them and claim their kinship in the way to shame them most, and the shock will kill her, kill her! There is only one earthly way. He will go for money."

"He can't, if he's a soldier. It's desertion. It's—why, they follow them, capture them and it means state prison or something for years."

"I know nothing of that—I know I'm only a helpless, distracted woman, but drink and money are the two things he worships. For them he will risk anything. I can see him this night. He is this moment on post, out here on the bluff. You know him. It's the man they call Tom Graice."

Ormsby's hat fell from his hand. "My heaven! That man here again?"

"Here, here, and I have known it only for a few hours. See what I am suffering. Do you not see what it means if Royle Farrar makes himself known? —and he is capable of anything. Shame to Will, shame to Ellis, heartbreak—death perhaps—to Mrs. Farrar. Do you not see you must help me get him away from here? You must for all their sakes and— keep his secret and mine."

"It is my secret, too, Mrs. Farrar," said poor Jack, rallying to the rescue now that danger threatened. "I will do whatever you wish, whatever you say. You shall have whatever money I have here and more can follow. You're a brave woman. Forgive me that I doubted you."

"Oh, never think of that now. Only keep my secret yet a little, and let me see you before ten to-night. That's the hour that relief goes on again. I've watched them so often. And—and all the money you think—even a hundred—two hundred dollars. Oh, God bless you for the help you give me! Now, I know you wish to see her, and I must get into the open air awhile."

Calling the maid servant, she bade her take Mr. Ormsby's card to Miss Farrar, then hastened from the house.

But the answer brought to honest Jack—poor fellow—was that Miss Farrar begged to be excused.

## CHAPTER X.

A SNOW-CLOUD was hanging over Fort Frayne that lovely Christmas Eve, and the moon shone down through a filmy veil of lace and cast black shadows on the dazzling surface. Everywhere about the post lights were twinkling in the quarters, and sounds of soldier merriment and revelry came from the barracks. Over at the assembly room Rorke and his party were still busily at work hanging festoons of green and completing the decorations for the morrow, while in the several households among the officers dinner parties or similar entertainments called together under one roof or another almost all the families, as well as the bachelors of the garrison. The children were rejoicing in their great Christmas tree at the chapel. The colonel had bidden them all to his big house for a Santa Claus party after the public ceremony of the post Sunday school, and Aunt Lucretia, a garrulous, flighty, feather-brained fairy of forty summers or more, was doing her best to get the little gifts in proper order against their coming, being aided in her perplexities and complications by the dreamy, but devoted, Wayne. Kitty was dining at the Farwells'—a temporary truce having been patched up between her and Will about sunset—and Ellis, too, very, very much against her wish, was one of this party. Ormsby was, of course, bidden, and had been placed next the lady of his love, but averted eyes and monosyllabic answers were the only returns of his devotion. Grieved and hurt at first, the sterling fellow was finally stung to reprisals. He was guilty of no wrong. He was worthy far kinder treatment at her hands, and, noting her apparent determination to talk only with the men across the table, or with Captain Amory, who had taken her in, the New-Yorker presently succeeded in interesting the lady on his right, and, when dinner was over, and the women passed out into the parlor, was enabled to make way for Miss Farrar with a very courteous but entirely ceremonious bow. Ellis, flushed, but inclining her head, passed him by without a word.

It was then nearly 8:30 o'clock, and the gleeful voices of the children could be heard returning from the chapel, and, mindful of his promise to Helen Daunton, Ormsby was already figuring for an opportunity of temporary escape. It had been arranged that most of the officers and ladies were to gather at the hoproom after ten, "just to see if the floor was in good shape for to-morrow," and Jack well understood that Ellis did not mean that he should be her escort, and, as matters now stood, he did not desire her to suppose that such was his wish. Even as he was pondering, over the cigarettes and coffee, how he should manage the matter, and, giving but absent-minded attention to the cheery chat about him, Captain Amory suddenly lifted his hand and said: "Hush!"

Out across the parade, quick, stirring, and spirited, the cavalry trumpet was sounding "officers' call," and every man sprang to his feet. "What can it mean?" "What has happened?" were the questions that assailed them as they came streaming out through the parlor in search of their great-coats.

"Did you ever know such a regiment?" exclaimed the hostess, impulsively. "I do believe we never get through Christmas without a tragedy of some kind!" and then she bit her tongue as she caught sight of Ellis Farrar's startled face.

"I think if you will excuse me, Mrs. Farwell, I will go to mother a moment. She is at the chaplain's by this time, and Mrs. Daunton is with her. Still, I feel anxious. All this may excite her very much."

And so, while the officers went hurrying away across to the adjutant's office, Ormsby found himself, after all, tendering his arm to Miss Farrar. He was the only man left. Kitty, excited and agitated, she knew not why, had made some comical attempts to detain Will, but his long legs had by this time carried him half way to the scene of the sudden summons.

"Thank you, no. I do not need it," said Ellis coldly. "Indeed, I do not need escort at all to go so short a distance."

"It seems to be the post custom none the less," was the grave answer. "Besides, I think I am justified in saying you have treated me with aversion so marked of late that I am entitled to know the cause. What can I have done to deserve it, Ellis? Let us understand each other."

"There is only one way, then, Mr. Ormsby," she answered, with sudden impulse. "Who is Helen Daunton?"

"Ellis, I cannot tell you now," was the sorrowful, gentle answer. "Be patient with me yet a little while."

"Yet you know?"

"Yes—I know."

"And you say let us understand each other," she answered, bitterly.

"Ellis, I said to you before when we spoke of this, there are secret orders a soldier must obey and not explain. In these last few hours secret orders have come to me."

"And you accept secret orders—from her?".

"I accept them from my honor, Ellis, for I have given my word. No," he implored, as she hastened as though to leave him, "listen, for it may be my last opportunity to-night. I know it seems hard and strange to you that when I would lay my whole life open before you, I must not yet tell you this. But, Ellis, I give you my honor, I am hiding nothing shameful to that poor woman, nor to me. It is only for a time I must be silent. When I can speak you'll forgive me, dear. You will thank me that I do keep silence now. Trust me, Ellis. Can you not look up at me and say you trust me?"

Ah, how pleading was his tone, how full of love and fire and tenderness his manly face, as in that still winter night he looked down into her eyes. Over at the barracks there was a sudden stop to all the music, but men's voices could be heard in excited talk. Along officers' row many a door was opened and women and children were peering out in search of explanation of the unusual summons. Over at the adjutant's office a dark throng had gathered, the officers of the garrison and other knots as of soldiers or Indians could be seen, but Jack and Ellis, saw, heard nothing of this. Her voice had the ring of steel to it as she answered.

"If it were just a question of my own happiness, I might trust you, but it is my mother's happiness —perhaps her life. I must know all there is to know about that woman whom my mother trusts so blindly, I must know for myself. In the name of the love you offer me, will you tell me the truth about her?"

"Ellis, I cannot to-night. I have given my word."

"Then keep it," said she with sudden passion. "Keep it and keep your love," then turned and fled within the chaplain's gate, leaving him standing on the snowy walk without, sorrowing, yet determined.

For a moment he stood there following her with his eyes. Never stopping to knock or ring, she turned the knob and let herself into the brightly-lighted hall. He caught a glimpse of the gray-haired chaplain bending over a womanly form. He caught one fleeting view of Helen Daunton's anxious face. Evidently the call had been heard there, too, and, coming as it did in the stillness of the holiday evening, it boded no good. Only on rare occasions or some sudden emergency was Fenton known to call every duty officer to his presence, even by day, and he would be almost the last man to break in upon the festivities of the season with a stern call to arms unless arms and men both were needed somewhere. The day had been one long trial to Mrs. Farrar, and since noon one long torture to her cherished friend. And so, as they were seated about the chaplain's fire and the trumpet notes were heard, and a servant hastening in said, "It's officers' call, sir," just as Ellis feared, her mother was seized with sudden faintness. "My boy, Willy! They won't take him," she faltered, and then sank back nerveless into her chair.

Ormsby turned and sped away for the office. At least he could ascertain the cause of the summons and bring them tidings if it meant no move, but the first glance through the window at his uncle's face, as he stood surrounded by his officers, told the New Yorker, already experienced in frontier garrison life, that something imminent was in the wind. Fenton was talking rapidly, as was his wont when roused, and the only faces in the group that did not seem to kindle in response to the light in his keen, sparkling eyes, were those of two heavily-blanketed Indians standing sullen and imperturbable beside him. Out in the snow half a dozen non-commissioned officers were gathered in a group by the little knot of Indian ponies and cowboy broncos. An Indian boy lolling in his saddle, replied in monosyllables to their eager questions. A brace of cowboys, one of them obviously in liquor, sought to impress upon all within hearing their version of some row that had evidently taken place. Among the bystanders was Ormsby's old friend, the sergeant major, and to him he appealed.

"What's up, sergeant?"

"Been a fight, sir—cowboys and Indians. Christmas drunk, I reckon. The cowboys were having some fun with their lariats and they roped old Big Road off his pony and shot at him when he showed fight. Then his two sons shot Laramie Pete, and it looks like a general scrimmage. Big Road's whole village is camped only ten miles down stream, and they're war dancing already. There's a lot of drunken cowboys over at town and they swear they'll rouse the county and clean out the whole Indian outfit."

Thanking the staff sergeant for his information, Ormsby pressed on to the crowded room and stood in the outskirt of the throng of officers. Fenton was speaking as he entered the hall, and his voice had no uncertain ring. He had been questioning one of the cowboy leaders, a scowling, semi-defiant, but splendidly built specimen of frontier chivalry, and it was evident that the verdict of the commander was against these turbulent gentry, and in favor of the Indians.

"By your own admission, Thorpe, your fellows are on a tear, and whether they meant it as fun or not, it was rough fun at best, and nothing less than a mad-brained trick in my eyes, and an outrage from the Indian point of view. Big Road would have been no chief at all if he hadn't resented it furiously. It may be, as you say, that he was first to pull his gun, but you pulled him off his horse. The men that did it deserve to be shot, and I'm sorry he missed. You say there are cowboys enough in the county to clean out a dozen such bands as his, and that Laramie Pete's friends won't rest until they've done it. Go you to them right from this spot and say for me there are not cowboys enough in all the territory to lick this regiment, and you've got to do that before you can raise one scalp in that village."

"All right, Colonel Fenton. In the old days we used to say blood was thicker than water, and in many a tough place we've stood by the soldier against the savage. There was never a time we went back on you, and this is the first time I ever heard of an officer who would go back on us—"

"Don't distort things now, my friend," said Fenton, coolly. "I never would go back on you, as you say, if you were the assailed and the wronged. This is a case of simple justice, and I interpose to keep the peace until the rights and wrongs can be sifted and settled. Take my advice and keep away from the village."

"There's a higher power in the land than the military, Colonel Fenton, and that's public opinion, and public opinion says Big Road's people murdered Laramie Pete. Public opinion says we want the murderers, and by God! we mean to have 'em even if we have to clean out the whole village. We want no fight with you, but, through the press and Congress, we'll use you up till there won't be as much left of you as the Sioux left of Custer's crowd. Take my advice and keep away from us."

And so saying big Ben Thorpe, "king of the cowboys," as they called him on the Platte, strode angrily out of the room, the officers parting in silence to let him go. At the threshold he turned and once more faced the post commander.

"Another thing, Colonel Fenton!" and as he spoke Ormsby could see how the strong frame was quivering with excitement and wrath. "You say we're not the sheriff's posse and we cannot act in accordance with law. There's no sheriff in all Wyoming nearer than Rock Springs, and I'm sheriff in these parts until he comes. I'm sheriff enough to hunt murderers, and sheriff enough to run down horse thieves, and do it without waiting for warrants either, and that damned redskin whom you're protecting there by your side is one of the four that shot Pete Boland. I'll send a sheriff's posse here in ten minutes, and I'll give you warning here and now we mean to have the law on him or you, and you take your choice. Will you surrender him?"

Ormsby felt his nerves and muscles quivering. This was indeed bearding the lion in his den. It was a new thing to see a post commander braved in his own bailiwick. Fenton, however, never showed the faintest irritation. Checking with a gesture the indignant move made by some of the younger officers, he turned quietly to the officer of the day.

"Captain Amory, let a file of the guard escort that gentleman off the reservation."

"So be it, Colonel Fenton, and let the country know I was thrust off the post at the point of the sabre. I'll wait for my escort."

He had little time to wait. Almost at the doorway already, the corporal's guard, obeying the impatient summons of the young officer in command, came trotting up at double quick, a non-commissioned officer and two troopers. One of the latter, stocky, heavily bearded, slouchy, with furtive, blood-shot eyes, looked uneasily about him as the detail halted, and, springing up the steps, the corporal lightly touched the cowboy on the shoulder. Thorpe had turned back as though to hurl some parting shot or sarcasm at the oppressor, but at the touch of the corporal's hand looked coolly around. "Well, sonny, what do you want?"

"Come along, Ben," said the corporal, quietly, then started back involuntarily at the expression of amaze and wrath that shot suddenly into the cowboy's face.

"What!" hissed Thorpe, striding a pace forward. "You here? You officiating as policeman to show me off Uncle Sam's jailyard. You, you sneak and scum!" he shouted, shaking a fist in Graice's sodden face. "You, you braggart and blackguard—you coward, who left poor Crawford's wife without a defender; you cur you stole the last cent he had, and then betrayed him to the Indians; you liar who brag of being an officer's son, and dare not own your own name. Stand back!" he fiercely cried, as the corporal once more strove to place a hand upon his shoulder. "I've no quarrel with you, Reddy, or with this other poor devil, who can only do as he's ordered, but I'd die in my tracks before that white-livered hound should escort me off this post. Out of the way!" he cried, and with one magnificent bound reached his horse, leaped into saddle, and dashed a few yards away. Then, whirling about, he swung his hat in air. "Good night to you, gentlemen. Merry Christmas to you, one and all. You've got one of those bloody murderers here, so keep him if you choose, but we'll have the other three before the sun rises in spite of all the thugs and thieves like that fellow you can muster in the cavalry."

And with a parting malediction at Graice and a lash of the stinging quirt, he whirled his bronco and dashed away at the gallop.

"Damn that fellow!" said Fenton. "I like him in spite of all his deviltry. There's no help for it gentlemen, the Twelfth has got to spend its Christmas standing between those rough riders and the very band that killed our colonel—three long years ago.

## CHAPTER XI.

Just as first call for tattoo was sounding (no one having thought to tell the orderly trumpeter that, both on account of the holiday and the unexpected duty for the garrison, "the rules were suspended,") a long column of cavalry wound away through the shimmer of the snowy moonlight and disappeared from sight along the flats below the post. Fenton and Wayne, with four of the six troops, had ridden down stream for a ten mile march. His object was to bring Big Road, with his little village, warriors, women, children, ponies, dogs, dirt, and all within the lines of the reservation of Fort Frayne. Once there even cowboy dare not molest them, and no self-appointed sheriff could impose his authority. With all Thorpe's bluster, Fenton felt reasonably assured that even in so turbulent a corner of Wyoming, the hustlers could not muster in force sufficient to warrant an attack that night. Big Road's braves were few in number, but they were fighters to a man. Their sins, like those of all their tribe and kindred tribes, had long since been forgiven them by Uncle Sam, and it was not for his vassals to keep up the feud. Rare, indeed, are the cases when the soldier has long cherished a grudge against the Indian. The Twelfth had fought like devils after the murder, as they could but regard it, of their beloved colonel, but when the opposing band had finally surrendered and accepted the situation, all rancor speedily died away.

It seemed to the regiment, therefore, a perfectly natural and obvious thing that it should hasten forth to protect this little remnant from the revenge of the whites. Laramie Pete, with all his faults, was a frontier hero whose popularity was second only to that of Thorpe, and at the latter's call, from far and near, cowboy, ranchman, miner, and prospector, would hasten to join forces under his leadership, and in twenty-four hours or less he could count on five hundred determined followers, fearless as they were reckless, and defiant of any law that was not of their own devising.

In the selection of his troops Fenton had been governed by the time-honored tenets of the Twelfth. Leale's men, having returned but a month before from a tour of detached service, escorting a Government survey through the lands of the Shoshones far to the west, were therefore the ones designated to remain in charge of the post, being supported by what was left of the so-called Indian Troop—Crow Knife's company, a band of swarthy cavalrymen that took to Uncle Sam's clothing, pay, and rations with avidity, and even to his drill and discipline, so long as it was a new toy; but little by little the innate sloth and restlessness of the savage nature prevailed, and, one after another, non-commissioned officer and private, the Sioux soldiery had been discharged until nearly all were gone. Of the dozen that remained, however, were some of the noblest specimens of the race, men, who, like Crow Knife, seemed determined to rise above the apathy of the past into some position of power and influence for their people in the future, and it was almost unspeakable grief to these that they should be told that they could not go with the command. Yet Fenton's decision was a wise one. Ever since Big Road's messengers (White Wolf and Pretty Bear) dashed into the garrison at eight o'clock, claiming the intercession of the Great Father's soldiers, the excitement among the remnant of the Indian Troop was furious. For a moment it looked as though they might cast off their uniforms and, turning out in breechclout and paint and feathers, indulge in a genuine old-fashioned war dance on the parade. They were wild to get their arms and horses and to gallop to the succor of their kinsmen down the valley, but the lieutenant commanding was a cool hand, and, aided by the persuasive talk of one or two older warriors, measurably quieted the disturbance. Then, as most of the men on guard begged to be allowed to go with their comrades, seven of the Indians were distributed among the three reliefs, and Leale's men filled all the other gaps. It was about 9:30, as has been said, when the column marched away. It might be back before Christmas night. It might not be back for a week. No one at the moment could say because, even now, Big Road could have broken camp and started with his whole village on a night march for the fastnesses of the mountains, uncertain what fate might be in store for them if he remained. With the column went White Wolf and Bear, the former generally believed to be one of the four Indians engaged in the fracas that wound up the earthly career of Laramie Pete. Ahead of the column, full gallop, with only a single orderly, but with instructions to tell Big Road and his people to stay just where they were, as the Great Father meant to come to their protection, went Lieutenant Warren, and the maddest, "miserablest" man in all the garrison was Lieutenant Will Farrar.

When a young fellow is full of soldierly ambition, when he knows he is master of his work and is eager for an opportunity to prove it, when everybody has been treating him as a boy and he knows he has all the ability of a man, when his sweetheart, even, has been teasing and twitting him upon his apparent lack of consequence in the eyes of the garrison, and he is therefore all the more mad to prove at any hazard that it contains no more daring and spirited an officer, such an opportunity as was here afforded Mr. Farrar was not to be lost. He had implored Colonel Fenton to let him be the bearer of the message, and was broken-hearted at the kind but firm refusal. "The Indian is peculiar, Will," said the old soldier, gently. "He never forgets or forgives. If his father had been killed as yours was he would hold it something to be avenged, although resentment had to be concealed, perhaps, for years. They know you are his son. They know that the white men are leaguing now to avenge the death of Pete. They cannot understand such a thing as white soldiers, from sheer sense of duty and justice, interposing against their own kind to save the red man. In your coming they would read only treachery, and would argue that you came to urge their remaining so that we might join our white brethren in surrounding and wiping them out of existence. Whatever you urged, even in my name, they would be sure not to do. No, I must send Warren. They know him well and trust him." But Fenton was thankful he had so good an excuse, for even without it he could not have brought himself to send Marjorie Farrar's only remaining son upon a mission that might prove perilous—that would certainly seem perilous in her eyes.

Hastening to the chaplain's as soon as Thorpe made his melodramatic exit, Ormsby was met at the door by the good old dominie himself and begged him to say to Mrs. Farrar that there was no cause for alarm: there had been a fight between Indians and cowboys several miles away, and Colonel Fenton had decided to send a force out to keep the peace. She heard his voice, and faintly but eagerly asked that he should come in. It was Helen, not Ellis, who bore her message, Helen, who noted with comfort, and Ellis, with mixed emotion, that the mother had learned to lean upon this stanch and devoted friend. Mrs. Farrar took his hand and looked appealingly up into his face as he briefly told her what had happened and what the colonel had decided to do.

"Will Willy have to go?" was her one question,

and, ignorant as yet that Leale's troop would be designated to remain, Ormsby gravely answered that he presumed the entire command was ordered out. "But," he added, reassuringly, "that fact itself is the surest guarantee of peace. There can be no further disorder in face of so strong a force."

For all answer she bowed her head and hid it in her slender white hands. No wonder it seemed as though Christmas ever brought its tragedy to her at old Fort Frayne.

And then came diversion that was merciful. There was a rush of light footsteps, a flutter of silken skirts on the porch without, a bang at the door and in came Kitty, flushed, disheveled, tearful, indignant.

"What's this about Willy's going?" she demanded. "Where is he? What business has he— Why! he *cannot* go, Mrs. Farrar. He's engaged to me for the german to-morrow night."

There was something so comical in her utter inability to understand the gravity of the situation, to realize that a soldier's duty far outranked even so solemn a compact as an engagement to dance with his sweetheart that even Mrs. Farrar forgot her grief and apprehension for the moment and opened her arms to the imperious little lady and drew her to her heart.

"Ah, Kitty, you have the same lesson to learn that I had long years ago" she cried, as she sought to soothe and console the child, but Miss Ormsby was in no mood for petting. She was up in arms.

She was being defrauded. Uncle Fenton had no business whatever to send Willy away on such a quest at such a time. It was worse than inconsiderate. It was outrageous, and then Mrs. Farrar's face went white again as she asked what Kitty meant, and then Kitty's nerve gave way and she buried her bonny face on that motherly shoulder and burst into tears.

"I thought you'd heard," she sobbed. "They have only just told me. Captain Farwell came home to change his dress, and I asked him where Will was, and he said he left him offering his services to Uncle Fenton to ride ahead to the Indians, and he wanted to know if I didn't think Will was a trump. I don't!—I didn't!—I think it's simply h-h-heartless in him!"

And then Mrs. Farrar raised her eyes appealingly to Ormsby, and he went without a word. He knew what she needed, and hastened in search of Will. He found him at Fenton's, whither he had accompanied the colonel, and where he was still pleading, and tugging at his tiny mustache and tramping up and down and biting his nails, while Fenton, in the adjoining room, was calmly getting out of his dress clothes and into winter field garb.

"Would you mind dropping this and going down to the chaplain's and comforting your mother and my sister?" said Ormsby, as soon as he could get in a word edgewise.

"Yes, go, Will," said Fenton, "and tell her that there is nothing whatever in this affair to worry about. We're merely going to bring old Big Road up here to take Christmas dinner at the fort. There's no chance for a fight, or you should go along. No; it's useless arguing, my boy. I'd do anything for you that's right, but this is absolutely unreasonable on your part. Now go and tell those two blessed women that you're to remain on guard over them, and they'll rise up and call *me* blessed—at least they ought to.

And so, finally, Ormsby got the peppery young fellow out of the house and fairly started, Ormsby keeping pace with him as he strode excitedly from the room.

"I want you to do something for me, Will," said he in a low tone, as they hastened along. "I'm going with the command, and I haven't a moment to spare. Give this note to Mrs. Daunton for me as soon as possible after you reach the house. May I rely upon you?"

And as he spoke he held forth an envelope, evidently snugly filled, and Farrar took it mechanically, and without reply. The boy was thinking only of his own disappointment. "Do you understand, Will?" persisted Ormsby. "It is of great importance that she should have it before ten o'clock. You won't forget?" and wondering now, Farrar promised, and Ormsby turned abruptly back.

"I wish to the Lord I were in your place," was poor Will's parting shout, as the guardsman hurried back to dress for the night ride. Already the four troops had marched to stables and were saddling.

Already there were sounds of excitement over across the river, and much scurrying through the straggling street of the cattle town of well-mounted ranchmen and "cow punchers." Thorpe was as good as his word. He was rousing the county with a vengeance, hoping to ride down the valley in strong force within the hour and "wind up the whole business" before the cavalry could come to the rescue of the offending band. Will could hear the occasional whoop and yell that came ringing over on the still night air, and he was in a petulant mood, bordering on exasperation, when admitted at the chaplain's and ushered into the parlor, where Kitty still lay, clasped in the mother's arms.

She scrambled to her feet the instant he entered and began an energetic outburst, but the sight of his woe-begone face checked her suddenly. Mrs. Farrar read instantly the cause of his gloom, and her eyes brightened with rejoicing.

"Willy, my boy, then you don't have to go?"

"Don't *have* to go!" was the wrathful answer. "Don't have to go! I've been on my knees to that stony-hearted old rip for the last ten minutes, and he won't let me go!"

"God bless him!" were the mother's fervent words. "He knew—he well knew what it would cost me to have my only boy torn from me at this time," was the thought that flashed through her mind, and her eyes welled with grateful tears, though she could say no more. It was Kitty who restored the social equilibrium. "I won't have you speak of Uncle Fenton in that disgraceful way, Mr. Farrar. You ought to be thankful you don't have to go, as you put it. Have you totally forgotten our engagement for to-morrow night?"

"Oh, for heaven's sake, Kitty! What is that at such a time as this? There won't be a sign of a dance, unless they all get back in time, and I'd rather be dead than left here the first scout the regiment has after my joining it." He threw himself disgustedly into a chair, refusing to see his mother's outstretched hand, and for the time being absolutely indifferent to Kitty's reproaches. It was the discovery of this fact that taught her how thoroughly in earnest he was, taught her that there was something alive in his heart of which she might well be jealous, and for the first time in her life the girl stood a little in awe of him, and, relinquishing her purpose of upbraiding, she turned back, baffled and defeated, and took refuge by the mother's chair.

"Tell us who are to go, Willy," said Mrs. Farrar, entreatingly.

"Everybody but me—and Leale. They'll be off in ten minutes, too. Even Jack Ormsby goes, and I'm ordered—absolutely ordered—to stay here, as if I were some—some baby in arms, unfit to do duty with my fellows. I'll never forgive Fenton as long as I live."

"And I'll never forget it," murmured the mother, as she gently checked Kitty, once more about to burst into impetuous speech. "I'm sure Colonel

Fenton had grave and good reasons for keeping you here, my son, and if so tried and brave a soldier as Captain Leale can remain without reproach, surely you can."

"There's just the difference," answered Will miserably. "Leale has been under fire and on trying duty time and again. His reputation was assured long years ago. I'm treated as a boy by—by everybody in this garrison, high or low, and forbidden a chance to do a thing. If you folks want to see that command off the sooner you get out to the bluff the better."

"But you are going to take us, Willy," said his sister, sympathetically, "Kitty and I, at least, wish to see the regiment. Do you care to go, mother, dear?" she asked anxiously, and, then, crossing over to her mother's side, bent down and kissed her, but the question was no sooner asked than she would gladly have recalled it—"or will you come home now with me?" she hastened to say.

"I'll take mother home," said Will. "Go on if you want to see them start. I don't. That's more than I could possibly stand. The chaplain will take you gladly enough."

And so at last did Miss Ormsby begin to realize that even in the eyes of the man she had captivated she was for the time being of no account.

It was one of Fenton's fads to have out the band when the regiment or any considerable detachment of it marched away, and now, even at night, he did not depart from his practice. The chaplain had opened the door to note the progress of the preparations across the parade. Orderlies with the horses of the officers were trotting past. The non-commissioned staff were already mounting at the adjutant's office, and over at the band barracks the gray chargers, the music stools of the musicians, were being led into the line. A mounted band was something that Kitty had never seen, and curiosity and coquetry combined, led her to lend her ear to the chaplain's suggestion that she should come out and see the column ride away and wave good-bye to her admirers among the subalterns. If Will persisted in his ill temper there was no sense in staying there, and perhaps the quickest way to bring him to terms was to manifest interest in his fellows. So, leaving him to the ministrations of his mother, she danced away to the front door, Ellis promptly following. The night was still and beautiful, softly hazy, and not very cold, and the scene across the snow-covered parade was full of life and animation. Lights were dancing to and fro among the company quarters. Two of the designated troops had already marched up from the stables, formed line in front of their barracks, and dismounting, were awaiting the sounding of adjutant's call and the formation of the squadron. Officers were mounting every moment along the row and trotting out to join their commands, and presently, from the colonel's big house on the edge of the bluff came three horsemen clad in heavy winter field garb, and even in the dim light there was no difficulty in recognizing Fenton's soldierly form. These were joined by the adjutant as they rode out upon the parade, and then one of the group came jogging over towards the chaplain, followed by an attendant orderly. It was Jack Ormsby, and Kitty fluttered down to the gate to meet him.

"You and Aunt Lucretia will have to keep house by yourselves to-night, little sister," said he laughingly, as he bent to kiss her good-bye. "Corporal Rorke is to sleep at the house so that you will not lack for guards. Where's Will?"

"He's with his mother in the parlor, and just too miserable for anything," said Kitty, who, now that she could see for herself the preparation for a march, began to feel far more sympathy for her lover, if not actually to wish that she were a man and could go too. Ellis, quick to notice Ormsby's coming, had slipped back within the hall and partially closed the door. Glancing over her shoulder she could see that her mother had left her reclining chair and was bending fondly over Will, smoothing his tumbled hair and striving to soothe and comfort him, but it was evident that Will was sorely hurt, for he turned away in irrepressible chagrin and distress and covered his face with his hands. Helen Daunton, forgetful for the moment of her own bitter trouble, had sought to aid her friend in consoling the boy, but it was her first experience in such a case. She had never realized what it meant to a proud and ambitious young soldier to be held in garrison when his comrades were being sent to the field; and finding presently that she could be of little aid, she drew away toward the window to join the chaplain and his wife, who were gazing out upon the parade, when the stirring notes of adjutant's call came trilling through the hazy moonlight, and with a groan that seemed to rise from the depths of his heart, poor Will threw himself face downward upon the sofa, utterly refusing to be comforted.

"Come," said the chaplain in a low tone, "They will be better left to themselves. Let us go out and see the troops form line," and hastily quitting the parlor they came suddenly upon Ellis lingering at the outer door.

"Mr. Ormsby was saying good-bye to Kitty," she nervously explained, "and I remained here for a moment. He is still there."

Yes, still there, although he had said adieu to his little sister and the squadron was rapidly forming on the parade. Still there, and looking now and then beyond Kitty's pretty, pathetic little face, clouded with a trouble altogether new to it. Still there, and longing for a sight of the face he loved as he did no other, despite all its coldness and aversion. Then they came hurrying forth—the old dominie and his faithful helpmeet, the two young and beautiful women—and at sight of them Ormsby suddenly dismounted, and passing the reins to his orderly, ran nimbly up the steps and extended his hand, " Good night, chaplain—Good night, Mrs. Ransom. We count on eating our Christmas dinner here, despite the night march. Good night, Miss Farrar," he added, gravely, gently. "We still hope to be here to wish you Merry Christmas. Please extend my sympathies to Will. I know how hard it is for him to stay. Good night, Mrs. F—— Mrs. Daunton," he stumbled on, and extended to her the hand which he had withheld from Ellis. "Oh, pardon me. Did Farrar give you a note I intrusted to him for you?"

"Not yet, Mr. Ormsby. He has hardly thought of anything but his grief at being retained here."

"Well, ask him for it before ten o'clock. It"— and he was halting painfully now, for Ellis, withdrawing a pace from the group, was gazing straight into his face—"it—it explains itself. You'll understand it. Good night, good night, all. I must hurry." And with that he ran down the steps and out of the gate, mounted quickly, and without a backward glance rode quickly away to take his place by the colonel's side. Another moment, and the adjutant, galloping out in front of the long line of horses, had presented the squadron to Major Wayne, and that distinguished officer, unexpectedly awake and lively, lost no time in preliminaries, but broke his command at once into column of fours, and with the band playing its joyous march music, and with old Fenton himself in the lead, away they went down the winding road to the flats to the east. Once out of the garrison, the band wheeled out of column and played the troopers by, then trotted back to unsaddle for the night. Men, women and children, the populace of Fort Frayne, gathered along the eastern edge of the plateau, and silently, and in not a few cases, tearfully, watched the column out of sight in the dim, ghostly light, and then little Trumpeter Meinecke came out from the guardhouse and trilled the martial curfew that sent them shivering homeward— an ominous Christmas eve tattoo.

## CHAPTER XII.

TEN o'clock and no one yet came riding back from the column with later news. Almost as soon as the command had disappeared from view Mrs. Farrar had gone home, Helen, Ellis, Kitty and Will in close attendance, and there they were presently joined by Aunt Lucretia, whose volubility even calamity seemed powerless to check, and then to the relief of all the women, Captain Leale knocked and was promptly admitted.

"I am in search of my right-hand man," said he, with his bright, cordial smile. "They tell me he is playing Achilles and sulking in his tent, but I have work for him to do," and then once more did Kitty look remonstrance, for she could form no idea of work for him that did not involve deprivation for her.

"You are not going to send Mr. Farrar away after all," she began, but Leale laughingly checked her.

"Far from it," said he. "I need him at the guardhouse, and mean to put him in charge of the prisoners when they come in. The chances are that the colonel will have to arrest not a few of those fellows, and he'll do it in the interest of peace and good order, despite the fact that he has no warrant. Are you ready, sir?"

"I'm ready and willing to do any duty, Captain Leale," answered Will, ruefully. "But I was the first to volunteer for that courier ride to Big Road, and I think the colonel ought to have given it to me. I'll be officer of the guard to-morrow, anyhow, and would just as lief begin now. Shall I come at once?"

"Yes, the second relief goes on in a few minutes, and you would better inspect them. Everything is started right. You have a capital sergeant of the guard. I want the sentries on the north and east bluffs instructed to listen for all sounds from the east, and to keep a close watch on that plant of Bunco Jim's. Watch every movement in that rowdy town over yonder, though I believe most of the populace has already ridden away at the bidding of the so-called cowboy king."

Will bent over and kissed his mother's forehead, "I'll get my sword and go at once," said he, "and I'll be back as soon as I've made the rounds of the second relief. I suppose nobody here means to turn in for an hour yet. We ought to have news of some kind before midnight." With that he quickly left the little parlor, and vaulting the low fence, let himself in at his own door in the adjoining bachelor roost. Mrs. Daunton, who had been occupying herself close to Mrs. Farrar, presently arose and stepped into the hallway, took a heavy wrap and noiselessly quitted the house. Surprised, Captain Leale looked about him for an explanation. Ellis had drawn aside the curtain, and with pale, set face, was gazing fixedly out upon the parade. Kitty looked bewildered. It was Mrs. Farrar who spoke

"This has been a trying day for Helen. She is

not strong, I fear, and to-night she is so nervous and unstrung that she seems to shrink from company or conversation. I have never known her so distracted. I fancy she wants to be alone a few minutes and to take the fresh air on the gallery." Ellis moved impatiently, but said not a word. She could see that so far from having stopped on the gallery, Helen Daunton had hastened through the gate, and, turning to Will's quarters next door, was there awaiting his reappearance. The boy came out in a moment, his sword at his side, and wrapping his cloak about him, stopped short in evident surprise at sight of Mrs. Daunton. Ellis well understood the purport of the conversation that ensued, though she could hear no word. Will searched one pocket after another, then ran back into the house, came forth again in less than a minute, handed a square white envelope to Mrs. Daunton, and, raising his forage cap in farewell, hastened away across the parade. Ashamed of her espionage, yet fascinated, Ellis lingered at the window and saw Helen tear open the envelope, and draw forth a little packet or roll, which she closely inspected and rapidly counted over. Money! Treasury notes beyond question! Money, and paid her by Jack Ormsby! Ellis dropped the curtain and turned away. She cared to see no more.

Over at the guardhouse the second relief was being formed as Farrar reached the spot—seven soldiers in their fur caps and gloves and heavy winter overcoats and arctics. The corporal had just reported them all present, and the lieutenant quickly yet closely inspected their equipment, then stepped to the front again.

"In addition to the usual orders," said he, "Numbers Six and Seven are cautioned to keep a sharp lookout and to listen attentively for anything at the eastward. In the event of any unusual sight or sound, call for the corporal at once. Who is Number Five?"

"Graice, sir," said the corporal.

The young officer's face darkened a bit. He had no trust in the man whatever and knew well his evil reputation. "Graice," said he, "you have double functions to-night. You have not only the same orders as Six and Seven, but the commanding officer directs that you keep a special watch over the settlement across the river, particularly of the plant of Bunco Jim. I believe you know it."

"There are plenty of others that know it as well," was the surly and unexpected answer.

"That will do, sir," was the stern rejoinder. "You were asked no questions, and will keep silent until you are. Do you understand your instructions?"

"I am not deaf," was the sullen response.

"Answer my question, Graice," said Will, tingling with indignation, but keeping his temper. There was a moment's silence, then—

"I 'spose I do."

"There appears to be some doubt, however," said Farrar, coolly. "Post your relief, corporal, and we will look further after Number Five. Has that man been drinking again?" he turned and asked the silent sergeant, as the relief marched away.

"It's hard to say, sir. He's one of those steady soakers. It would be difficult to find him when he hadn't been drinking more or less. I think he has been drinking all day, but he knows what he's doing, and is as sober as he is at any other time."

Farrar gazed doubtfully at the relief as it trudged away through the misty moonlight; shook his head in some dissatisfaction, then turned in at the doorway of the tower.

"I will look over the guardroom and cells," said he, "and visit sentries later," and, taking up his lantern, the sergeant followed.

A big stove burned brightly in the center of the guardroom, and the men of the third relief, sitting or sprawling about, sprang up and stood to attention as the officer looked in. Another stove, the mate to it, was burning almost at red heat in the general prison room, across the hall. Here were confined some half dozen poor devils, the scapegraces of the command; some drink-sodden and stupid, others merely reckless and "ne'er do weel." Following the spirit of holiday decoration, and never expecting the visit of an officer that night, one of the number, with a fine sense of humor, had induced a comrade to fetch him a parcel from the barracks, and now on the bare wooden wall opposite the entrance there hung a chromo with a flowery border and the pious sentiment, "God bless our happy home." Will's eye caught it at the instant. "Take that down!" said he, with manifest indignation. "There is to be no burlesque business here to-night." There was a faint odor of dead tobacco about the grimy room. "You'll have to search those men and that room," said he to the sergeant, as they turned away. "There must be neither pipes, matches nor anything with which they can start a fire. If this old rookery ever flames it will go like a flash. Do it at once! Any men in the cells?"

"None, sir, and none in the outer prison room."

"Keep the other empty, then. The chances are it'll be filled to-morrow when the column gets back. Remember the orders about fire."

"No man's like to forget that, lieutenant, with the powder stored there on the second floor."

"I know," answered Will, gravely. "How much powder is there there?"

"Only a dozen cartridges for the reveille gun, sir, but that's enough to blow the place into flinders."

"There's no one in the light prison room on that floor?"

"No one, sir. That floor is empty. There's no fire up there at all."

Presently the tramp, tramp of martial feet was heard on the crunching snow, and officer and sergeant both stepped forth to receive the relief of sentries just taken off post. One of them was Crow Knife. He gravely saluted as he passed his officer, and placed his carbine in the arm rack, then went out on the east side of the little building and stood there, silent, listening for sounds from the distant east.

"May I have the lieutenant's permission to go out on the bluff awhile?" he asked, as Farrar came by him. "I can hear the call of the corporal if we are wanted for anything, and I am very anxious." And Will, who at first would have said no, saw the anxiety in the Indian's face and consented.

"Crow is strangely superstitious," said the sergeant, after a moment's silence. "He has been like that ever since he came on guard. He says the ghost dogs were howling the death song last night, and that somebody's to get his death blow to-night. We can't laugh him out of it."

Will turned away and watched the rapidly-retreating form, growing dimmer every second. "I suppose he dreads trouble for his people, and this row makes him nervous," said he. "I'm going the rounds now, sergeant, and will leave you here in charge."

"It is just 10:30 now, sir. Shall we call off?"

"Ay, ay, let it go," was the answer, as the young fellow stalked away in the direction of the stables. It was his purpose to take the sentry posts in inverse order, so as to visit first those on the eastern flank.

Without a break the watch-cry went from man to man, Number Five shouting a gruff, stentorian, "All's well," that again directed the attention of the officer of the guard to his probable condition. The last sentry had called off and Number One had given, loud and prolonged, the final assurance that all along the chain was peace and security before Will reached the bottom of the slope and began his examination of the stables and corrals. The last thing he saw as he cast a backward glance northward along the snowy slope that terminated the plateau on its eastern side, was the solitary figure of Crow Knife standing mute, motionless and attentive, just at the upper end of the post of sentry on Number Six.

He was delayed unexpectedly among the stables, for one of the orderlies, in the absence of his troop and officers, had gone visiting among his associates in the adjoining building, and one or two spare horses were loose and roaming about the gangway. The next thing he heard of his sentries there were excited shouts for the corporal of the guard, and hastening out into the night to ascertain the cause, he nearly collided with little Meinecke, the trumpeter.

"Lieutenant," cried the boy, breathlessly, "Crow Knife's killed, sir. Stabbed to death!"

"My God!" moaned Will, as he hastened up the slope. "There's a curse on Christmastide at old Fort Frayne."

When ten,—twenty minutes had passed away and Helen Daunton failed to return, Mrs. Farrar had become anxious and ill at ease. Leale, too, had been listening eagerly for her step on the porch without, and, unable to control his longing to see and speak with her, despite her palpable efforts to avoid him, he had early taken his leave and gone forth in search.

Ellis, slipping from the parlor into the dining-room, had thence managed to go to her own little chamber, for a moment or two to herself. Whatever doubt remained as to the justice of her suspicions up to dinner time that evening, it was banished now and her heart was hard against Ormsby that he should have so braved and deceived her. Looking out from her window she could see much of the walk in front of Officers' Row, but not a sign of Helen Daunton. The clouds had thickened, the moonlight had grown dimmer all of a sudden. Once more the snow was sifting down. She could not dream where Helen had gone.

It was a desperate woman who stole silently out of the little army home and intercepted Lieutenant Farrar at the gate. In few words she made known her errand and asked for the note Mr. Ormsby had placed in his hand, and Will for the first time remembered it. He had stowed it in the pocket of the overcoat he was wearing as he returned with Ormsby from the colonel's, and was compelled to run back indoors again to find it. Absorbed though he was in his own trouble, Will could not but remark how strange it seemed that his mother's companion should be seeking, and Ormsby sending, those mysterious notes at night. He made such explanation and excuse as he could, however, then hurried away. With nervous fingers Helen counted over the money in the envelope. Two hundred dollars! Ormsby was indeed generous. Then desperate, determined, thoughtless of the military crime she was about to urge upon her husband, thinking only of the dreadful menace his presence was to the friends who had harbored and sheltered her, she sped away up the row, and turning through the broad open space near the colonel's quarters, came out upon the snow-covered brow of the heights overhanging the silent, ice-bound stream; and there, barely a hundred feet away, the dim outlines of that huge, hulking figure could be seen. She knew it only too well—knew it at a glance. Graice was standing on post at the moment, listening, apparently, to some faint, distant sounds of maudlin revelry that rose from the unhallowed walls of Bunco Jim's, beyond the Platte. With one brief muttered prayer to heaven for guidance and strength, she sped across the snowy expanse and was at his side before he could either halt or challenge. He never had time to speak before impetuously she began:

"Royle Farrar, I must speak to you here and now. If your being here meant only danger and harm to me, you might do your worst and I would bear it. You are under a false name. Your life has so changed you that as yet no one has recognized you, but it cannot last, and then there will be bitter shame and, perhaps, death that would lie at your door—your mother's; your poor, gentle mother, Royle, who holds her life only through the belief that you are no longer alive to bring further disgrace to your father's name."

But now he had partially recovered himself and angrily interrupted: "Is it my fault I'm here?

Did I suppose of all cursed places they'd send me to it would be here, to be ordered about by my cub of a brother, to see my noble captain making love to my—"

"You dare not say it!" she cried.

"You've had some experience of what I dare, my lady, and one thing I dare and mean to do is to stick it out right here and take my chances at Frayne. There's no other post where I'd find so many friends at court if things go wrong."

"You shall not stay here if I have to buy you to go," she cried, but she shrank even as she spoke, as though dreading a blow, for, with uplifted hand he sprang to her side; then roughly, savagely, seized her slender wrist.

"Who are you to pose as guardian angel of the Farrars? Who are you to say shall to me? Do you realize, my love, that your place in the army is not in officers' quarters, but down yonder in Laundresses' Alley? By the Lord! I've a mind—"

But here a dark shadow fell between him and the slender writhing object of his brutal rage; an iron grasp was laid in turn on the hand that so cruelly crushed the white wrist. A deep voice, eloquent with wrath, controlled, yet boiling, seemed to ring in his ears the two words, "Let go!" and then, releasing perforce his hold on the shrinking, startled woman, Graice writhed in furious effort to free himself from the clinch of Malcolm Leale, and writhed in vain.

"You've the devil's own grip," he savagely hissed through his grinding teeth.

"I've a grip, my man, that won't loosen till you are past doing further mischief here," was the stern, relentless answer. Then uplifting his voice, Leale shouted for the corporal of the guard, and at the instant the cry went echoing over the posts of Six and Seven. The sentry still writhed in impotent rage. Finding his struggles futile, he once more lashed with his tongue.

"Don't be too sure of that, captain. There are some kinds of a hold even your grip can't loosen."

"No insolence! You go from here to the guardhouse, as it is."

"Damn the guardhouse and you, too!" raged the soldier, hurling down his carbine. "If I'm to spend Christmas in limbo, I'm cursed if you shall spend it making love to my—" and here, with a tigerlike bound, his free hand brandishing a glistening knife, he lunged at the officer's throat. A lithe form had come leaping like a panther up the path, and even before Helen's cry had died away, Crow Knife had hurled himself between the men, and the shining blade was buried out of sight. There was a moment of furious struggle, and then the sentry lay felled like an ox in his tracks and Leale's foot was at his throat. The knife, blood-stained, had dropped in the snow. The Indian, his hand pressed to his side, was swaying slowly back, as the sergeant of the guard, with a brace of men, came running to the spot.

"Take this man to the guardhouse!" was the brief, stern order, as they lifted Graice, stunned and sodden, to his feet. Then the captain turned to Crow Knife. "Did that crazy brute strike you? Are you hurt?" he asked, in deep concern.

"Captain," said the Indian, slowly. "I believe I'm killed."

Leale sprang to support him. Other men, running to the scene, linked their hands and made a chair and raised the poor fellow from the ground. "Carry him gently to the hospital, lads. I'll be with you in a moment," said Leale, and then he turned to where, trembling, terrified, Helen Daunton still stood as though powerless to move.

"Helen—Mrs. Daunton! First let me see you home. I ask no confidence, no explanation, but this is something in which I must help you. I have guessed the truth, have I not? That man is your brother?"

"My brother, Captain Leale? God pity me—that man is my husband!"

For a moment not another word was spoken. Leale had recoiled—staggered—as though struck a mortal blow. Then, in hoarse whisper, so choked and broken seemed his voice:—

"Your husband! Your husband, Helen? Oh, my God! And I had thought you free to be loved, as I have learned—as you have taught me—to love you."

"Captain Leale!" she cried. "In pity say you do not believe that. Oh, hear me! Do not turn from me," she implored, for in his misery he had averted his face. "You shall not think me so vile," she went on, desperately. "I never knew until to-day that you had learned to—care for me. I thought all that had gone with my youth—oh, so long ago! I only asked of life a place where I could be useful and safe, and where, by and by, perhaps I could forget. I have seemed to myself so old and dull and sad, so different from the women men love that I never dreamed it my duty to say I was not free. Oh, I thought you were my friend. My heart has been so heavy and so numbed I have thought it dead since that Christmas Eve, four years ago. Ah, let me tell it to you and you will understand. Four years ago this night my little sick baby woke and wailed with pain. That man—my husband—was in a drunken sleep on the floor. The baby's cry woke him. He swore a dreadful oath at the little weak, white thing in my arms and struck it hard across the mouth. I don't know what wild words I said to my husband, but I told him I would never see his face again. Then I caught my baby to my breast and I ran and ran through the cold Christmas streets, and the stars went out, and the lights went out in the houses, and the little baby on my breast grew heavier and heavier, and by and by it was dawn, and, oh, so cruelly cold, and I—I opened the shawl and saw—" Here, overcome by the recollection the poor woman covered her face in her hands and burst into wild sobbing.

And then the captain turned. "Helen, Helen, my poor, poor girl! Hush! I spoke like a brute, but I was hit hard. I was your friend—I am your friend. It is late. You must go in. Take my cloak, you are shivering."

With that he turned and led her to the angle by the colonel's quarters, and there she looked up one instant into his sorrow-stricken face. "Do not come further with me," she implored. "You have been so good to me," and, bowing to her will, he let her go, and stood, following her swiftly retreating form with his longing eyes. And then, soft and sweet and clear, as though rising above all surrounding of crime or sin or sorrow, there floated on the night the prolonged notes of the cavalry trumpet sounding the soldier lullaby—"Lights out."

"Lights out," murmured Leale. "Lights out— ah, God help me—for life and love it is, indeed, lights out."

## CHAPTER XIII.

CLEAR and sparkling Christmas morning dawned on old Fort Frayne. The clouds that obscured the moon at midnight sent fluttering earthward a fresh fall of snow and spread a spotless coverlet over the valley of the Platte, softening rude outlines, capping with glistening white roof and chimney, tree and tower, and mercifully obliterating the unsightly streaks that led across the frozen river, and the deep red blotches that smeared the post at No. 5.

Two discoveries had been made by the officer of the guard in his search after the removal of Graice, struggling and cursing savagely to the prison room on the second floor, where Leale himself directed him placed, instead of among the garrison prisoners in the general room. One was that the sentry had received from some source a flask of whiskey, after being placed on post, for, half emptied, it was found in a woodpile back of the officers' quarters. The other was that he had more than once meandered from the beaten path to the rear gateway leading to the Farrars' quarters, as though some powerful attraction drew him thither.

Even before the tragedy which had shocked the garrison at taps, busy tongues had everywhere been telling of Thorpe's furious denunciation of Graice and of the statement as to his claim to being the son of an officer. Members of the guard had noticed the fury that seemed to possess Graice after that episode. He slunk away from his kind as though unable to face them after having passively received such a scoring. He had twice been refused by the sergeant permission to leave the guardhouse, as it was surmised he had liquor hidden somewhere, and was craving its fiery comfort and stimulant now. So strong was his conviction on this head that the sergeant had searched him before letting Graice parade with his relief at 10:15. But Graice knew too much to conceal a flask about his person. Looking only for liquor, the sergeant unluckily had failed to notice the keen knife that was secreted within the breast of his overcoat, and that knife had done bloody and disastrous work. It was evident to all that he must have been drinking heavily after taking his post, for he was reeling when led to the guardhouse, and the mad imprecations on his lips were frightful to hear.

Up to reveille Christmas morning not a word had come from Fenton's command, but soon after stable call a courier rode in with a note to Leale. "All right," it cheerily read. "We found the whole band spoiling for a fight and ready to clean out half the county anyhow, but the cowboys kept at respectful distance until we got there. Then when they knew a fight wouldn't be allowed they came charging down and demanded battle or the surrender of White Wolf and his three pals. Two of the latter were half way to Crazy Woman's Fork by this time, and I do not officially know the other, so the whole village moves up under our wing and will camp on the low ground to the west of the fort. Then, when the civil authorities come with warrants and the assurance that the two shall have fair play and a square trial, Big Road will surrender the alleged murderers. Meanwhile no cowboy shall be allowed on the reservation. We should be back by noon." 'Signed', "Fenton."

And by noon back they came, the big squadron of regulars, the motley village of Sioux, followed at very discreet distance by an equally motley array of cowboys and citizens, and all Christmas afternoon the industrious squaws were pitching the tepees on the westward flats, herding the ponies and cooking for their lords, while most of these latter were loafing about the post, glad of a chance to prowl around the quarters and storehouses and beg for anything they saw or fancied. As for "society" at Frayne, it accepted the bliss of the situation as readily as it had mourned the necessity that sent the command away, and, except in one or two households, all thought was centered in the briefly-interrupted preparations for the festivities of the coming night.

Wyoming winter days were short enough, yet this, almost the shortest of the year, had already proved too long, too trying, to more than one comparative stranger within the gates of Fort Frayne. The story of Graice's furious outbreak, of Crow Knife's devotion and dangerous wound, had gone like wildfire over the once more crowded garrison. The former, as has been said, was safely locked in the smaller prison room of the old guardhouse, where for a time he had been heard savagely raging at his bars and kicking at the resounding woodwork; Crow Knife, borne on a blanket to the hospital, lay silent, patient, and hovering between life and death, the captain whom he loved and for whom he had periled his life, sitting steadfast by his side.

Night came on strangely still. The boom of the sunset gun,—the evening chorus of the trumpets and the voices of the men at roll-call all muffled by the fleecy fall of snow,—yet there was premonition in the air, and old-timers glanced at the sky and at the yellow sunset, gloomily predicting ugly weather before the coming morn. Within the cheery mess-rooms, where the troopers were wont to flock with bustle and "chaff" and all manner of fun, mingling with the clatter of plate and knife and spoon, among the cozy homes across the parade, where the families of the officers gathered at dinner, the gloom of Graice's drunken crime, merged in the shadows of the wintry gloaming, seemed to oppress every heart, killing joyous laughter, saddening soldier tones, stifling merry quip and jest, strangling every effort to throw off the weight that had settled on old and young, on one and all. Even among the more reckless and indifferent of the men, Leale's impartiality and justice had won respect that outlived their dread of his stern and unyielding discipline. Even those who had suffered at his hands could not but admire more than they hated him. Among nine-tenths of the troopers he was held in solid esteem, among very many in almost enthusiastic affection, but one and all they united in praise of his conduct on this trying occasion, and in deep, if not loud denunciation of his brutalized assailant. As for the other, the more reputable if red-skinned savage, the soldiers had but one opinion: Crow Knife was the whitest Indian in Wyoming, and they meant it as a compliment despite its unflattering possibilities.

Graice himself had made no friends. A man with a grievance is never popular among soldiers, high or low, and Graice's sullen, surly ways had estranged even those in whom his mouthings against his superiors of every rank, from colonel to corporal, might possibly have responsive echo. That there should be talk of lynching was characteristic of the time and neighborhood and the associations of frontier life, and that it would come to nothing in a military garrison, its most strenuous advocates fully realized.

And all the same, despite the prevailing gloom, the preparations for the dance went on. Battle and murder and sudden death from which we worldlings so earnestly pray deliverance, were matters that might mar, but could not down, the soldier love for social gayeties. Were it otherwise there would have been many a year in the history of our little army wherein no music sounded save the dirge, and the only answer to the battle volley was its measured echo at the grave. Just as the bandsmen peal their most joyous strains as they lead the funeral column on the homeward march, so must there be the merry sound of music and the dance in every garrison of the far frontier, or the wolf's long howl and the savage war whoop, the battle cry, and dying moan live unbanished from the tortured memory, and mind and matter both give way under the ceaseless strain. The morbid curiosity that brought shivering little squads of children and delegations from Sudsville and the stables, ay, from Officers' Row, to peer at the scene of the fierce and sudden affray still sent its victims thither, and questioners were perpetually bothering Rorke and his assistants as they were putting the finishing touches to the decorations and lighting the lamps about the ballroom.

"G'wan out o' this, Finnigan," said Rorke, flourishing his broom at the little group. "Go to your quarters, Collins. Divil knows there was no persuadin' on ye to come a-visitin' here when wurrk was on hand; but now ye shmell the spread, an' drame o' crumbs and heel-taps, ye're as privilent as poor relations at a wake. Arrah, go talk to me ould helmit over at the barracks yonder—me head's tired. Shure I've tould yer lasht night's dark shtory tin toimes over, an' there'll be no more shtory to tell till we know whether it's loif or death for Crow Knife —poor soul—at the hospital yonder, an' a rope or a penitentiary cell for that drunken divil in the guardhouse tower."

"What's he in the tower for?" asked Trooper Martin. "All by himself is he? Too fine for the general room?"

"Too fine? Too wise, crazed as he was," answered

Rorke, "as to thrust himself in the general prison room. Sure he begged pitiful to be shut up by himself and not put loike an onrighteous Daniel into that din o'lious—maniu' two Indians an' a woild Irish prisoner or two, an' they knowin' him to have his comrade's blood, not dhry on his hands."

"Yes, and if things go wrong with Crow,' said Martin, reflectively, " I reckon Graice will wish fire would stand his friend again, as he was telling us it did in Mexico."

"Arrah, if foire were to visit him this night it's him wad visit the divil in short order," said Rorke, looking out of the window. "There's purgathory's own wind that'll be abroad presently, an' a fire sntarted anywhere in the post wad foind thim cartridges in the guardhouse before we cud say our prayers. G'wan out of this, ye omadhauns," said he, flourishing his broom again at the crowd that gathered about him. "Shcat down to Sudsville wid ye before your betters come to foind ye disfigurin' the landscape. Off wid ye, ye son av a soap dish," he cried to a laundress's child, "and tell yer mother she ruined my best shtable frock wid her bluin' lasht week. Faith, it ran loike the legs in yer father's breeches the lasht fight we were in,—bad scran to him for the worst cobbler in the cavalry. Out wid every mother's son of ye," he cried, driving them all out but Kraut and Martin. "Shut that dure now, Kraut, and bar it wid the broad av yer back, till I get the schrane before the enthrance."

But Martin still had other questions to ask. "They

say the Indians of Crow's troop will be neither to hold nor bind if that's his death wound that Graice gave him. I'm told there's mutterings about their having Graice out of the guardhouse to-night, tower or no tower."

Rorke turned and gazed out of the window to where the lights were beginning to burn in the little building. "I pity the man," said he, "that thries to have him out whin Captain Leale's there to watch him and says he shall sthay in."

"Will Crow Knife die, do you think, corporal?" asked Martin.

"Oi don't know. The doctor believes it, an' for the besht reasons,—shure he knows what he's been giving him."

The voices of ladies could be heard at the moment at the vestibule, and presently, with their escorts, Mrs. Farrar and Ellis came hastening in as though they had come purposely to have one look at the old colonel's portrait before the gathering of the rest of the party. A little behind them, pale and with an expression that seemed to tell of the strain through which she had been passing, Helen Daunton came, leaning on the arm of Major Wayne, whom she led to one side, as mother and daughter stood in front of the picture.

"The light seems perfect," said Mrs. Farrar. "I'm sure I see your hand in all this, Rorke, and I want to thank you not only for myself, but for your old colonel. It's many a Christmas we both of us have seen with the old regiment, and the first of them I was a girl bride and you a wee boy trumpeter."

"Indade, ma'm," answered Rorke, "those were merry Christmases that came afther, whin you used to come to the min's dances there a-ladin' little Masther Royle—plague on me tongue! Phat am I sayin' of?"

"Speak of him when you will, Rorke," she answered, gently. "I love to have him brought before me, as we remember him then; my Royle— my brave boy!"

"Dade, an' he was worth remimberin', ma'am. The handsome wild young rider—free wid his money and free wid his fists. Many's the toime I've had to shtand betune him and his little brother—him as is my shuperior officer this day,—Oh, but it's a foine officer he makes, does Masther Will! I never see him so sthrait an' handsome and martial on parade—loik his father before him—him that's gone to glory wid the love av ivery soldier that iver knew him, that I don't remimber thim days whin I was a recruit an' he was the colonel's kid. Och, what days—what days!" and, lost in the enthusiasm of his reminiscences, Rorke failed to notice that Lieutenant Farrar and Kitty had come quietly in and were standing but a little distance behind him. "Do ye remimber, now, ma'am, the Christmas Masther Will mounted his little pony, ahl dressed up to kill, an' 'twas to take the docther's daughter out ridin' he wud, an' tin minutes later we brought him home ahl dhrippin' and rippin' and ragin' ahl along av Corcorin's ould billy goat havin' butted him into the ditch back o' Company D's quarthers an' him ready to kill me for burstin' wid laughin'. Oh, he was a foine boy—." And here Will came furiously forward, and Rorke, horror-stricken, stiffened up to the salute. "I beg yer pardon, Masther Will."

"Your reminiscences are ill timed, corporal, to say the least. If you've quite finished, you'd better follow your men—unless—" and this he added with scathing sarcasm, and glancing at Kitty, who was convulsed with laughter—"unless, perhaps, Miss Ormsby desires you to further entertain her with anecdotes of my childhood," and here Kitty burst in.

"I? Mercy, no! My constant effort is, out of respect to you, to forget your youth, not to recall it. Surely, you're not going to put on that horrid thing again?" she exclaimed, as Will, who had laid aside his overcoat and sabre, now buckled on the weapon.

"Are you afraid I'll injure you with it?" said he, with deep sarcasm.

"Oh, not a bit," said Kitty. "Nor anybody else —unless you should happen to cut yourself."

"Gibe away, Miss Ormsby," said the officer of the guard. "You cannot gibe me into laying aside my sabre. As duty forbids me to appear without it, even your wishes cannot be regarded."

"What? *You* officer of the guard?" exclaimed Kitty. "Ah," with sudden change of manner, "then for one night the post is safe." Here she seized Rorke's broom and took the position of charge bayonet. "Who comes there?" she cried. "The enemy a million strong! Halt, enemy and tremble! Run for your lives! Do you know who is officer of the guard? It's Masther Will." And then, turning from him in saucy imitation of his swagger and stride, with her broom at right shoulder, away she marched for the dressing-room.

"She's past patience," said poor Will to himself, justly wrathful at such ignominious treatment at the hands of his love, and what made it worse was that numbers of people were rapidly arriving and that many had witnessed and enjoyed Kitty's saucy mockery; but right in the midst of these new arrivals came an orderly trumpeter with a note which he lost no time in delivering to Mr. Farrar with the brief announcement: "The officer of the day's compliments, sir, and he said the lieutenant should have it immediately."

Helen Daunton was among those who marked the swift coming of the messenger, and it was impossible for her to resist the impulse that drew her toward the young officer. Intuitively she knew that that message in some wise concerned her wretched husband, now the object of the wrath and curses of the whole command. Breathless she watched Farrar as he tore open the envelope and rapidly read the brief inclosure.

"Crow Knife is dead. There is intense excitement among the men, especially the Indians, and threats of lynching have been heard. Graice knows his peril, and may try to escape. Look well to your guard. Farwell, Officer of the Day."

"Escape from my guard," Helen heard him say, "*Not if he were my own brother!*"

The next minute Will had caught up his cap and overcoat and started for the door.

But Kitty had already begun to repent of her experiment and to question whether she had not hazarded too much in thus provoking her devoted but none the less peppery lover. Peering from the dressing-room, she saw him dart past Helen Daunton, giving very brief answer to some question asked, saw him pick up his cap and coat, and that was more than enough to bring her to terms. Unaware of the coming of the orderly, she looked upon Will's preparations for departure as proof positive that he was so angered against her as to have decided to quit the ballroom for good and all. In an instant she came fluttering to his side, catching him only at the very doorway.

"*Where* are you going, Mr. Farrar?" she demanded, aggrieved and imploring, both. "You're engaged to me for the very first dance, sir. Surely you're not going out?"

"I regret to have to ask for my release, Miss Ormsby," answered Will, with infinite dignity, "but duty of unusual importance calls me at once. My sabre and I made sport for you a moment ago, and now we are going where both are needed," and, bowing very low and looking very majestic, the officer of the guard turned and abruptly left the room, leaving his late tormentor gazing after him with eyes that suddenly filled and lips that quivered suspiciously. Ellis saw through it all at once and came to comfort her.

Strange to say, the young officers were gathering but slowly to-night, and several of their number had not yet arrived. The musicians were in their places and already awaiting the signal of the floor manager, but Leale's absence was remarked by many of those present, and when Fenton entered, his face, usually so jovial, was clouded and anxious. Ormsby was with him, and his eyes seemed to seek and find Ellis at once. Kitty was just turning away as they came. She had watched Will's tall figure disappear in the gloaming toward the guardhouse, and now precipitated herself upon Uncle Fenton to demand an explanation of Will's mysterious references to important duty, and once again, therefore, Ellis was alone. Ormsby stepped quickly to her side. She would have escaped to the dressing-room, but could not do so without passing close beside him. She could not be deaf to the mingling of reproach and tenderness in the tone with which he spoke.

"It would be advertising our—difference were you to deny me a dance or two, Miss Farrar, and I have come to remind you of your promise. You have not forgotten?"

"I think all promises are at an end between us," was the cold, constrained reply. "I forget nothing. I remember only too well."

"Ellis," said he, with sudden impulse, "these are the last words we can have alone, for I have determined to go, and by the very next train. I appeal no longer for your love. The girl who has not learned to trust cannot learn to love, but I do appeal to your sense of justice not to pass blind, cruel judgment on the innocent woman whose secret I am shielding at the cost of what is dearest to me in life."

But she was immovable. Like the soldier's daughter she was, she looked him squarely in the eyes as she answered:

"Neither an innocent woman nor an innocent secret can need shielding at such a cost."

"Ellis," he began, his voice trembling with emotion, as he stepped close to her side, but she recoiled from him, and, noting it and the entrance of new arrivals, he strangled the impulse that swayed him, and, after a moment's silence, continued, in a tone as cold as her own: "No; I see it is useless. The last word is said; but we cannot forget the world is looking on to-night. You will give me—this dance?"

She inclined her head in assent, but would not trust herself to speak. Even now, when angered and full of jealous distrust, she cared for him far too well not to note the sudden change in tone, not to feel vague yet deep distress that he had taken her at her word—that he had determined to leave her this very night—that he would plead no more.

## CHAPTER XIV.

An hour later and the long-expected Christmas ball was in full swing, but the late comers entered snow-covered and buffeted, for, just as Corporal Rorke had predicted, a howling blizzard was sweeping down from the gorges of the Rockies, and whirling deep the drifts about the walls of old Fort Frayne. Leale had come in about tattoo, grave and taciturn, his fine face shadowed by a sorrow whose traces all could see. He had come for no festive purpose, was still in undress uniform, and, after a brief, low-toned conference with his colonel, had turned at once in search of Helen Daunton, who, ever since the dance began, had hovered near the windows that looked out toward the guardhouse, barely one hundred yards away, yet now, even with its brilliant light, only dimly visible through the lashing storm. Twice had Mrs. Farrar essayed to draw her friend into the little circle by which she was surrounded, but Helen had speedily shown she was unable to give her attention to what was being said or to take any part in the conversation. It was at the window Leale found her, and gently but firmly drew her to one side and closed the shade.

"I have felt in every fibre," said he, "how you were waiting, watching, and agonizing here for news from—from him. There is no news, Helen, except

—you know the man he stabbed—who gave his life for me—is dead?"

"I know," was the shuddering answer. "Has he heard? Does he realize?"

"Possibly not. He seems to be sleeping. But he will know it soon enough. Helen—do you know this—that to-morrow we must give him up?"

"Give him up?" she asked, unable to comprehend his meaning, and looking with new dread into his compassionate face.

"Yes, to the civil authorities. He has—I cannot choose words now—he has committed murder and must be tried by a civil, not a military, court."

"You must give him up," she moaned. "Oh, what can we do—what can we do?" and, fearfully she glanced to where Mrs. Farrar was seated, chatting blithely, even joyously, now, with her garrison friends.

"Yes," he answered, "and well I know now why you gaze at her. I know all the miserable truth. Ormsby told me when he came to ask my counsel and my help. He has only left me a short time since. I was pledged to help your husband, Helen, and I am doubly pledged to help that dear, dear woman's son. I must protect Royle Farrar to the utmost of my power, but, Helen, in this last half hour, by the bedside of the brave fellow who gave his life for me, I have looked life and my own soul in the face. I know what I must do and what I cannot do. I am not strong enough to play at friendship with the woman I love with all my soul.

I can only be your friend by serving you from far away. When what is coming to Royle Farrar has come, I shall take leave of absence and go over the sea. It is good-bye between us now. To-night I look my last upon the face of Royle Farrar's wife. What? You want me, Will?" he suddenly turned and asked, for at this moment, throwing back the snow-matted hood of his overcoat, Farrar entered and came quickly to them, unseen by his mother.

"Yes, sir. The news of Crow Knife's death is all over the garrison, and the men are fairly mad over it. They won't try lynching, but the sentries at the guardhouse are doubled, front and rear. Graice is sleeping yet, or else shamming. I don't think he's too drunk not to realize what would happen if Crow Knife's people got at him."

"Then your duty is doubled, lad," was Leale's low-toned answer; "to hold the prisoner and to protect him, too."

"I understand," said Will, firmly. "The man who gets at him to-night, sir, will have to go through hell first."

And then he turned to find Kitty standing, smiling in saucy triumph at his elbow, leaning on the colonel's arm. Still angered against her and deeply impressed with the importance of the duties devolving upon him, Farrar would have hastened by them with only brief and ceremonious salutation, when Fenton stopped him.

"Where did I understand that you were going, sir?" said he with mock severity of manner. "I gave you permission to remain here, sir, and you'd better jump at the chance. Here's my niece telling me that you are engaged to dance with her, and at this moment it seems you are about to leave the room. Off with that overcoat, or it's your sabre that will come off, sir, in arrest. What! Slight a member of your colonel's household? Lord bless me, sir! it's tantamount to mutiny!"

"But colonel," responded Farrar impetuously, "the officer of the day—"

"Not another word, sir. Here is your officer of the day," said he, indicating Kitty, "and you will report for duty instantly."

Irresolute, rejoicing, disappointed and perturbed all in one, Farrar stood one moment hardly knowing what to do, when Kitty seized him by one arm, and Lealc, noting his embarrassment, stepped to his aid.

"I am going to the guardhouse, Will, and I will look after your duties there. Have your dance and return at your convenience. The colonel will let you go after awhile."

And then Kitty resumed her sway. "I shan't dance one step with you until you take that dreadful thing off," said she, indicating his dangling sabre, and utterly ignoring his protest that, as officer of the guard, it was an essential part of his uniform and equipment. Her only response was that he was to remember that he was then on duty to her. "Take off that sword, sir, and hurry about it, for there goes the band." And so unslinging the heavy weapon, he handed it submissively to his imperious queen, who promptly stowed it away under the wooden settee against the wall, and then, curtesying to her partner, indicated to him that at last he was at liberty to lead her to the dance.

And now, smiling, joyous, and once more thrilling with mischievous delight, as she bore her sulky prize across the room, Kitty came suddenly upon the major standing mooning and preoccupied, gazing, apparently, at the portrait of Colonel Farrar, yet, as was equally apparent to the little knot of laughing lookers-on, seeing it not at all. Kitty was on the point of accosting and bringing him to himself, but with eager whisper and gesticulations Amory, Martin and others called her to them.

"Don't wake him," they murmured. "Do let Aunt Lou have that comfort. See, she's coming to him now," And, as what Kitty most wanted at that moment was an opportunity to restore her interrupted dominion over her angered lover, and as he was blind and deaf to anything but the consideration of his own grievances, personal and official, Wayne was left to become the central object of interest, while Kitty drew her deposed officer of the guard to a distant corner.

Wayne was a study. That he was struggling to recall some important matter was evident to all who had long known him, and for the time being he was lost to all consciousness of surrounding sights and sounds, and had floated off into that dreamland of reminiscence in which only he was thoroughly at home. One or two of the ladies who were at the moment resting from the dance, stood leaning on the arms of their attendant cavaliers and watching with them the result of Lucretia's timid, yet determined, approach. Almost tiptoeing, as though afraid that her noiseless footfall might rudely awaken him, she was stealing to his side, and presently they saw her lay her hand upon his arm and peer trustingly up into his face. Thinking only of him and for him, she, too, then was almost unconscious of any observation, kindly and good-natured though it was.

Unwilling to interrupt too suddenly the current of his meditations, she hesitated before speaking. Then, half timidly, she suggested: "You like the picture, major?"

Slowly his gaze came down from the flag-draped portrait, and through his eye-glasses Wayne benignantly regarded her. Finally his wandering wits returned and he aroused himself to faltering answer to her repeated question. "It makes him look too old," he said. "I can't bear anything that looks old, don't you know?" Then, dimly conscious of something he might have put in far happier form, he quickly strove to recall his words. "I—I don't mean women, of course—I like old women. You know I liked you twenty years ago."

"You left me to guess it, then," murmured she, vaguely grateful for even this admission and desirous of encouraging avowals even thus late and lukewarm.

"Yes," he went on, "you know it seems to me—

wasn't it that last night we danced together at Jefferson Barracks? That was every day of twenty years ago."

"Ah well," answered Lucretia, "you know it is so very difficult to reckon from, because that was the 29th of February, and that coming only once in four years, you—"

"Hah!" Wayne laughingly interrupted, and then suddenly fell back again into his old moaning way. "And yet, you know, there was something I wanted to ask you that night, and I was so confoundedly absent-minded—"

"Oh, very," said she, "for you mentioned that there was something you wanted to ask me and I have—I've been wondering what it could be for twenty years."

"Do you know," said he delightedly, "so have I—so have I." And here he leaned beamingly over her, and his eye-glasses fell off and dangled at the end of their cord. "It was only to-night," he went on, "it came to me that it was something connected with this ring—my class ring, you know. It's odd I can't think what it was. Why, your hand is trembling!" Coyly she upraised it to meet the coming ring, and then again he faltered.

"I remember I was holding the ring just like this, when somebody called to me that I'd better hurry—"

"Yes," she said, breathlessly. "Indeed you'd better hurry." But he was still wandering in the past.

"It seems to me—oh! they'd sounded officers' call,

and that meant the devil to pay somewhere, don't you know?" But Lucretia was wilting now, despondent again, for still he went on: "You know, I fancied until the very next day that I'd left the ring here," and, suiting the action to the word, he slipped it on her finger, "and yet the very next day, when I was on scout, I found—I found it here," and with that he again replaced it on his own finger. Lucretia's face was a sight to see. There was an instant of silence, and then, failing to note the expression of her face, looking into the dim recesses of the past, he again wandered off. "Of course I might have known I couldn't have left it on your finger without even seeing—without even seeing if it would fit—without—" and here he lost the thread of his language entirely, and, groping for his glasses, finding them, distractedly he tried to fit their spring on Lucretia's finger. Fenton, who had joined the group of onlookers, could stand it no longer. Bursting into a roar of laughter, he came toward them and, thus interrupted, poor Wayne dropped both hand and eyeglass, madly trying to fit his own ring into his own eye, and look through that under the impression that it was a monocle.

"What on earth are you people laughing at?" he inquired.

"Laughing at? At your trying to make a spectacle hook of Lucretia's hand, you inspired old lunatic," was Fenton's unfeeling answer, and poor Lucretia, unable to stand the raillery at the moment, turned and fled to the dressing room, leaving Wayne to confront his tormentors as best he might.

But while music and laughter reigned within the wooden walls of the assembly room and many young hearts were able to cast aside for the time being the oppression that had settled upon the garrison earlier in the evening, and while in some of the barracks there were sounds of merry-making and Christmas cheer, there was raging in many a breast a storm as wild as that that whirled the snowdrifts in blinding clouds all around and about the guardhouse, where a score of seasoned troopers, silent, grim, and by no means in love with their task, were keeping watch and ward over their little batch of prisoners, especially of the cowering wretch who had been stowed away in the upper room, an utterly friendless man.

Over across the wind-swept parade, among the rows of wooden barracks, was one building where no laughter rang and about which, wary and vigilant, three or four non-commissioned officers hovered incessantly. Here were quartered Crow Knife's few remaining comrades of the Indian Troop. Here were gathered already a dozen of his kindred from Big Road's transplanted village, forbidden by the fury of the storm to return to their tepees up the valley, banished by the surgeon from the confines of the hospital, where they would fain have set up their mournful death song to the distraction of the patients, and refused by the colonel the creature comforts they had promptly and thriftily demanded, except on condition that they consume them in quiet and decorum at the Indian barracks and deny themselves the luxury of their woe. Tomtom and howl were stilled, therefore, while the funeral baked meats went from hand to mouth, and disappeared with marvelous rapidity, and, indeed, but for its exciting effect upon the warriors, the colonel might as well have accorded them the right to lament after their own fashion, since the howling of the tempest would have drowned all human wail from within the wooden walls. But while they had promised to hold no aboriginal ceremony over Crow Knife's death, and meant to keep their word, they had refused to pledge themselves to attempt no vengeance on his slayer. Well they knew that, throughout the garrison, nine out of ten of the troopers would have cared not a sou had some one taken Graice from the guardhouse and strung him up to the old flagstaff without benefit of clergy, but this would not have satisfied Indian ideas—hanging according to their creed being far too good for him. Two of the best and most trustworthy Indians were placed by Leale, with the surgeon's consent, as watchers by the bier of the soldier scout, but the others to a man were herded within the barracks and forbidden to attempt to set foot outside. Close at hand in the adjoining quarters the men of two troops were held in readiness, under orders not to take off their belts, against any sudden outbreak; but the few who first had talked of lynching or other summary vengeance had soon been hushed to silence. What was feared among the officers was that Graice had been told by some of the guard that the Indians were determined to have his scalp, and that the soldiery so despised him that he could not rely upon them to defend him. Sergeant Grafton was confident that Graice hoped in some way, by connivance, perhaps, of members of the guard, to slip out of the building and take refuge among the outlaws at the groggery across the stream. Having killed an Indian he had at least some little claim, according to their theory, to a frontierman's respect.

Returning to the guardhouse, as he had promised Will, Malcolm Leale was in nowise surprised at Grafton's anxiety, and even less to learn that Graice had begged to be allowed to have speech with his captain.

It was a ghastly face that peered out from the dim interior of the little prison in answer to the officer's summons. At sound of footsteps on the creaking stairway Graice had apparently hidden in the depths of the room, and only slowly came forward at the sound of the commanding voice he knew. Hangdog and drink-sodden as was his look, there was some lingering, some revival, perhaps, of the old defiant, disdainful manner he had shown to almost every man at Frayne. Respect his captain as even such as he was forced to do, look up to him now as possibly his only hope and salvation, there was yet to his clouded intellect some warrant for a vague sentiment of superiority. Outcast, ingrate, drunkard, murderer though he was, he, Private Tom Graice, born Royle Farrar, was legal owner of all that his captain held fairest, dearest, most precious in all the world. Leale's love for Helen Daunton was something the whole garrison had seen, and seen with hearty sympathy. It would be something to teach this proud and honored officer that he, the despised and criminal tough, was, after all, a man to be envied as the husband of the woman his captain could now only vainly and hopelessly love. It was his plan to bargain with him, to invoke his aid, to tempt the honor of a soldier and a gentleman, but for a moment, at sight of that stern, sad face, he stood abashed.

"You wished to see me," said Leale, "and I will hear you now."

"I've got that to say I want no other man to know," was the reply after an interval of a few seconds, "and I want your word of honor that you will hold it—sacred."

"I decline any promise whatever. What do you wish to say?"

"Well, what I have to tell you interests you more than any man on earth, Captain Leale. I'm in hell here—I'm at your mercy, perhaps. My life is threatened by these hounds, because by accident that knife went into that blind fool's vitals. It was only self-defense. I didn't mean to hurt him."

"No. I was the object, I clearly understand," said Leale, "go on."

"Well, it's as man to man I want to speak. You know I never meant to harm him. You can give me a chance for justice, for life, and I—I can make it worth your while."

"That will do," was the stern response. "No more on that head. What else have you to ask or say?"

"Listen one minute," pleaded the prisoner. "They'd kill me here if they could get me, quick enough—Indians or troopers either. I must be helped away. I know your secret. You love my wife. Help me out of this—here—this night, and neither she nor you will ever—"

"Silence, you hound! Slink back to your blanket where you belong. I thank God my friend, your father, never lived to know the depths of your disgrace! Not a word!" he forbade, with uplifted hand, as the miserable fellow strove once more to make himself heard. "For the sake of the name to which you have brought only shame, you shall be protected against Indian vengeance, but who shall defend you against yourself? I will hear no more from you. To-morrow you may see your colonel, if that will do you any good, but if you have one atom of decency left, tell no man living that you are Royle Farrar," and with that, raging at heart, yet cold and stern, the officer, heedless of further frantic pleas, turned and left the spot.

But at the porch the captain turned again. Wind and snow were driving across his path. The sentries at the front and flank of the guardhouse, muffled to their very eyes, staggered against the force of the gale. It seemed cruelty to keep honest men on post a night so wild as that for no other reason than to protect the life of a man so criminal. The members of the guard who had resumed their lounge around the red-hot stove the moment the captain disappeared, once more sprang to attention as he re-entered and called the sergeant to him.

"I am tempted to ask the officer of the day to relieve those sentries, and let Number One come up into the hallway," said he. "I believe that, with the watch we have on the Indians, there is no possibility of an outbreak on their part."

"There isn't, sir," was the sergeant's prompt reply. "But every man in the garrison knows by this time that it was the captain that blackguard aimed to kill, and it is not the Indians alone that would do him if they could. I find that, whenever I have had to leave the guardhouse, some of the men have talked loud, for him to hear, swearing that he would be taken out and hanged at daybreak. Others want to tempt him to try to escape, so that they can pursue him over to town and hammer him into a jelly there. The tower is the only place where he can be unmolested, sir. I couldn't guarantee his safety from some kind of assault, even if I had him right here in the guard-room."

And just then a corporal came from the little office.

"Sergeant, its 10:25. Shall I form my relief?"

The sergeant nodded assent. "I'll inspect it in the guardroom," said he, and, as Leale turned shortly away, intending to go in search of the officer of the day, and the sergeant opened the door to let him out, Graice could be heard on the upper floor, savagely kicking again at his bars.

"That man has more gall than any man I ever

met, sir," said Grafton. "He's kicking because we refused to send to the barracks for his share of the Christmas cigars."

"Did you search him before he was sent up there?" asked Leale. "Has he matches or tobacco?"

"Nothing I could find, sir, but other and sharper men have been confined there, and I'm told that somewhere under the floor or inside the walls they've hidden things and he's hand in glove with all the toughs of the garrison."

"Very well. I'll notify Captain Farwell," said Leale, briefly, "and he will attend to it," and he left the building on this quest, just as the second relief came tramping out into the storm, leaving the guardhouse, its few minor prisoners on the lower floor, and that one execrated criminal, his old colonel's first born and once-beloved son, cursing at his captors in the tower, all to the care of the members of a single relief; and the sentry on Number One set up his watch-cry against the howl of the wind, and no one a dozen yards away could have heard, nor did it pass around the chain of sentries, nor was there other attempt to call off the hour that memorable night. For long days after men recalled the fact that the last hour called from under the old guardhouse porch was half-past ten o'clock.

Meantime, having had two dances with his now pleading and repentant sweetheart and having been cajoled into at least partial forgiveness, Will Farrar had sought his colonel to say that he really ought now to return to his guard at least for a little time, but Fenton, conscious of the shadow that had overspread the garrison earlier in the evening, seemed bent on being joviality itself. He bade the boy return to his immediate commanding officer and obtain her consent before again coming to him, and Kitty flatly refused. She was dancing with Martin at the moment, and that left Will to his own devices, and, after a fond word or two from his mother, he had stepped back of the seat occupied by her little circle of chosen friends, and was standing watching the animated scene before him. Close at hand, not a dozen feet away, stood Helen Daunton, partially screened from observation of the dancers. It was at this moment that Leale again came striding in, glanced quickly around until he caught Will's eye, and the young officer promptly joined him.

"Is Farwell here?" he asked.

"He came in a moment ago. Yonder he is now, sir," answered Will, indicating by a nod the figure of the officer of the day in conversation with some one of the guests at the other end of the room.

"Then ask him if he will join me in five minutes at the guardhouse. I need to see him," said Leale, and the youngster sped promptly on his mission.

The music had just sounded the signal for the forming of the sets for the lancers, and with soldierly promptitude, the officers, with their partners, began taking their positions. Floor managers have little labor at a garrison hop. Ellis Farrar, who had reappeared upon the arm of Captain Vinton, mutely bowed her head and accepted Ormsby's hand, as he led her opposite Will and his now radiant Kitty, and Malcolm Leale, halting at the screened threshold before taking his departure, turned for one long look at Helen Daunton's face. Some intense fascination had drawn her once more to the east window, and there, as the dancers formed, alone, almost unnoticed, she slowly turned and her eyes met his. One last, long, intense gaze and, in one impulsive movement, as though he read in her glorious eyes the kindling light of a love that matched his own, he would have sprung to her side, but, with sudden recollection of the barrier between them, he gathered himself, lifted his hand in gesture of farewell, and turned abruptly away. The music crashed into the opening bars of the lancers and the dance began.

For a moment longer Helen stood there. Again that powerful fascination seemed to lure her to draw aside the curtain and gaze forth across the white expanse of the parade, to where the guarded prison stood within whose walls was caged the savage creature whose life was linked so closely with those of many there besides her own. Then the thought of that other—the man whose love, all unwittingly, she had won, and the fear that, glancing back, he might see her shadow as when he came—caused her to draw hastily away. In all that gay and animated scene, as once more she faced the merry throng, Helen Daunton stood alone. The dance went blithely on. Chat and laughter and the gliding, rhythmic steps of many feet mingled with the spirited music of Fort Frayne's capital orchestra.

Even Mrs. Farrar's sweet face, so long shadowed by sorrow, beamed with the reflected light of the gladness that shone on many another. Longing to be alone with her misery, Helen turned to seek the seclusion of the dressing room, and had almost reached its threshold, when over or through the strains of the lancers and the howl of the wind without, there came some strange sound that gave her pause.

Somewhere out upon the parade she heard the distant, muffled crack of the cavalry carbine. Another —another, farther away, and then, mingling with them, hoarse, low murmur as of many voices and of commands indistinguishable through the gale. Louder grew the clamor, nearer came the sounds; then the added rush of many feet in the adjoining barracks of "K" Troop, the quick, stirring peal of trumpet, sounding some unfamiliar call. Overstrained and excited as were her nerves, fearing for him against whom the wrath of the garrison was roused, she could only connect the sounds of alarm and confusion with him and his hapless fate. She started forward to call the colonel's attention, for among the dancers the sound was still unheard. Again the shots and shouts, the rush of hurrying feet on the broad veranda without. Again and nearer, quick and imperative, the thrilling trumpet call. Then, close at hand the loud bang of the sentry's carbine and the stentorian shout of "Fire!" And then, just as the music abruptly ceased in response to the colonel's signal, bursting in at the door, followed by a couple of troopers, came **Rorke**, rushing for a ladder that had been in use during the day.

"It's that madman, Graice, Sorr!" he cried in answer to the look in his commander's face. "He's fired the tower and he's burning to death."

Springing to the window, Helen Daunton dashed aside the curtain, and, all one glare of flame, the guardhouse burst upon the view. A black ladder, silhouetted against the blaze, was being raised at the instant the curtain fell from her nerveless hand. Will seized his cap, made one leap to the door, despite Kitty's frantic effort to seize him; then, missing his sabre, whirled about and rushed from point to point in search of it. Divining his object, the girl threw herself in front of the settee, behind which she had concealed it, and, when he sought to reach around her, desperately, determinedly fought him off. Seizing a cap, the colonel vanished into the night. Throwing over his shoulders the first mantle he could lay his hands on—which happened to be Lucretia's—Wayne followed his leader. Will, delayed and maddened, only succeeded in capturing his sabre by forcibly lifting Kitty out of the way; then he sprang to the doorway to join the men hurrying from distant points to the scene. Ormsby, too, had rushed after the colonel, and only women were left upon the floor. These, horror-stricken, yet fascinated, had gathered about the eastward window, where Helen Daunton crouched, unable to look again upon the frightful spectacle. It was Ellis who hurled aside the curtain, just as old Rorke, re-entering, sprang to the middle of the hall.

"Come away, ma'am! For the love of God, Miss, stand clear of that window! The poor divil's climbed to the top, and the cannon powdher's in the tower."

With a moan of despair, Helen burst through the group and toward the open doorway, as though she herself would hie to the rescue. Rorke, with one leap, regained the threshold, and thrust her back.

"My God, can no one save him?" she cried.

"Save him, ma'am! It's sure death to the man that dares to try it. Any moment it may blow up. They're rushing clear of it now. The colonel's ordered them all back. No! God of hivvin, some one's climbing the ladder now! It's Captain Leale! Oh, don't let him, men! dhrive him back! Oh, what use is it? Did man ever live that could turn Malcolm Leale from the duty he deemed his own?" And away rushed poor Terry. Ellis sprang to her mother's side just as, to the accompaniment of a shriek from Kitty's lips, there came a dull roar, followed by a sudden thud and crash of falling timbers, and the hoarse shouts of excited men. An instant later, Ormsby, nearly breathless, leaped in at the door.

"They'll have to bring him in here. Leale would have saved him if he hadn't jumped. Ellis, your mother must not see his face. Take her into the dressing room."

"And why?" cried Ellis. "The lives of our best and bravest have been risked to save that worthless life? This is no place for him. He shall not be brought here."

"Hush," said Ormsby, in a low, intense tone. "In God's name, Ellis, hush! The man on that litter is your mother's son—your own brother—Royle Farrar. That is the secret I was guarding for Helen Daunton—your brother's wife."

A moment later as the women gathered about Mrs. Farrar, obedient to Ormsby's murmured injunction to keep her from seeing the face of the dying man, lest it prove too severe a shock to her weakened heart, the men came solemnly, bearing a stretcher on which lay the blanket-covered form, followed by a silent group of officers. The doctor simply touched the wrist, gave one glance into the scorched and blistered face, shook his head, and drew the blanket. Kitty, sobbing, clung to Willy's arm, their quarrel forgotten. Helen, who had thrown herself almost hysterically upon her knees at the stretcher's side, turned in added terror at the words of the colonel, "Another patient, doctor," for at the instant, supported by Wayne and others, Malcolm Leale was led within the doorway, a handkerchief pressed to his eyes.

"He got the full flash of that explosion in his face," murmured the old soldier, as the doctor met them. Then, in the solemn presence of death, in the hush and silence of the throng, Mrs. Farrar stepped forward and laid her white hand gently, reverently upon the lifeless breast.

"Reckless and hardened he may have been," she

said, "but somewhere — somewhere, I know a mother's heart is yearning over him and a mother's lips are praying for the boy she loves."

And so it happened that only one or two could hear the single, whispered word with which the doctor turned to his commander after one brief look into Malcolm's eyes.

"Blind!"

## CHAPTER XV.

JACK ORMSBY did not go East by the first train after the Christmas ball, as had been his purpose, but he saw no more of the lady of his love. Late that dreadful night, rousing for a few moments from the stupor into which she had been thrown by the announcement that it was her own brother who lay there downstricken in the midst of his career of crime and shame, Ellis Farrar, little by little, realized the whole miserable truth—that he, her brother, was the man who had wrecked Helen Daunton's life—Helen, who to spare that invalid mother an added sorrow, had hidden from her the name of the man whose brutal blows and curses had rewarded her love. More than all did Ellis realize that the lover, whose loyalty and devotion she herself had repaid with scorn and contempt, had suffered her words in silence rather than betray another woman's confidence and thereby divulge a truth that would overwhelm with shame all who bore the name of Farrar. Then it was that, hysterically weeping, she broke down utterly and before the setting of another sun the mother and all the household learned from her lips that it was all that was left of Royle Farrar that now lay there, cold and stiff and still in that bare, echoing ward of the old hospital, awaiting the last volleys and the solemn trumpet salutation to the soldier dead.

Only a corporal's guard formed the firing party,

when, just before sundown, the remains of "Private Graice" were laid in the bleak, snow-covered cemetery out on the rolling prairie, but more than a dozen men in the crowded garrison knew by that time that the folds of the flag were draped over the mortal remains of a colonel's son.

It was an awe-stricken group that gathered about the hospital when the bearers came forth with their burden and placed it in the waiting ambulance, and the firing squad presented arms. The idea of the recreant—the would-be murderer, Tom Graice—being buried with military honors had not occurred to the garrison as a possibility. Yet here was the little escort, here were the trumpeters, (the band had been mercifully excused), here were pall bearers from his troop instead of from among the garrison prisoners, as might have been ruled when one of their number died; here were old Terry Rorke, and some of the senior sergeants of the regiment; here, indeed, with pallid face was young Lieutenant Farrar, with him Mr. Ormsby, the adjutant, quartermaster, the surgeon, and one or two veteran captains, Major Wayne, and even Colonel Fenton himself! Who ever heard of such an array as that attending the obsequies of a criminal? Fort Frayne was mystified and talked of it for hours, but the story told itself before tattoo and the mystery was done.

They had buried the first born of the colonel whom all men loved and honored and mourned, and old Fenton had himself decided that, as Graice had never yet been tried and convicted, and could never appear before an earthly tribunal, he must be considered as innocent, and so issued the order that no military honor should be denied, except the band. It was too bitterly cold for them to attempt to play, for the valves of the instruments would freeze at once, and it was deemed best that no sound of the dirge music should reach the ears of Marjorie Farrar. Neither she nor Ellis knew when the funeral took place—Mrs. Farrar learning only on the following day, Ellis not until weeks thereafter, for, as a result of all the long, gradual strain, culminating in the shock of that tragic night, and the realization of the wrong she had done the honest man who had so loved her, her strength gave way, and brain fever and delirium supervened. In the week that followed that hapless holiday, Ellis hovered on the borderland 'twixt life and death, and no man could say that the fatal Christmastide might not claim still another of the Farrars.

And that week was one of woe to poor Jack Ormsby. He haunted the neighborhood of the Farrars; he hung about the gateway, importuning the doctor, the colonel, Kitty, Will—anybody—for tidings of the girl he loved. His fine, alert, intelligent face was clouded with the dread and sorrow that overcame him. He could not see Mrs. Farrar—she rarely moved from her stricken daughter's side—but twice he saw and talked with Helen, and once, with her, walked out to visit the new-made grave. All that week the shadows cast by the glare of the guard-house flames seemed to wrap Fort Frayne in gloom, and people gazed upon the black ruins only with a shudder. The Indians, ever superstitious, had professed to see the hand of the Great Spirit in the clouds, pointing remorselessly at the spot, and warning them of further wrath to come, as a consequence of the unavenged murder of a chieftain's son. Cowboys and "hustlers," angered against the garrison because it had interposed between them and their purposed punishment of Big Road's band, saw here a capital opportunity of embroiling the red men with their white defenders. By dozens, in shivering silence, wrapped in their blankets and seated on their scraggy ponies, the warriors had looked on at the solemn little ceremony, and within another day by scores the cowboys and settlers were spreading the story that the white chief had buried Tom Graice, with all the honors of war despite his crimes and misdemeanors, simply because he had killed the son of an Indian chief—the son of the chief whose people killed the colonel of the Twelfth when he attacked the fleeing village on the Mini Pusa three long years before. It was the white soldiers' way of taunting the red man. It was proof of his real feeling toward the Indian.

"Look out for yourself, Big Road!" said these astute, frontier statesmen; "Chief Fenton and his soldiers have only lured you here within range of their walls, that they may the more readily swoop upon you some bitter morning, and put you and your warriors, your women and children to the sword." In the intense cold of the three days that succeeded the blizzard, there was no interchange of visits, so to speak, between the fort and the Indian village, but the emissaries of Ben Thorpe had been busily at work. Big Road and his warriors had been bidden to attend the stately funeral of their kinsman and friend, Crow Knife, on the morning after Christmas, and had flocked to the scene and lifted up their mournful chant when the volleys flashed and the crowd of attendant soldiers bowed their heads in mingled homage and sorrow. That was as it should be, but what did it mean that his slayer should then be accorded equal honors—aye, that more officers—chiefs—were present at Graice's grave than when the son of a Brulé warrior was laid to rest? This they could not fathom, and this, despite the strained relations that had resulted in the death of Laramie Pete, the cowboy emissaries proved eager to explain in their own way and to explain to attentive ears.

"Old Fenton thought he'd done me when he moved that bloody band up here to the fort," said the cowboy king to his admiring audience, over at the saloon across the Platte. "If I don't pay him off with compound interest within the month and make him wish he hadn't monkeyed with my business, call me a coyote. He and the stuck-up gang he heads will wish to God they'd left those Indians where they were."

And five days after Christmas Colonel Fenton heard of goings on within the village that gave him cause to summon his adjutant and officer of the day, to double his sentries on every front, and to realize how much in these few years he had learned to lean for counsel and support on Malcolm Leale, for now the colonel was forbidden, as was everybody else, to see him, even for a moment. Not only had the flash of the explosion wrecked his eyesight, but there was grave reason to fear that he had inhaled the flame. Captain Leale was suffering torment, yet bearing his burden without a moan.

A troubled man was the veteran post surgeon all that woeful week. Ellis Farrar, delirious in burning fever, Malcolm Leale prostrate on a bed of pain, blind, and breathing only in agonized gasps; Mrs. Farrar looking so fragile and weak that it seemed as though a breath might blow away the feeble flicker of her life; others of the women more or less overcome and shocked by the events of the last few days, and now, right in the midst of it all, came indications of trouble in the Indian village up the stream—powwowing, speechmaking, and dancing by night, runners flitting to and from the Big Horn, messengers darting in from other tribes—and, when Fenton sent for Big Road to come into the office and explain the chief temporized, expressed himself as suspicious of some plot to separate him from his people and to hold him as hostage at the fort. If Colonel Fenton desired to talk let Colonel Fenton come to the council lodge at the village but leave his soldiers behind. Big Road's old men had seen visions and had heard warnings; his medicine chiefs had been signaled by the Great Spirit; his young men were excited and alarmed; his women were weeping and gathering their children to their knees. If the white chief meant peace and friendship, let him show it by coming to his lodge with gifts in his hands, instead of guns. He, the white chief, was rich, and his horses and his young men were fat and strong. Big Road was poor and his people were hungry and cold; his ponies dying. Fenton, indeed, would have gone with only his adjutant and interpreter and a single orderly but for the warning of a Brulé girl, who had left her people a few years before to follow a soldier lover, and had made her home among the whites, a patient, sorrowing woman, ever since his untimely death. The Amorys had provided for her in every way, for the soldier was one of the captain's troop, and she had grown deeply attached to them, even though now occasionally visiting her kindred.

It was at luncheon, talking to his wife, that Amory told of Colonel Fenton's purpose of riding over to the village that very afternoon, and the story was repeated in the kitchen, where it reached the ears of the Indian girl. In an instant she had darted out of the house and gone to the colonel's, where she frightened Lucretia out of her seven senses with the first words she uttered: "They kill the colonel! He no go!" Luckily, Wayne was at hand to soothe, support and explain. Other officers were sent for, and, despite Fenton's pooh-poohing, so strong were their arguments that at two o'clock a messenger was dispatched to Big Road's bailiwick to tell him the colonel had heard that which made him say to the Indian chief that now the only way in which he would meet him would be at the adjutant's office, as originally proposed, or else alone and unarmed midway between the fort and the village, no soldiers or warriors being allowed to approach within two hundred yards, unless, indeed, Big Road himself should propose an adjutant for each. If this was satisfactory, let the time be set for three o'clock and Fenton would be there. The half-breed messenger came back in half an hour. "Big Road would send his answer by a squaw," and that was Big Road's way of saying that the white chief was an old woman. Utterly forgetful now of the service Fenton had rendered his people and him, duped by the visions of his medicine men, and fuddled with the liquor lavished on him by the cowboys, Big Road was hot for war.

No squaw came; no conference took place. Darkness was settling down upon the post when at last the westward sentries reported a small party of Indians riding out from the village toward Fort Frayne. The trumpeters were just scattering after sounding retreat, when the officer of the day conveyed the news to Fenton, and in two minutes an officer, with a dozen men, trotted out from the stables of Troop "K" and four hundred yards beyond the sentry post signaled to the advancing warriors: "Halt!"

There were ten in the party, and Big Road was not among them. The officers, returning from stables and retreat roll call, had gathered about the colonel on the westward bluff, and field glasses were brought to bear on the opposing parties, now only dimly visible in the gloaming. Over at the barracks the men were still gathered about their respective parades, despite the fact that supper was ready and they as ready for supper. All over the garrison had gone the rumor of Big Road's hostile and defiant message, and the troops were wrathful at the indignity put upon their colonel. Some of them had stepped inside the quarters and were quietly examining their belts and equipments, and counting the cartridges in their boxes. Ormsby, sharing the suppressed excitement, had hastened out to join his friends of the Twelfth, his nerves tingling again at the thought of the possibility of a skirmish, and now he stood with Fenton close at hand, waiting eagerly for the first developments.

But little time was wasted. There was a brief parley between the lieutenant with the troopers and a formidable-looking Indian who seemed to lead the others. Then the officer turned and sent a man galloping back to the post. In four minutes he was in the colonel's presence, dismounted, and making his report.

"Big Road's compliments—I mean, the lieutenant's compliments, sir—and Big Road sends his delegation for three wagonloads of meat, flour, sugar, and coffee, sir, and says as the colonel hasn't come to see him, he's going to move."

The colonel laughed—the first laugh since Christmas, somebody remarked at the time. "Are you sure there's no mistake, Fallon?" he asked the messenger.

"That's what the lieutenant asked the Indians, sir, but we have two of "L" Troop with us—what's left of 'em—one Brulé and t'other Ogallalla, and they both translate it the same way, and Bat is with us, too, sir; and he says it's like Big Road when he gets liquor in him. He thinks he's lord of the earth. Bat says he's drunk now, and believes the colonel will be glad to do as he demands for fear of him."

"Well, who brought the message? Who's that big buck in the lead there?"

"That's One-Eyed Bull, sir—him that was nursed in the hospital here after the fight three years ago."

"Bull? He ought to know better than to bring any such message," said Fenton, reflectively. "I presume he dare not refuse, however. Mr. Adjutant, mount Fallon's horse, gallop out there, and tell Bull to tell Big Road to go to the devil. That's all on that head. Captain Farwell, as soon as your men have had supper, let them saddle and be ready for night work. Orderly, have my horse sent up in half an hour. That's all for the present, gentlemen. Come, Jack—Lou's waiting dinner for us."

It was the first time that any one had seen Fenton mad, as Amory put it, when the group broke up. "Either Big Road will come down off that high horse or the old man will snatch him, and within the next few hours, too. Ormsby brings us luck. He never comes out here that we don't have a shindy of some kind."

More than one officer was thinking of this remark of Amory's as they scattered to their homes. Many a dinner was kept waiting and many a housewife had to be placated when the lord and master hurried in, and tongues that were primed with wifely reproof were stilled by the tidings that quickly spread from door to door. Big Road had made an insolent demand, and coupled with it a defiant message. Big Road was drunk and had threatened to move with his village, and then it would become the duty of the Twelfth to surround and herd him back. Under the stipulation of a late treaty, he was allowed for his winter range only the south bank of the Platte, from Frayne to the breaks of the Medicine Bow. If he crossed the Platte and struck out for the Big Horn, he invaded the cattle lands and laid himself open to attack from the "hustlers." If he dove into the mountain range to the south, he left his reservation and forfeited the rations and supplies which the agent at Fetterman Bend was bound to issue at regular intervals. He had quarreled with the agent and moved his village up stream to within ten miles of Frayne—which he had a right to do. He had quarreled with, and on good grounds, the cowboys, and then taken under the wing of Uncle Sam for safety, and now he proposed quarreling with his benefactors and launching out on forbidden territory, and that meant business for all at Frayne.

But One-eyed Bull was no truculent warrior. He had delivered his message in accordance with his chief's demands, and in far more civil tone and terms than it was consigned to him; then had waited in dignified silence, confronting the somewhat flippant blue coats from the fort, refusing to make any response to the jocularity and ridicule in which some of their number indulged, or to enter into any discussion with Bat or the two Indian soldiers as to the probable inspiration of Big Road's bombast. Well enough he realized when the adjutant arrived upon the scene that the "bluff" had totally failed, and before a word was spoken read contemptuous refusal in the young officer's face. They were indeed cold and hungry over in the village, and he himself and the warriors with him would have been glad of a feast on army rations. Nor were the warriors at all satisfied with the judgment and discretion of their chief, but one and all the Indians were now imbued with the warning of their medicine men, and expected nothing less than some sudden act of hostility on the soldiers' part. If there ever was a time in Big Road's history when a clear head and cool brain were needed, it was now, just when he had succeeded in getting drunk, and well had the cowboys reasoned. While some of the number lured the chief to the banks of the Platte and plied him with lies and whiskey, others were scurrying up and down the valley, routing out the ranchmen, settlers, and "hustlers," and warning them to be in readiness to gather at the given signal, for there was no telling what would be the first consequence of their diplomacy. If Big Road simply broke camp and started with his whole village in the dead of night in hopes of leading the soldiers a stern chase to the Big Horn, they could stumble in his way, impede his fight, and bring on a row in which, with vastly superior numbers, they could at least rob the red men of their pony herd. That would be part satisfaction for the death of Laramie Pete. Then, when the soldiers came up, they could sail in after them and claim such spoil as was worth having and all the credit of having brought the chief to bay. If, on the other hand, Big Road became so crazed with their fire-water as to go down and beard the lion in his den and defy the cavalry at the fort, then there might be a pretty scrimmage right over on the flats when the colonel ordered the chief's arrest, and when the soldiers were tackling the warriors in the open and having a nip-and-tuck fight of it the frontiersmen could surround the village and help themselves. There would be only old men and women and children to defend it. There was gloom, therefore, in Bull's sole remaining optic as he received in majestic silence the adjutant's indignant rendering of the colonel's message, and, motioning to his blanketed braves to follow, he turned about and rode away.

"What do you think they'll do?" was the eager question asked the adjutant on his return to the post. "Is he mad enough to mean fight?"

"He is, if he doesn't get any drunker," was the answer. "More whiskey would be the surest way of settling the question now, but it would rob us of the pleasure of knocking him out—and be damned to him for spoiling my dinner!"

At eight o'clock that night, with one platoon in dispersed order well to the front, and others in reserve, while the garrison of Fort Frayne stood by their arms within the fort, Captain Farwell's troop moved slowly up the dark valley, along the snow-covered flats, out beyond the point where the delegation was met at dusk and held at bay, and, though the stars were glinting in the frosty sky and not a breath of air was stirring, and the night was still as solitude itself, not a whisper could be heard from the direction of the village, not a spark of fire could be seen. Over against them on the northern shore were sounds at times as of rapid hoof beats, muffled by the snow. Half a mile out a horseman loomed up at the front, and in a moment was merged in the advancing line.

"What is it, sergeant? What news have you?" asked the young platoon commander.

"They're off, sir! A whole gang of old folks and women on ponies and travois has started across the Platte. The warriors are all there yet. You'll hear Big Road shouting in a minute. He's fighting full and is urging on some deviltry—I can't make out what, but from all we can understand of it he wants to lead a rush through the stables to capture or kill the horses. He's just drunk enough to try, but the others won't let him. They declare they won't follow him. They know too much. What they want to do is to get out and reach Trooper Creek to-night, I reckon."

"Ride back, then, and let the captain know. Who else are out at the front on watch?"

"Only Rorke and two or three of the Indian troop, sir. They are taking care of themselves, though."

And then for a moment the forward movement ceased. "Halt! Halt!" were the low-toned orders of the non-commissioned officers dispersed along the line, and, under the twinkling stars, dim, ghostly, and silent, the extended rank of riders seemed as one man to rein in and wait. Here and there an impatient charger began to paw the snow, and others sniffed suspiciously and cocked their pointed ears in the direction of the unseen village. Some young troopers, tremulous with excitement and cold combined, began to slap their fur-gloved hands on breast or thigh and had to be sternly called to order. Presently a muffled horseman came riding up from the rear, a trumpeter in his tracks.

"That's right, Martin. You did well to halt a minute. I've sent back word to Colonel Fenton. He had wired to the agency before we pulled out."

"Can't we turn. 'em back without his authority, sir?"

"No; even when we know they mean to cross the Platte. But orders will come to-night. The wires are working well."

"Captain, did you hear what Captain Amory said this evening?" asked the youngster, as he edged in closer to the elder's side, "that Ormsby never came out here that we didn't have a shindy with the Sioux?"

"Yes; but poor Jack is out of the dance this time and can't be with us, as he was before."

"I don't understand," said Martin, having some vague theory that the illness of Miss Farrar was at the bottom of Ormsby's inability to take part in the promised chase. "I—didn't suppose anything could keep him from taking a hand in soldier service."

"Well, that's just it! Those fellows in the Seventh are as punctilious on a point of duty as any man we know in the army. Ormsby promised to be back with his company for some review or ceremony within this week. He's got to go. They've telegraphed to remind him, and he has just time, barring accident, to make the trip."

## CHAPTER XVI.

Nine o'clock, ten o'clock of that wintry evening came, but no orders. Fenton had reported the situation by wire to department headquarters late in the afternoon, and had twice sent messages to the agency. In answer to these latter came characteristic appeals to do nothing to excite or exasperate Big Road, but to induce him to remain where he was until he, the agent, could come and confer with him,—he'd be along the first train in the morning. To this Fenton responded that, unless he was permitted to go out, surround, and arrest him and his principal braves at once, Big Road would break camp and be off before the rising of another sun. Fenton felt sure of it. To this came response that such a course would only anger the Indians, who were very sensitive to anything that looked like coercion, and that until they had actually crossed the Platte no steps such as were indicated by Colonel Fenton should be taken. Still, they should not be allowed to attempt to cross.

"Now, how on earth," said Fenton, "am I to prevent their doing that without something that looks like coercion? If I can't stop them, I at least won't lose touch," said he. And so, while the rest of the command was held in readiness, Farwell's troop had been dispatched, as we have seen, with orders to observe and follow—but not to interfere with the movements of the village. Up to ten o'clock, as he learned through Indian scouts, only women and children, old men, old ponies, and dogs had been spirited away. With them went perhaps half a dozen warriors as guards against night attack from hostile white men, but the main body still hung about the site of the dismantled village. Big Road wanted more talk with the cowboys—and more firewater.

Now was the very time to attempt the arrest since none but warriors remained—none but fighting braves would suffer if they resisted and opened fire, and, all eagerness, Farwell sent back messengers explaining the situation and asking from his colonel authority to do something. Eleven o'clock came and still no orders reached Fenton, either from the general commanding or his chief of staff; no further authority from the agency. It looked as though the wintry night would be allowed to slip away, and the Indians with it, and that meant that more of their Christmas holidays would be lost to the Twelfth through having to go campaigning in the biting cold. Taps sounded at eleven, and Fenton, disgusted, gave orders that the command should unsaddle and go to barracks, but practically to sleep on their arms. Meanwhile luckless Farwell and his fellows would have to make a night of it up the Platte, and already two poor boys were sent in, numb and more than half frozen.

The waning moon was not yet risen, and the darkness was intense, but for the glinting of the stars on the snowy surface; yet keen-eyed scouts hung close to the site of the Indian camp and sharp ears noted every sound. There was a guffaw of derisive laughter among the blanketed warriors in answer to the faint, far-away sounding of "lights out."

"Small use to sound 'lights out,' whin it's lightin' out thim blackguards are doing already," growled old Rorke to his fellow-trooper. "It's many a Christmas they've spoiled for me and mine, and now they do be drawin' on the New Year's party, too. It's in the Big Horn we'll be against Sunday next, or I'm a Jew."

"That's the prettiest country in the world for fishin' and fighting," was the answer, "but I've no likin' for it when the cowld would freeze the soup twixt the mug and the mouth. Who's yon?" he broke off suddenly, bringing his fur-guarded thumb to the hammer of his carbine and indicating with a nod of his head a dim, dark shape coming crouching toward them through the starlight.

"Halt, there!" was Rorke's gruff, muttered challenge, at the instant. "Rise up, you, and say who ye are. Oh, it's you, is it, Pollywog? Come in from under yer head an' explain what keeps your brother night owls yonder—why don't they start, if ever they're going?"

Obedient to the order, given in soldier terms he could not use, yet sufficiently understood, an Indian scout—an Arapahoe boy—whose big shock head seemed twice the size of his lean torso, straightened up from his catlike crouch and came swiftly toward the two troopers.

"Big Road going—plenty quick," he muttered. "Heap whiskey now—Bunco fetch 'um!"

"Ah, that's what kept him, was it? Run back, Clancy, and tell the captain he's fired up, and I'll creep in closer and see if he's started." So saying the old trooper doubled up over his huge, moccasined feet and, carbine in hand, crept stealthily onward toward the point where last the tepees had been seen at dusk, Pollywog excitedly shuffling by his side. For fifty yards or so nothing could be heard or seen in front, then they came upon a dark object kneeling under a stunted cottonwood, close to the bank of the frozen stream. It was one of the Indian troopers, and at Rorke's muttered summons he raised his hand as though to caution silence, and again bent his head attentively,

"Heap whiskey!" was his whispered verdict. "Pretty soon fight. Listen!"

There were sounds of turmoil in the Indian ranks —harsh, guttural voices and much shuffling about. Every now and then the thud of pony hoofs could be heard, as the nimble little beasts went scurrying over the snow; then muffled shouts across the stream in impatient hail and excited answer. One party of warriors was evidently on its way, and its rearward members were striving to induce the laggards at the village to come in.

"Bedad!" said Rorke; "John Barleycorn has laid some of thim buck blackguards by the heels already, and they can't rouse 'em up. Go you in there, Pollywog. They won't see you this night.

There isn't one in that gang could tell a 'Rappahoe from a raw recruit with six fingers av Bunco Jim's jig wather in him. G'wan in, boy. Harass the inemy all ye can, without bringin' on a general engagement—by which I mane any kind av a fight that's too big for a corporal. Did ye find the captain?" he asked, turning suddenly to Clancy, who came steadily up from the rear.

"Whist! he's right here, an' Mr. Ormsby with him."

Surely enough, crunching through the snow, making as little noise as they could, yet stumbling painfully at times, two burly forms could be seen creeping toward them, and presently Farwell was near enough to whisper an inquiry as to how far the village was ahead.

"Not fifty yards, sorr," said Rorke. "But you needn't fear to wake 'em. There's only wan word what's left of Big Road's people can understand now and that's whiskey. It's my belief there's a dozen bucks over there too drunk to ride, and they've sent all the travois ahead and don't know how to lug 'em along. They haven't all the plainscraft in the world, sorr, and the Twelfth could give 'em a line or two of lesson on that score."

"Damn the luck!" said Farwell, heartily. "My orders are not to interfere or to follow until they're all across the Platte. How many are holding back there, corporal?"

"Faith, I don't know, sorr, but ivery man that's

left sees double, and I've told Pollywog to count 'em. How far back are the men, sorr?"

"They're close at hand now. We moved forward after getting your message. Listen to those beggars!"

Through the still night a wild, mournful howl was uplifted from the direction of the village. "A cross betune the yelp of a coyote and the howl of a keener," said Rorke. "Bedad, they may talk Sioux when they're sober, but Irish is the universal language when they're drunk. Hark til 'em now." Another howl went up. Somebody was making a speech, and presently, as the orator warmed to his subject, the sonorous tones rang out over the frozen valley and came thundering back from the echoing bluffs.

"That's Big Road himself," muttered Terry. "He's too crooked to-night to see his own way, but he can steer the others all the same. What's he saying, Bismarck?" he inquired of the silent Indian trooper.

"He says Big Road's village reaches from the Medicine Bow to the tops of the Big Horn, and there are not enough white soldiers or cowboys in all the land to take him. He says he's going to ride with his six sons and fight Fort Frayne at sunrise."

"Then I'll have time to see the fun," said Ormsby, with a laugh that had no mirth in it. "My train goes at eight, and I should hate to miss the entertainment. I've come out to say good-bye to you,

Terry," he continued, as he held forth his hand to the surprised corporal.

"Shure, Misther Ormsby is not goin' to lave us—now—with all the new trouble—and Miss Ellis down sick?"

"I'm of no use to them, Rorke," said Ormsby, sadly, as Farwell edged on to the front as though to give him a chance to talk to this faithful old henchman of the Farrars. "Indeed I'm getting superstitious. I bring them nothing but ill luck. I've never come that it wasn't like some bird of ill omen. First it cost them the blessed old colonel's life, and now that scapegrace son is brought back into their world just long enough to reopen all the old wounds, and the poor mother is bowed with new shame and sorrow and with new anxiety since Miss Ellis is down. The doctors say the danger is past and she will soon rally. You and Lieutenant Will are all they need. So—take good care of them, Terry, and of yourself, too, and don't forget we've had one or two good rides together, even though I can't be with you in this—and—I've left a little remembrance for you with 'Master Will'—only don't you dare call him that again."

"Sure, no man in the Twelfth will ever need a rememberance of Mr. Ormsby that saw him that day we jumped Kill Eagle in the snowstorm, but whisper," he murmured, wistfully, "who's to tell Miss Ellis? The roses will be slow coming back to the blessed face av her—whin she finds you're gone."

"I've got to go, Rorke," said Ormsby, briefly. "In all my years in our regiment, I've never missed an inspection or a review, and mighty few drills have I failed to be there. They'd forgive me for staying here for the honor of the Seventh, and a sure thing of a fight, but nothing less, and the colonel says there is no fight here—only another surround and capture and escort home. Why, Big Road's drunk!"

"Ay, ay, sorr, and if the colonel was Irish, as was him that preceded him—by brevet annyhow, and the love of ivery Irishman in the Twelfth—he'd know that an Indian's never so full of fight as whin he's full of whiskey. There isn't room in Big Road's skin for another noggin', sir. His people will drag him after the village. The cowboys will jump them up the range. It'll bring on a general row, and our carbines will be crackling along Trooper Creek by noonday to-morrow, or I'm worse than a Jew—I'm a bureau agent!"

"How'd you get out here, any way? You're in Captain Leale's troop."

"True, sorr, but the colonel put me on jewty wid the few Indians that's left since Crow Knife died, and by regimental orders I'm timporariously a Sioux sergeant. It's an Irishman over the Indian. That's poetic justice, sorr—the green above the red."

"May you win the chevrons this night in your own troop, Terry, and I'll send you the handsomest pair to be made in New York. Good-bye, old friend. Take care of them—all. I must ride back now."

And so with one long clasp of the hand the two friends and fellow campaigners, oddly mated, yet closely allied, turned slowly away from one another.

Rorke to take up once again his post of duty, Ormsby to mount and, riding in silence past the shivering groups of soldiers, huddling about their horses and dancing and stamping to keep from freezing, to hie him back to the fort and for a parting word with Will.

Far up on the snow-mantled bluff the ruddy night lights were burning in the colonel's quarters. Far above them, the brilliant stars were twinkling in the sky. Over across the stream the bale fires burned like wreckers' luring signals on the shore among the dingy clusters of wooden shacks where Bunco Jim had undisputed sway. Away out northward across the frozen steppe there sounded once in a while some bacchanalian whoop, for savages red and savages dirty white were riding in parallel parties, and beginning now to shout drunken defiance at one another over the intervening mile. Behind him, as he swiftly rode, Ormsby could hear, with increasing frequency, the whoops and yells of Big Road's stragglers, still anchored south of the Platte, but evidently getting slowly under way. Then straight ahead, up along the plateau, in ringing, fearless tone, the sentries began their midnight call, and all the valley re-echoed to the stirring assurance that, so far as Frayne and its sleeping populace was concerned, it was twelve o'clock and all well.

And then somewhere across the stream among that cluster of ramshackle hovels there flared a sudden light, a single, instantaneous flash, followed in a few seconds by a loud bang that revived the echoes of the watch-cry, just as the last, in faint aerial ripple, seemed dying miles away, and then Jack Ormsby struck spurs to his horse and galloped to the post. Even though no answers came from the sentries on the bluff, he knew that shot was no empty, meaningless, reckless deed. It was a signal to some distant watcher and was answered, just as Ormsby expected, by a faint, far-away crack of rifle, miles perhaps to the silent north.

A corporal came running to meet and identify him when he was halted by the westward sentry on Number Three.

"Have they started, sir?" asked he.

"Yes; all but a few are gone. What are the lights about? Anything astir at the post?"

"'K' Troop ordered right out, sir. The wires quit working twenty minutes ago, and they're cut along the railway to the east."

Throwing himself from his horse when he reached the colonel's quarters, Ormsby hastened in and found that energetic warrior saying things that impelled Aunt Lou to stop her ears and lift up a plaintive voice in vain protest. The adjutant was there, a sympathetic listener, however, and the orderly had gone for the officer of the day—the official who, next to the adjutant, was always sure to be summoned when anything of unusually exasperating character had happened.

"Did you ever know anything more contemptuously impudent in your life, Jack?" said his uncle. "They've let me wear these wires hot sending all manner of prayers to be allowed to do something, and, just so long as the replies were orders not to interfere, our friends and fellow-citizens have let them through. Now, the moment the tide begins to turn, and the agent or the general, or somebody else, has a lucid interval, and things begin coming our way, they find it out and clip the wires. How could they find it out? Why, they have more friends at court than we ever could hope to have. I'll bet six months' pay the order for us to move is sizzling in the snow somewhere east of Cañon Springs. I've sent half a dozen of the best light riders in 'K' Troop east to find the break, but it will be broad daylight before a word can reach us, and by that time that whole outfit will be at Trooper Creek. Were there any left when you came away?"

"Just a few, sir. They've been supplied with whiskey from Bunco Jim's, I fancy, and some of them seem very drunk. Farwell thinks the village is strung out over as much as a dozen miles. You heard that shot a few minutes ago, did you?"

"The sentry did, and reported it—Number Five—and he said there were others far to the north. I'm told that there isn't a man left in that hell-hole across the creek—all gone to take part in some prearranged scrap with Big Road's people, and here we are, powerless to do a thing."

"Well, said Ormsby, after a minute's reflection, "on general principles, don't you think it rather a good thing to let them scrap? It will only result in a number of very objectionable characters, red and white both, being cleaned out, and for once the Twelfth will have no losses to mourn. I'd let 'em fight, and say, bless you, my children, if I had anything to do with it."

"Oh, so would I, if I weren't a 'regular', and therefore blamed, no matter which way the thing goes. If the Indians get the worst of it, the Interior Department, the peace societies, the Y. M. C. A.'s, and God knows how many other pious people all over America, will be howling 'Abolish the army' for looking on and allowing this wholesale slaughter of innocent and helpless wards of the Nation, and if the wards come out atop and clean out the cowboys, the press of the country will ring with accounts of how the gallant frontiersmen sent courier after courier to the fort, praying for aid, and the cowardly commander and his dude cavalry were most of them helplessly drunk, and couldn't do or wouldn't do a thing. I agree with old Kenyon down at Fort Russell, by Jupiter! We'd have Inspectors and courts of inquiry and all that sort of thing, and by the time the lies had saturated the whole country and the truth was beginning to come out, the papers would say it was no longer a matter of sufficient interest to publish. No, Jack; you thank God you're in the Seventh, even when you're being brickbatted. I'm going to launch out after that gang, orders or no orders. So that's the end of it. Ride after Farwell," said he to his silent staff-officer, "and tell him to follow close on the heels of Big Road, and I'll back him with all we've got. Tell him if he hears firing ahead to stop it, if he can, but if he can't, then, by thunder, to help the Indians—they're the injured ones in this deal!" And with those memorable instructions on his lips, Fenton strode forth upon the porch of his quarters, out into the still and starlit night, now faintly illumined by the rays of the waning moon, and in another moment the trumpets were blaring "To horse," and all Fort Frayne sprang to life.

It was but a little after midnight, and many of the men were still awake. Others, lying down on their bunks without removing boots or blouses, had fallen into an uneasy doze. It seemed but a minute before, full panoplied, they were streaming down to the stables, where the horses were already pawing and snorting excitedly as though the sound of this midnight alarm had conveyed its full meaning to them. At any other time Jack Ormsby would have found keen delight in watching the prompt, soldierly style in which the troopers sprang to their work, and the swift, deft saddling and rapid formation of troop after troop, but to-night his heart was leaden. Not for.him the rush and vigor and exhilaration of the sudden start and sharp pursuit. While they, the men among whom he was proud to be hailed as friend and comrade, were speeding on their ride to the rescue, he, summoned by a duty as imperative and held as obligation every bit as sacred, would have to turn his back on the bounding column, on Fort Frayne, with all that was dearest, fondest, fairest in life, and hasten eastward by the morning train, or be held as having broken the spotless record of his company.

Even as the men were leading into line and the stern voices of the troop sergeants could be heard calling the roll, and lights began to gleam in the lower windows of the officers' quarters and pallid women appeared at the doorways, clinging to the very last to husband or father hastening to his duty, poor Jack stood in front of the little gateway of the Farrars', gazing aloft at the window of Ellis's room, where the dim night light told of the sad and anxious watch maintained, and with all his soul he longed to follow the buoyant, bounding footsteps of the gallant boy who had just come rushing by from the adjoining quarters, admitted at the hallway for the mother's parting kiss and blessing, and long, long clinging embrace. With all his heart bound up in that little household, Jack stood there at the threshold, unbidden, yet longing to enter. Not once had he set eyes on the face of the girl he loved since the night of his startling announcement. Only once had he caught sight of the mother's pallid, patient features at the window. Had he no rights, no welcome there—he, who would serve them with his heart's blood, if that could save them from ill or suffering? Booted men in rough campaign dress brushed him by with unheard, unanswered words of soldier greeting, and the surgeon, hurrying past, stopped to say: "Leale begs you will come to him a moment, and I can't forbid it now."

Ormsby bowed assent, yet hardly knew to what. He was waiting only for Will, and presently the boy came springing forth and, as Ormsby stepped eagerly forward with inquiry for Ellis and her mother, the words died on his lips, for, dashing his hand across his eyes, Will sped swiftly by, with only this for greeting: "Hello, Jack! Don't stop me now, for God's sake. I've just time to see Kitty," and more than half the words came back over his shoulder.

It was Helen Daunton who, peering forth from the doorway, saw him standing there and mercifully bade him enter—Mrs. Farrar would be only too glad to see him—and gratefully Jack obeyed. The squadron was forming on the parade as Ormsby entered the little army cottage and was ushered into the parlor. There at the window, with tears still streaming down her gentle face, stood Mrs. Farrar, gazing out over the dim expanse at the dark ranks on the opposite side, and longing for one more peep at her boy, whose horse had been led away up to the colonel's quarters. She partly turned as Jack tiptoed in, and a wan, sad smile flickered one moment about her lips.

"You, too, are going," she said, "and I know how busy you are, but I could not let you go until I had told you—as I told Willy to tell you, if I did not see you again before the start—that from Helen I have learned how true, how noble a friend and helper you have been to her and how you strove to shield my poor, poor boy. God bless you, Jack—I shall always call you that now, for you seem like my own to me. God bless you for all you've done and tried to do for me and mine." She had clasped both his hands now, and the tears were raining down her face.

Before he could answer, a little knot of horsemen rode past the gate. One of them reined aside and waved his hand toward the window where the mother stood. Again she turned thither with love and dread, with pride and sorrow and yearning in her gaze. Then a trumpet sounded, and the tall young soldier spurred suddenly away.

"Forgive me, Jack, I know you have to go. Don't let me keep you now," she sobbed, and Helen came and twined her arms about her, and Ormsby bent and kissed the fragile hand and went noiselessly out into the night. Twenty minutes later, when once again he gazed upward at the little dormer window of the room where Ellis slept her fevered sleep, the squadron had gone, the parade was deserted. There were bright beams from the windows of the colonel's quarters, but all was darkness in his heart and here in the little army home where were left only women now, bearing the name and the sorrows of the Farrars.

## CHAPTER XVII.

"A HAPPY New Year to you," said the conductor of the "Limited," as Jack Ormsby was whisked away eastward from Chicago, after sixty hours of incessant railway riding from Fort Frayne. Happy New Year, indeed! It sounded like mockery.

Turning away with a sigh from the gateway of Will's quarters, he had gone at last to Leale's, and bitterly did he reproach himself that so little thought had he given to the appeal of that stanch and loyal friend. The attendant ushered him in to where, with bandaged, sightless eyes and painful breathing, the stalwart soldier lay, heroic in his endurance. Their interview was brief, for Leale was forbidden to talk more than was absolutely necessary, and only in a hoarse whisper could he talk at all. Bending over his bedside, Jack had taken the captain's hand in his and told him that the troops were gone on their stern chase in default of orders to the contrary, and that Fenton hoped to overtake the Indians and interpose again between them and the cowboys before the latter could gather in overwhelming strength, and then he briefly gave the reasons which compelled him to take the morning train for the East. Even under the bandages Ormsby thought he saw an instant shadow of disappointment.

"What is it, Leale, old chap?" he asked. "Had

you any plan?—anything in which I could serve you?"

"I must go—too—but they will not let me move —yet," was the whispered reply.

"Man and boy," cried poor Jack, "I've been in the Seventh ever since I was old enough to enlist, and never until this night have I known what it was to wish I were free to stay away, but dear old fellow, I thought it was costing me more than I could bear before seeing you, and now—Leale," he broke off impulsively, "I'm turning my back on everything I hold dear in this world to-night—my sister, my heart's love, my trustiest friend when most he needs me—everything but one, and that is the old regiment in New York. You're a soldier, Leale, if there ever lived one. You know our record and our traditions. So long as I hold my warrant in the Seventh, is it not my bounden duty to go to them and go at once?"

A clasp of the hand with a movement of the lips was the only answer for a moment, and then "You're right, Jack—go! I'm coming—soon."

"Then I'll come half way to meet you, Leale. I'll join you in Chicago. If there be time I'll come 'way back here, and, unless your doctors say you must go into hospital, my house is to be your home, and the specialists can see you there. I have said good-bye to Mrs. Farrar—to Will's mother, and to—Helen. They think I went with the command. Will you promise? Will you come to my roof, Leale, and let us nurse you there to sight and strength again?"

But Leale slowly shook his head. "I must go home, Jack, a little while, and then—to Europe."

And so the friends had parted—each aware of the other's plight, yet neither able to help. Not until long after the train had gone whistling away did the Farrars know that it was back to Gotham Ormsby had been called, and then it was through Kitty. She came hurrying in to say that with their glasses they could plainly see some of the command riding homeward from the direction of Trooper Creek. And meantime the line repairers who had gone along the track from Cañon Springs had found the breaks—a dozen of them—and restrung their light copper wire, and, now that they were no longer of consequence, orders, injunctions and suggestions by the dozen were coming in. Wayne, left at the post in temporary command, opened, read, re-read and pooh-poohed the first that came—these being from the agency— but began to wake up in earnest as he opened the sixth or seventh of the brown envelopes. Then suddenly he hastened over to the colonel's house, leaving the clerks at the office to their devices, and with his field-glass and an attendant officer and orderly, began studying the northward stretch of snowy prairie while Lucretia wistfully watched him from the gallery. When a messenger came running up with, and Wayne opened, the next dispatch, she could not longer restrain her curiosity, and so came boldly forth to demand explanation.

Over across the Platte, among the shanties that surrounded Bunco Jim's establishment, there were signs of excitement and lively emotion. The sentries reported that ever since daylight, in squads of twos or threes, cowboys and ranchmen had been riding to and fro, and now there was much carousing about the bars, and no little scurrying hither and thither of slatternly women. Two teams had been hitched and driven away northward, and the few soldiers who swarmed out along the sentry post—forbidden to go beyond or to hold communication with the gang across the river—surmised that they were needed to bring in wounded, and that therefore there must have been a scrimmage. Old Jimmy Brewer, a frontier character to whom no few liberties were allowed because of his long-tried loyalty to garrison after garrison at Frayne, had been relied upon to come in as usual with his load of dairy goods and gossip, had failed, however, to materialize this morning, of all others, and Frayne was short of cream and news of the neighborhood just at the time when both would have been comforting.

But Wayne, as has been said, was a man who, once aroused from the dreamy abstraction of his daily life and thrown upon his mettle as commanding officer, had been known to display surprising energy, and here was a case in point.

"I wish you," said he to the post quarter-master, who was in attendance upon him at the moment, "to take a couple of men and find out what you can in the settlement yonder of what has been going on this morning. Then I need a first-rate rider to go at the gallop to Trooper Creek." Then he turned and bowed to the appealing face peering out at him from under its hood of fur so close at his side. "Let me put an end to your anxiety, Miss Fenton," said he, reassuringly. "Your brother, the colonel, will be on his homeward way just as soon as he gets those dispatches. So you and Miss Ormsby can breakfast in peace and comfort."

But Wayne, for once in his life, revealed no more than was his actual intention. Pouring forth her voluble song of thanksgiving, Lucretia talked a steady flow until once more he raised his cap to her at her door, and then, turning suddenly away, hastened to the office before she could recover from her astonishment at this unusually precipitate move. She had deprived herself of all opportunity of asking for particulars or for learning what Wayne himself was now to do. Hearing from his lips that her brother would soon be on his homeward way, she placed no other interpretation upon the news than that the regiment would be coming with him, that the war was over, and their troubles at an end.

But could she have seen Wayne's face as he hastened to his quarters, bade his orderly pack his field kit at once, and then get the horses, she would have known that a serious matter was in hand. From his own door the major hurried back to the office again, wrote three telegraphic messages, and summoned the orderly trumpeter.

"Give my compliments to the post surgeon, and ask if he will meet me at my quarters at once," he said. Then, directing the clerk to have the messages rushed, he hastened across the parade, and, ringing at the Farrars' door, begged to see Mrs. Daunton a moment. As luck would have it, Dr. Gibson himself was in low-toned consultation with Helen in the parlor, and he looked up with marked interest as Wayne was ushered in.

The major read the inquiry in the doctor's eyes. He greeted Mrs. Daunton with brief courtesy, and then spoke. "Yes. He's ordered in—relieved—and I'm ordered out. It's only another instance of the old story. I go in ten minutes, and have no idea at this moment what has been going on at the front—no more idea than Fenton has of what has been going on at the rear. If there's been a fight, cowboy and Indian, as is probable, and the band has slipped away to the mountains, then we will have to follow, and probably take up a fight we had nothing to do with at first and did our best to prevent. I came, Mrs. Daunton," said he, gravely, "to ask for Mrs. Farrar and Miss Ellis, as Will will be anxious to know, and I fear it will be some time before he can hope to see them again."

"That is what his mother feared, major, and it is that we have to contend with now. Miss Farrar is somewhat better, as the doctor will tell you, but, of of course, she is very weak, and knows nothing of the excitements of last night. But what am I to tell Mrs. Farrar?" she continued, with brimming eyes. "The servants have been saying in the kitchen that there has been a battle, but the corporal of the guard declared to us that the regiment could be seen coming home, and I have comforted her with that, and now—"

"And now I fear I'll have to say it is only some little detachment convoying prisoners," answered Wayne, "but the command itself will have to push on in pursuit. Tell her, though, there is no likelihood of our having any serious fighting, and that I'll watch over Will and care for him as though he were my own boy."

"I wish she could hear you," pleaded Helen, "but I made her go back to her bed a while ago, and you must start—"

"I must go at once," he answered, gravely. "Is there anything I can take for you or for her?"

"She is sleeping, I hope," said Helen, in reply, "for all night long she has hardly closed her eyes, but there will be other messengers, probably, during the day, will there not?"

"Yes, several, doubtless, especially after the detachment gets in."

"Well, then, I have one—packet; I hardly like to burden you with it, major, yet ought not, perhaps, intrust it to any one else. It can be ready in five minutes."

"Then I will call for it," he answered promptly, and, taking the doctor with him, retraced his steps to his own door.

Fifteen minutes later a motley little procession began straggling across the Platte and heading for the post—a small party of troopers escorting a bevy of Indians, some prostrate on travois, some astride of scraggly ponies, some shuffling along afoot, some few big-eyed, solemn little papooses on their mothers' backs, and with them came the first tidings of the events of the night gone by.

Long before Big Road's party had begun to reach the appointed rendezvous on Trooper Creek, there had been hostile demonstrations from white men out on the bluffs to the front and on their right flank;—that is to the north and east. There had been firing during the night. Now came serious action with the break of day. These men wore fur caps and gloves, soldiers' winter overcoats just like the regulars—and why shouldn't they, since Bunco Jim and his associates had long driven a thriving trade buying up such items of winter wear of deserters or drunkards from the post? They formed along the hillsides afar off, keeping up the semblance of cavalry skirmish order, and evidently striving to harass or delay the movement of the Indians as much as possible, and yet to keep well out of harm's way. There was also evident desire to convince the fleeing village that its assailants were cavalrymen from Fort Frayne, but even before the few young braves, riding valiantly out to interpose between their women and children and old folks and these, their aggressors, sent in word that no soldiers were among the enemy—that it was all a cowboy crowd—the older men who remained had discovered the fact, and dispatched runners to Big Road with the news. That redoubtable chief was still drunk, but the sound of firing had vanquished the stupefying effect of his potations, and, though two or three of his chosen followers were helplessly gone, he appeared with the first peep of day, aggressively hostile and eager to fight anything or anybody. Galloping forward, reeling in saddle, but hanging on as only an Indian can, he had marshaled and led his people, and the next thing the cowboys knew old Big Road had turned on them like a baited bull. Within half an hour after dawn the bluffs along Trooper Creek were ringing to the music of warwhoop and battle-cry, and the wintry air was throbbing to the swift rattle of musketry. With half a dozen of his prominent fellow-citizens stretched on the snow dead or crippled, Bunco Jim thanked God when some one shouted that the cavalry were riding into line not two miles away. Gathering up the stragglers of the village, old Fenton had pushed his skirmish line straight out across the frozen creek, and, while Big Road and most of his warriors went whirling up the opposite slope, backing away for the Big Horn with most of the village beyond them, and firing from a distance at the swift but regulated advance of the Twelfth, Fenton had swung his right wing in wide-spreading sweep across the snow-covered prairie, brushing aside, turning back, and in some few instances riding over the cowboys who wouldn't get out of the way.

"You tricked those poor devils into making a break," he furiously replied to the first plainsman who claimed to be fighting to help the soldier. "You lied them into leaving, and then attacked them on the run. Get out of the way, every damned one of you, or, by Heaven, there'll be war that'll make your head swim."

But, do his best, he was too late for the real object of his coming. Bunco Jim's strategy had prevailed. The Indians were in full flight for the mountains, and the onus of the whole business was satisfactorily transferred to the shoulders of the troops. Two of Jim's numerous allies had been knocked on the head, but as he sagely reflected, they were fellows from the Powder River country who didn't owe him a cent. Certain others were more or less severely wounded, and would have to be cared for at Jimtown, but, on the other hand, they had gathered in a number of Indian ponies, had shot a warrior or two and could easily swear they'd killed a dozen; but, best of all, they had embroiled Big Road with Uncle Sam, and brought on a war that might involve all Big Road's friends, Sioux or Cheyenne, call to the scene thousands of soldiers, and "bull the market" for beef cattle, provisions, and forage, on all of which Jim held a corner.

And so, when noonday came, his wounded were safely in hospital, within the log walls of his prairie town, and the Indians were far away northward toward Cloud Peak, the Twelfth following in steady pursuit, receiving shots from time to time from the daring rear guard of the redskins, who refused all efforts to bring them to a halt and parley. A dozen Indians, young and old, were once more huddled about the smoking fires on the flats above the post, and a few troopers were swearing and shivering on guard about them, while up along the plateau, from door to door flitted the wives and children of the officers thus summarily hustled away into savage campaign, and all thought of holiday rejoicing was at an end.

It was just eight o'clock when the major rode away, attended by a single orderly, leaving the post to the care of the few soldiers who remained. He had dismounted at the colonel's, ostensibly to ask if they had any messages to send before reflecting that, unless something utterly unforeseen should occur, the colonel himself would be there to hear the messages in person before the setting of the sun. The consciousness of this fact dawned upon him as Lucretia met him at the door and covered him with an embarrassment and confusion which made nothing short of ludicrous his farewell to the lady of his love. Kitty had gone to the Farrars, as has been said, to mingle her tears with those of Will's unhappy mother, and if there ever was a time when the coast was absolutely clear and all conditions favorable for a fond if brief avowal, it was this—it was now; yet such was Wayne's consternation at finding he had bethought him of no other excuse than his own longing for coming at all, and such was his unconsciousness of the fact that she would prefer that to any excuse he could possibly devise, the bedeviled major stared blankly at her as she opened the door, and—to this day they tell it in the Twelfth with renewed guffaws of rejoicing—the only words that rose to his lips were these:

"Er, ah—does—does Colonel Fenton live here?"

And Lucretia, bursting into tears, believed her beloved had gone stark, staring mad.

"He up and grabbed her by the arm," said Trumpeter Billy Madden at the bivouac fires that night, "and kind of shoved himself inside the door with her, and she a-cryin', and the next I see of him he come a-lungin' out, and, you hear me, her shawl was a-hangin' over his shoulders and never dropped off till he got to the gate. What'd that mean? Well, if you'd a seen the old man's face you wouldn't ask. I'd a mind to strike him for ten right then and there, but Mrs. Daunton she come a-runnin' with a big envelope just as we was startin' and says, 'Give that to Mr. Ormsby, please, and he swiped it into his saddle-bags, and says, 'You bet,' or something like it, when he knowed and I knowed Mr. Ormsby was a-scooting for Cheyenne fast as train could take him."

Indeed, it was not until after Wayne was a mile away across the Platte, riding with a light and bounding heart on a sad and vexatious errand, that Helen Daunton learned for the first time from Kitty's lips that poor Jack had had to hurry home, that he had promised to be with the Seventh early in the week, "and that," said Kitty, "is just the one thing no one can argue Jack out of."

And Helen's face, sad and pale as it had been for days, grew still more sad and anxious now. This would be hard news for Ellis when she waked from the stupor of her fever. He had gone without one word, and, as Helen well knew, with a shadow, black and forbidding between him and the girl he so fondly loved.

Meantime, spurring rapidly northward and passing every little while small parties of returning "hustlers," Wayne was in chase of the command. A swift courier had ridden ahead with certain of the dispatches that had been received, but those which came last of all the major bore himself. "They will serve in some measure to prepare Fenton for these," he said, as he rode over the last divide that separated him from the valley of Trooper Creek, and thanked his stars the winds were still instead of blowing, as ofttimes they were in midwinter, and with bitter energy, from the icy summits to the northward. Down along the frozen stream were traces of the morning fight. Scraps of Indian household goods and chattels, dropped in the hurry of their scramble for the bluffs beyond, an abandoned travois, a luckless dog, slain by a chance bullet, and here, there and everywhere, the trampled snow and the countless prints of pony hoofs. Over toward the west, farther up the valley, a gradual ascent to the bluffs was seamed with over a score of parallel tracks at regular intervals, as though scraped out of the snowy surface by some giant harrow. This was where some troop in extended order had swept up the slope, with Big Road's warriors scurrying hither and yon at the distant crest. Far up the heights, stiffening in death, lay one of Amory's beautiful sorrels, and Wayne's heart ached as he thought of the many miles he had yet to ride, the similar sights he had yet to see, and the galling tidings he had yet to deliver. He had known Fenton over thirty years, and he knew well his deep-rooted pride in his profession, and the rugged honesty which dictated his every move. He knew that now, as perhaps never before since the great days of the civil war, was Fenton enthusiastically bound up in his duties, for she who was the inspiration of his earliest ambition and to whom, through all these years, his loyal heart had clung, was there at Frayne watching, despite the sorrows of her widowhood, the shock and shame that followed upon the death of her reckless, sin-stained boy, and the deep anxiety for her surviving children—watching and cheering his steadfast effort to keep the standard of the Twelfth where Farrar had left it—foremost among the famous regiments of the army that had been her home.

And it was this loyal, sturdy soldier and gentleman, in the height of his duteous and most energetic service, whom Wayne found himself ordered to supersede—to relieve in the command of Fort Frayne and so much of the Twelfth as was there stationed, in order that Fenton might repair at once to the distant headquarters of the department, there to answer the charges and allegations laid at his door by officials of the Interior Department, and by so-called prominent citizens of broad Wyoming. Verily, the king of the cowboys had not made his threats in vain.

## CHAPTER XVIII.

JUST as Terry Rorke had said, the Twelfth had spent its New Year's Day hot on the Indian trail. Into the foothills it wound, tortuous and full of peril, for from every projecting point, from rock to rock and crest to crest, the warrior rear-guard poured their fire on the advancing line. Charges were fruitless. The nimble ponies of the Indians bore their riders swiftly out of harm's way, and only among the charging force did casualties occur. Still, Fenton had hung like a bulldog to his task, hoping before nightfall to catch up with the main body and the moving village, then to hem it in. Numerically, he was little better off than the Indians, and fifty Indians can surround five hundred troopers much more effectively than five hundred troopers can surround fifty mounted warriors. Through Bat and others he had vainly striven to communicate with Big Road, to assure him no harm would be done; that all that was necessary was for him to return with his people under escort of the regiment to the reservation. Up to 4 P. M. not a shot had been fired by the Twelfth, even in response to a sometimes galling fusillade from the Indians. By that time several men had been unhorsed and two or three wounded, and the thing was getting exasperating, yet was it worth keeping up, for Bat and other scouts declared the fleeing village to be less than three miles ahead now, and, with that overhauled, the warriors could be brought to bay well south of the mountains, and to the accomplishment of this without sacrificing men or horses to any great extent, Fenton was bending every energy when overtaken by the first courier from Frayne.

Wayne had marked the dispatches in the order in which they should be read, but the only ones which much concerned him now were from department headquarters. A new king who knew not Joseph, a new general with whom Fenton had never chanced to serve, was there in command, and he, coming a comparative stranger to the community, knew little of the merits of the politicians by whom he was speedily besieged. They were present in force, armed with letters and dispatches by the score from so-called prominent citizens resident along the Platte, and Fenton was practically unrepresented. It was in no spirit of unkindness, but rather that Fenton might have opportunity to come thither and confront and confound, if he could, his accusers, that the general had issued the first order, which was that Fenton should "immediately escort Big Road and his people back to the agency, and then report to these headquarters for consultation." That dispatch, if delivered, would have ruined all the plans of the plainsmen, and the wires were clipped the moment warning came, and it never got beyond the old sub-station on the Laramie until after the repairs were made, but other dispatches were wired back from below the breaks, alleging first, that so far from Fenton's doing as ordered, he was apparently bent on driving Big Road's people up the river or into the open field; then, that he had done so, and that the Indians were now raiding the scattered ranches, and driving the cattle into the foothills, while the settlers were fleeing in terror. Fenton's dispatches, wired before Big Road's escapade, had, of course, been received, but his report of the situation was at utter variance with that from the agency and those from the Thorpe party. Gross mismanagement and general incompetency were the principal allegations against Fenton, though the astute "hustlers" did not forget to add drunkenness to the list as one which the public would accept without question, he being an army officer; and when the governor himself was induced to add his complaint to those of his enterprising people, the general yielded. The dispatches sent by courier called for explanation of the charges made by the agent and civilians, intimated doubt as to the wisdom of Fenton's course or the accuracy of his information, and wound up with the significant clause: "Do nothing to provoke hostilities or arouse the fears of the Indians," and here he had been in hot pursuit of them all the livelong day.

Stung to the quick, Fenton nevertheless pressed vigorously on. The result would justify him, and he could wait for his vindication until the campaign was over. The village at sundown could not be more than three miles away, said his scouts, and the energy of Big Road's defensive measures was redoubled. Instructions to do nothing to provoke hostilities were dead letters now that hostilities had actually been provoked—not by him or his people, but, between them, by Big Road and the cowboys. There was only one course for Fenton to take, and that was to overhaul the village and peaceably, if he could, but forcibly if he must, escort it back within the reservation lines. Bat had ridden up just as the sun was disappearing, to say that the Indians seemed to be heading for a deep cleft in the foothills through which the buffalo in bygone days had made their way. Now, if Fenton could only send Farwell or Amory with half the squadron to gallop in wide detour to the west, under cover of the darkness, and seize the bluffs overhanging the cañon, meantime making every pretense of keeping up the pursuit with the remainder of his force, he might trap the village while most of its defenders were still far away. Darkness settled down over the desolate wintry landscape, and the two troops dispatched on this stirring and perilous mission were those of Farwell and Malcolm Leale, the latter led by its boy lieutenant, Will Farrar.

One hour later, as the advance was still groping along the trail and the weary troopers, alternately leading afoot and riding sleepily in narrow column, pushed steadily in their tracks, two horsemen on jaded mounts came spurring from the rear, and Wayne, with sorrowful face, handed his dispatches to the colonel. By the light of a little pocket lantern Fenton read, while in brooding silence a knot of half a dozen officers gathered about them. The closing paragraph is all we need to quote: "You will, therefore, turn over the command to Major Wayne and report in person at these headquarters without unnecessary delay. Acknowledge receipt." At any other time the colonel might have been expected to swear vigorously, but the trouble in Wayne's face and the unspoken sympathy and sorrow were too much for him. "All right, old boy," said he, as he refolded the papers. "Pitch in now, and finish up the business, with my blessing. Bat," he continued, turning to the swarthy guide, "how far is it over to the Allison ranch? I think I'll sleep there." And no further words were needed to tell the little group that their colonel had been removed from command just on the eve of consummation of his plans, and he was the only man of the lot who didn't look as though all heart had been taken out of him as the immediate result.

"Damn that fellow Thorpe! It's his doing," swore the adjutant, between his set teeth. "He has never forgiven us for spoiling his scheme to clean out the whole band."

"Don't waste time swearing," said Fenton, grimly. "I'll take that job off your hands. They're heading for Elk Springs, Wayne, and I've sent Farwell with two troops around to the left to find their way to the bluffs and get there first. Everything depends on that."

But even Fenton hardly realized how very much

depended. It was now about seven o'clock, and ever since the early dawn the cavalry had been pressing steadily at the heels of the Indian rear-guard, never firing, never responding to the challenge of shot or shout from the scampering warriors before them. Again and again had Bat and his half-breed cousin, La Bonté, striven to get Big Road to halt and parley, but, though the signals were fully understood, Old Road was mad with the mingled rage of fight and whiskey, and believed himself the leader of an outbreak that should rival that of 1876 and place him, as a battle chief, head of an army of warriors that should overrun the Northwest. Anxious only to get the women and children safely in among the fastnesses of the hills, he contented himself, therefore, through the livelong day, with holding the troops at long arms' length, opening lively fire when they sought to push ahead. It was glorious fun for him and his. Well they knew that so far, at least, the soldiers were forbidden to attack. With the coming of another day Big Road planned to have his village far in among the clefts and cañons of the range, where a few resolute warriors could defend the pass against an advance, while he and his braves, reinforced by eager recruits from the young men of other bands at the reservation, could fall upon the flanks and rear of Fenton's force and fritter it away as Red Cloud had massacred Fetterman's men long years before at old Fort Kearny.

Everything depended on who should get there first,

and, as the Sioux said of Custer's column, the bloody day on the Little Horn, "The soldiers were tired."

Extending southward from the peaks of the Big Horn was a wild range of irregular heights, covered in places with a thick growth of hardy young spruce and cedars and scrub oak, slashed and severed here and there by deep and tortuous cañons with precipitous sides. Somewhere in among those hills was a big amphitheatre known as the Indian Race Course, approachable in winter, at least, only through the crooked rift or pass known for short as Elk Gulch. In just such another natural fastness, and only a few miles away to the northeast, had the Cheyennes made their famous stand against five times their weight in fighting men the bitter winter of 1876—a battle the cavalry long had cause to remember, and now, with but a handful of troops as compared with the force led in by MacKenzie, Wayne had right before him a similar problem to tackle. The only points in his favor were that Big Road's braves were as few as his own and that Fenton had already sent a force to race the Indians to their refuge.

At eight o'clock the darkness was intense. There was no moon to light their way, and their only guide was the deep trail in the snowy surface left by the retreating Indians. The darkness was no deeper than the gloom in every heart, for Fenton was gone, a wronged and calumniated man, and they, his loyal soldiers obedient to a higher duty still, were forced to push on and finish his work without him. For an hour only at snail's pace had they followed the trail. Bat and his associates had had many a narrow escape. Lieutenant Martin, commanding the advance, had had his horse shot under him. Sergeant Roe had a bullet through his coat, and Corporal Werrick, riding eagerly in the lead, got another through the shoulder. Luckily it was not very cold, but all the same, most of the men were becoming sluggish and sleepy, and that was just about the time Wayne might be expected to wake up—and wake up he did.

"*I* have had no orders on no account to attack," said he, "and I haven't time to read all the rot they've wired to Fenton. Watch for the next shots ahead, there," he cried to the foremost troopers, "and sock it to them?"

Then it was beautiful to see how even the horses seemed to rouse from their stupor and apathy and something almost like a cheer burst from the lips of the younger men. Old hands took a "swig" of water from their canteens and a bite at the comforting plug. Out from the sockets came the brown carbines, and a fresh platoon was ordered up to relieve the advance, and Lieutenant Randolph took Martin's place at the front. Every little while through the darkness ahead had come a flash and report from the invisible foe, and, as these had been suffered unavenged, it was soon observed that the lurking warriors grew bolder, and that with every shot the distance seemed to decrease. For half an hour past they had been coming in from easy pistol range, and Randolph took the cue. Bidding his men open out and ride several yards apart, yet aligned as much as was possible, he ordered carbines dropped and revolvers drawn, and then, trotting along the rear of the dozen, gave his quick caution to man after man. "Watch for the flash and let drive at it. Even if we don't hit, we'll keep them at respectful distance," he said, and the words were hardly out of his mouth when a ruddy light leaped over the snow, a shot went zipping past his head, and then, followed by a roar of approval from the main column, the revolvers of the advance crackled and sputtered their answer. The landscape was lit up for an instant; dark forms went pounding and scurrying away from the front, and a moment later there uprose a cheer over at the right and Randolph galloped to the spot. An Indian pony lay kicking, struggling, stiffening in the snow, shot through the body, and the rider had had to run for it.

"That's right, Randolph!" said the major, spurring to his side. "Now keep 'em off, but don't push too hard. Remember, we've got to give Farwell time."

"How far ahead is that confounded cañon, Bat?" asked the adjutant at the moment.

"Not more than two mile now. I hunt buffalo all over here when I was a boy," was the answer. "Big Road's people all there by this time, I'm afraid."

"Then you think that they got there first—that they've got the bluffs?"

"'Fraid so. Big Road no fool. He wouldn't let his village drive into a gulch and not guard the bluffs. If the captain got there first, they'd have found it out by this time and signaled for help. The reason I believe they think they're all safe is that so many Indians hang around us out here."

And just then came a grunt of disgust from La Bonté. The corporal at his side said "Hell!" and an excitable young trooper called out, "Look there! What's that?" for, over at the northwest, all on a sudden, a brilliant column of flame had burst through the blackness of the night and sent a broad glare streaming over the snow-clad surface of the rolling prairie.

"They're on to us, by the Eternal!" cried the adjutant, who loved the Jacksonian form of expletive. "Listen!" But no one listened more than an instant. Even through the muffling coverlet of snow, the rumble and rush of a hundred pony hoofs, like low, distant thunder, told of the instant flight of Big Road's braves in answer to the signal. Wayne was ablaze in a second.

"Close up on the head of column!" he shouted to the troop leaders. "Come on, now, men, for all you're worth. There isn't a second to spare."

And as the amazed and wearied horses gave answer to the spur and broke into lumbering gallop, far over at the west the rocks began to ring to the crackle of musketry. Farwell and the Sioux had clinched on the bluffs to the south of the springs, and were fighting in the dark for the right of way.

Ten miles away, at Allison's Ranch, wearied with the sleepless toil of twenty-four hours, too weary to be kept awake even by the exasperating sense of his wrongs, the colonel was just rolling into his blankets for a much-needed rest before setting forth with the rising sun on his homeward road. Fifty miles away over the white expanse of prairie under the cold and glittering skies, Marjorie Farrar sat by the bedside of her beloved daughter, praying ceaselessly for the safety of an equally beloved son now riding, for the first time in his brave young life, to prove his worthiness to bear the father's name in headlong fight with a savage and skillful foe.

And if ever a young fellow, wearer of the army blue, realized to the full extent the hopes and faith and fondness centered in him this night of nights, it was Will Farrar. Barely arrived by man's estate, not yet a year out of the cadet coatee, with his mother, his sister, his sweetheart, all there at the old fort so long associated with his father's name, with that name to maintain, and not only that, but with Malcolm Leale's old troop as one man looking up to him as their leader, yet competent, down to the very last man, to note the faintest flaw should he fail them, the junior subaltern of the Twelfth, the "plebe" lieutenant, as his elders laughingly spoke of him, found himself, as though some special providence had swept from his path every possible barrier to danger and distinction, lifted suddenly to a command that seldom falls to army subalterns to-day even within a dozen years, and bidden here and now to win his spurs for the honor of the old troop, the honor of the Twelfth, the honor of the name his father made famous, and that he must maintain—or die in trying to. All this, and God alone knows how much more besides, went thrilling through his very soul, as, on Farwell's left and in utter silence, he rode swiftly onward at the head of the column. Leaving to his own first lieutenant the command of the grays, Captain Farwell had told him to follow close in the tracks of Farrar's men, and, with only one of the Indian company to aid and no other guide of any kind but his senses and the stars, had placed himself in the lead and pushed forth into the night.

"Swing well out to the west," were Fenton's last orders. "Keep dark, as you know how. Head for the hills as soon as you're sure you're far beyond hearing, and try to strike those bluffs a couple of miles at least back of the mouth of the cañon. You ought to get there ahead of the village. Halt it with a few men down in the gorge, but hold your main body on the bluffs. We'll keep Big Road busy."

Luckily the stars were brilliant in the wintry sky, and the constellations out in all their glory. The pole star glowed high aloft and held them to their course. Out in the advance, lashing his horse with Indian whip to keep him to his speed, rode Brave Bear, a corporal of the Ogallalla company, side by side with Sergeant Bremmer. Whenever the drifts were deep in the ravines one of them would halt and warn the column to swerve to the right or left. Only a yard or two behind the two officers—Farwell, grizzled and stout, Farrar, fair and slender—came loping or trotting the leading four, and, though it was not his accustomed place, there rode Terry Rorke, where, as he had explained to the satisfaction of the sergeant, he could be close to "Masther Will." The prairie was broad and open, and fairly level. There was no need of diminishing front. A platoon could have ridden abreast, and found no serious obstacle, except the snowdrifts in the deep coulées. Two miles to the west they sped, moving cautiously at first so as to give no inkling of their intent, and, for the first mile, almost doubling back upon their tracks, so as to keep well away from the Indian rear-guard.

Then in long curve, Farwell led them toward the low, rolling hills, now dimly visible against the firmament, and presently the ravines began to grow deeper but farther apart, the slopes more abrupt and the westward hills loomed closer in their path, and still the snowy expanse showed unbroken, and Bear, bending low over his pony's neck and watching for sign, declared that no Indians had crossed as yet into the hills, and that the entrance to Elk Gulch was now not more then a mile to the north. And here the hills rolled higher, both to their front and toward the west, but Farwell rode on up a gradual ascent until the slope began to grow steep; then, dismounting, led the way afoot, the whole column rolling out of saddle and towing its horses in his track. Up, up they climbed until, breathing hard now, but pushing relentlessly on, the captain reached the crest, and faint and dim in the starlight, dotted here and there with little clumps of spruce or cedar, the rolling, billowy surface lay before him, shrouded in its mantle of glistening snow. Leading on until the whole command had time to reach the top, he motioned Will to halt, while he, with Bear and Sergeant Bremmer, pushed a few yards farther on. The column took a breathing spell and waited.

Far out to the eastward and below them an occasional flash as of rifle or revolver sparkled through the night, and the faint report was presently borne to their listening ears. Big Road was still barring the way of the column then, and that meant that all the village was not yet safely within the grim walls of the cañon. Northward the snowy slopes rolled higher still, but it was northwestward among the clumps of trees that the leaders had gone. The steam from the horses' nostrils and from their heaving flanks rose on the keen air and the blood raced and tingled in the veins of the men. Not a whisper of mountain breeze was astir. The night was as still as the voiceless skies. Three—four minutes, with beating hearts, the little command watched and waited, and drew longer breath, and then a dark shape came jogging back from the front and Farwell's voice said: "Mount and come on."

Then came fifteen minutes' trot, winding snakelike and in long extended column of twos among the stunted trees, and then Farwell ordered "Walk," for once more a dark form loomed up in their path, and Bremmer wheeled his horse about and rode by the captain's side, eagerly explaining in low tone. Will caught the words, "Right ahead. You can hear them distinctly, sir," and for the life of him Will could not quite control the flutter of his heart. "Halt! Dismount and wait here," were the next orders, almost whispered, and again Farwell pushed out to the front and again the column swung out of saddle, watched and waited, and presently men began to stamp about in the snow and thrash their stiffening fingers.

"Are we close to 'em now, Masther Will?" asked old Terry unrebuked.

"Right ahead, they say, corporal. But this, remember, is only the women and children with a few of the old men."

"Ah, it's your father's son ye are, sorr—God rest his soul! If it was daytime, ye could almost see from here the breaks of the Mini Pusa, where we struck these Indians three years ago this cruel winter.

"I know," said Will, briefly, "and if — if it comes to fighting here, Rorke, remember father's last order. It may be harder than ever to tell buck from squaw in so dim a light, but I want the men to heed it."

"They will, sorr, as they would if the captain himself was at their head, and Masther Will, for the love of heaven, wherever ye have to go this night let me be wan of thim that go wid ye if ye only take wan," and there was a break in the old fellow's voice, as he began his plea.

"Hush, Rorke. We'll see to that," said Farrar. "Here comes the captain back!" And Farwell came with speed.

"Mr. Farrar," he said, an unmistakable tremor in his tone, "there's not a moment to be lost. They are passing through the cañon now. We can hear them plainly, but they have flankers out along the bluff. Two bucks rode by not a moment ago, and Bear says the whole outfit is pushing for the Race Track. I've got to head them off further up the gulch. Bear says we can get down in single file by an old game trail there, and I wish you to dismount right here, line this slope with your men, send at least a dozen down into the ravine, and stand off Big Road and his fellows while we corral that whole village and start it for home. They can't tell how few you are in number, and Fenton will be close at their heels. Between you they ought to be forced to the north side, while I'm driving the village out to the south. You understand, do you not? It's a fight in the dark, and they're afraid of it, anyhow. You've got a splendid troop, lad, and they won't fail you. Don't be ashamed to ask your old sergeants for advice. You understand fully?"

"I do," said Will, stoutly, though his young heart was hammering in his breast. "We'll do our best, sir. Form fours, sergeant, and link—lively," he added, then grasped the captain's hand one instant before the latter turned away. Silently, quickly, the men linked horses, and, leaving number four of each set in saddle, came running up to the front, unslinging carbine on the way. Farwell and his fellows went trotting off among the clumps of pine as the last man fell in on the left. Then, quickly dividing off a dozen troopers from that flank, Will placed the first sergeant in charge and bade him find the way down the steep incline to the bottom of the gorge, which, there, was not more than two hundred and fifty feet below, giving him instructions to be ready to sweep it with their fire when the warriors came, as come they speedily must. Next, facing eastward, he deployed his men, causing them to stand or kneel in the shelter of the little trees, but to keep vigilant lookout. Another little squad was strung out down the face of the bluff, to keep connection with the men descending to the depths of the cañon, and these preparations were barely completed, when riding at rapid gait, two horsemen came lashing up the eastward slope. The panting of the ponies could be heard before anything could be seen, but the instant the vague shapes appeared, two sudden shots rang out on the night and then a dozen —a sputtering volley—flashed from the line.

Down went one pony, struggling and rolling in the snow. Away sped the other back into the blackness of the night. Then a dark object seemed to disengage itself from the struggling pony and go crouching and limping away. Two or three excited young soldiers banged their carbines without the faintest aim. Then it seemed as though the hillsides woke to a wild revel of battle, for, behind them, far up the cañon there rose a wail of terror from the fleeing squaws and shouts of the few old braves left to guard them, resounding war whoops of younger Indians somewhere, anywhere, everywhere, down the slopes to the east. Then a bright column of flame shot high in air over among the rocks to the north of the gate, and afar out over the eastward prairie Big Road and his braves came dashing, driving, thundering to the rescue.

"They'll not try the gulch, sorr," shouted Rorke. in his ear. "Only a few will push in there, most of 'em will come this way and get around us to our right."

"Open out, men! Push out southward there as far as you can," shouted Will, as he ran bounding through the snow toward the right of his invisible line. "Watch for them! They'll come with a rush, when they come at all!"

And Rorke, whose business it was to remain with his "comrades in battle" where first he was posted near the brow of the steep, went running after his young commander as hard as he could go, with no man to stop him.

In the excitement and darkness, in the thrill of the moment, some of the men seemed disposed to huddle together rather than to increase their intervals, for plainly now could be heard a dull thunder of hoofs—the roar of the coming storm. Then, too, shadowy spectres of horsemen could be dimly seen darting into partial view and out again like the flash that greeted them. But far up the gorge, behind Farrar's line the sound of battle grew fiercer and louder. Then down from the depths of the cañon there came sudden clamor of shot and cheer and challenge and yells of rage and defiance; and then all on a sudden, out from among the stunted trees, with panting, struggling, bounding ponies, with lashing, bending, yelling braves, there burst upon them the main body of the Indians, three-score warriors at least, and, despite the ring of shots, on and through and over they rushed the slim and extended skirmish line, and Will Farrar, springing for the shelter of a little cedar, was struck full in the breast by a muscular shoulder and knocked backward into the snow. He struggled to his feet, groping for his revolver, just in time to meet the dash of half a dozen racing braves, all yelling like fiends. Something crashed upon his skull and struck a million sparks or stars, and everything whirled out of sight and sound and sense as the young officer went down, face foremost, into the drifts.

## CHAPTER XIX.

"THE Battle of the Ghosts"—so Big Road's people called it, long months after—fought late at night and far up the slopes of the Elk range, was reported at Fort Frayne before the rising of another sun. The mysterious system of signaling which enabled the Indians of the reservations in Nebraska to know the details of the Custer massacre before they could be wired from Bismarck, was here in use again, and stragglers from the band far back at Trooper Creek, and even the cowboys and ranchmen carousing about Bunco Jim's in honor of the triumph of their plans, knew all about Farwell's overtaking the village, of Farrar's desperate stand, and Wayne's long gallop to their support before the first tidings were whispered within the silent walls across the stream, or even guessed at by the grim old soldier, rousing from his sleep barely ten miles from the seat of action. The first news to reach the garrison came from "Jimtown," and was laughed to scorn by members of the guard. The next words went fearfully along among the kitchens of Officers' Row, and speedily reached the ears of the anxious wives and children of the soldiers in the field, and still the surgeon left in charge at Frayne refused to believe the rumors and hastened to forbid that any one should speak of them where they could reach the ears of the household of Farrar, for the croakers told of fell disaster and of the death of the last soldier of that honored name.

But bad news travels fast, and the direful tidings reached Lucretia Fenton's ears while Kitty still slept the sleep of the young, the innocent and unsuspicious, and what Lucretia knew she could never conceal. The morning gun had failed to wake Will's dainty ladylove; the trumpets rang no reveille, for there was no garrison to rouse, and only one trumpeter remained to sound the calls, but people were up and astir and hurrying from house to house long before the usual hour, and Marjorie Farrar, watching by the bedside of her stricken daughter, heard with straining ears the excited tones of the servants at the back doors, and but for Helen Daunton's vigilance would herself have gone to ascertain the cause. Stipulating that her friend should not go down stairs, Helen had hastened forth finding their own kitchen deserted, and, as the colonel's house was but a few rods away, and Lucretia was there at the gate in vehement recitative with Mrs. Amory, and certain of the younger belles of the garrison as listeners, Helen hastened thither, only to see the party scatter at her approach. This in itself was ominous, but it was no time for hesitation. Some of the party were evidently in tears. The old chaplain was rapidly approaching from his quarters on the westward side; the doctor, field glass in hand, was studying the snowy expanse to the north from the edge of the bluff. With him stood the sergeant of the guard, and another non-commissioned officer was hastening toward him up the sentry post of No. 5. It was to them she appealed, and in their faces she read the first intimation of ill news.

The doctor turned, as though he had been expecting her, and held forth his hand. "I am glad you are here," he said, "for I have reason to disbelieve the news that has been frittering in ever since dawn, but I wish it kept from Mrs. Farrar as long as possible."

Helen's face had turned white as the snow. He saw it and drew her arm within his own. "Stragglers from Big Road's band say—those that were left at Trooper Creek, at least—that there was a fight last night. Part of the village was captured, and part of the band broke through and got away. The Indians claim to have killed several of our people, but they are the biggest boasters on the face of the globe. The cowboys over yonder believe it, because they hate Fenton and the Twelfth, and wouldn't be sorry to have them worsted, because that would bring on a big war and lots of troops. We would have heard it by this time, in some way, had there been serious disaster."

"But, doctor, Miss Fenton and others with her hastened away when they saw me coming, and they were in tears."

"Oh, they've got hold of some silly story that the servants have been gabbling, and that I've tried to test, that Farrar is among the injured. It all comes from that vile roost over there," said he scowling malignantly at "Jimtown." "No! don't you give way, Mrs. Daunton," he continued, as she seemed to shiver and tremble. "I shall need all your strength if there be trouble coming. But, if my opinion is not sufficient, let me tell you what Captain Leale thinks. He says that the Indians wouldn't fight in the dark except at long range, and the story is that Will was tomahawked. Keep everything from her, therefore, for the present. Colonel Fenton will be here by noon."

"Keep everything from her, doctor! A mother reads faces as you do books. No one can conceal from Mrs. Farrar that ill news is in the air, and that it is of her boy. Is there no way we can find the truth? Anything, almost, would be better than suspense!" she cried, with breaking voice.

"I know of none, my poor friend," he gently answered. "All over there at the settlement is riot and confusion. They believe everything and know nothing. It may be hours before we can get details, for the Indians say the fight took place away in among the hills through Elk Springs cañon, over fifty miles north of us, and the telegraph line from Laramie to the old post follows the stage road from Fetterman far to the east. If any reports, however, had gone in by way of Laramie they would surely have been repeated up here for our benefit."

And just then a man came hurrying to them from the line of officers' quarters. It was Leale's attendant. "The captain says, sir, that he thinks if you wire through Laramie they will be having news by this time at Buffalo or McKinney stage stations."

"That was like Leale," thought the doctor, "and he must have heard she was here with me." "It's worth trying," he said, aloud. "Will you go with me to the office?"

"I must. I cannot return to her—with such news as I have heard." And so, together, they hastened over the snowy parade, and Marjorie Farrar, watching from the dormer window of Ellis's little room, saw them and read the motive of their going.

Ten minutes later a dramatic scene occurred in that shabby little office—one that Frayne has not yet ceased to tell of, and will long remember. Kurtz, the operator, was clicking away at his instrument as the doctor entered. "I've got Laramie, sir, now," he answered in response to the first question asked him, "and he says Buffalo knows nothing yet. The first news ought to come through the stage station near Allison's ranch. Colonel Fenton was over there last night, but nothing has been heard this morning. The operator is there now."

"Wire to him, then! Urge him to find out whether there was a fight in the hills—whether Colonel Fenton is still at Allison's, and get any authentic news he can and send it here at once."

And even as Kurtz began clicking his message there was some sudden check, an eager light shot into his face, an expression of keen, intense interest. He let go his key and sat listening to the quick beating of the tiny hammer of the instrument, then seized a pencil and began to write just as a faltering step was heard on the creaking woodwork of the piazza. The door burst open, and in, with wild eyes and disheveled hair, a heavy cloak thrown about her, but without overshoes, without gloves, all oblivious to the bitter cold, Marjorie Farrar rushed in upon them.

"Tell me instantly," she began; but the doctor, an inspiration seizing him as he read the operator's face, turned with uplifted hand, with reassuring smile as Helen opened her arms to receive her friend. There was a moment more of breathless, harrowing suspense, of swift clicking at the table, of swift skimming pencil, and then Kurtz sprang to his feet and placed in Mrs. Farrar's trembling hand the yellow brown sheet. With eyes that seemed starting from their sockets, she read. Then, with one glad cry, "Thank God! Oh, thank God!" threw herself on Helen's breast. The doctor seized the fluttering paper ere it reached the floor and read aloud:

"My congratulations on Will's gallant bearing in his maiden fight. He merits the name he bears. Expect us home to-morrow night, very hungry.

GEORGE FENTON."

But that was only a part of the story.

What Leale said was true enough. The Indians would not fight in the dark except at long range but that did not prevent their taking advantage of the dark for a sudden rush that would enable them to burst through what they well knew could only be a thin and widely dispersed line. It was easier to do it in the dark, as the warriors well knew, than in broad daylight, and so, learning from their vigilant scouts about where Farrar's men were deployed, they rode forward in noiseless array until close upon them, then at given signal, and with full understanding that no one was to stop for anything, they dashed forward over the snow at headlong speed. The few shots fired whizzed by their ears without checking them in the least, though two Sioux saddles, by great good luck, were emptied, and when the pony of one low-bending warrior collided with Farrar and keeled him over, others following behind raced through just as he was scrambling to his feet, and one of the riders had struck wildly with his war club at the dark object and downed it again. The whole band was out of sight in less time than it takes to tell it. The crash and sputter of hoofs could be heard as they thundered away and then the loud crackling of rifle and revolver, as the band reached the descent to the cañon farther to the West and found Farwell's led horses on the bluff.

It was then as the sergeants were raising Will, stunned and bleeding, to his feet that they realized not an instant must be lost in hastening to Farwell's aid, and, while one bathed with snow the aching, bewildered head, and another gave the young officer water from his canteen, a third helped place the boy in saddle and gave the word to the men to follow. Another minute and Leale's men, led by their lieutenant—grasping at the pommel, all the same, to steady himself in his seat—went charging through the wooded highland and tumbled in on Farwell's assailants just in the nick of time. With every minute Will was reviving and pulling himself together again, and by the time Wayne and his fellows came riding in to their support through the fire-spitting clumps of evergreen, the boy was shouting his orders and cheering his men as though no blow had ever downed him. But Wayne's coming relieved him of all responsibility on that side, secured Farwell in his grasp on the village, and when at last Big Road's sullen, beaten braves slunk away through the timber, leaving the greater part of the village, women, children, old folks, and a few disgusted warriors in the hands of the troops, Will's frantically aching head reminded him that he was in need of attention, and then it was discovered that he was literally bathed in blood, and it was time for him to faint from the loss of it.

Heavens! what a to-do there was at Frayne when that boy was brought home with the setting of the second sun thereafter, his head bandaged and his shoulder sore and his hurts severe, and yet with the record that despite it all, he had fought his troop like a veteran—"like a Farrar." Fenton handed him over to his mother, after their long ride in the ambulance sent out to meet them, and went on by first train to comply with his orders, and Marjorie took her boy to her rejoicing arms, forgetful for the moment of Fenton, of Kitty, of all else in the world.

And then, in a few days more, came the major back with his squadron and his recaptured village, and more than half the recalcitrant braves, tired of their mid-winter spree and quite ready to be taken back to Abraham's bosom, to be forgiven, and, what was more to the purpose, feasted. And by this time Will was well enough to be out again and to ride to meet them, and to welcome Wayne with especial enthusiasm, for the major had reinforced his ragged line just in time to save him from another rush such as had burst it and downed him on the slopes a mile to the east, and Kitty, no longer imperious sweetheart, but devoted love, had found it high time to take no further chances, and so had named the day, and had amazed the dreamy major by her declaration that she would be married only where Uncle Fenton could give her away and Major Wayne, who had "saved her Willy," could be best man. There was one blissful episode, therefore, in that sad and sombre winter.

But so far as our friends the Farrars were concerned, it was about the only one. Not until the day after honest Fenton had gone did it occur to Mrs. Farrar to inquire how and why it was the colonel left the command and spent that night at Allison's ranch, and then as the story was unfolded by Will, her sympathy and indignation knew no bounds. Even at such a time, when wounded and maligned, when robbed of his command at the very moment when it was dearest to him and when he must have been burning with eagerness to face and confound his accusers, Fenton had turned back to learn the truth about the fight at Elk Cañon and wire to her—to her—the glad news of her boy's safety, the proud news of his spirited and soldierly behavior. If Fenton could have seen her emotion when from Wayne and Will she learned the whole story, he would have found his trials easier to bear.

He had gone, however, to department headquarters, and there his accusers were missing; not one remained to face him, and when called upon to substantiate their statements, as they had eagerly declared their readiness to do, one and all, they had business elsewhere. The chief conspirators had achieved in part, at least, the ends for which they were striving—a row with Big Road's band that would enable them to get square with White Wolf, Pretty Bear, and the other alleged assailants of Pete Boland, replenish their stock of ponies and other spoils of Indian war, and double the price of forage, and though the alleged murderers escaped them, and the village in great part fell into the hands of the Twelfth, and Fenton came back from headquarters a vindicated man, still they had given him and his regiment far more trouble than the regiment had ever caused them, so honors were more than easy. "We've larned the old man not to monkey with the cowboy again."

There was a sweet, womanly, grateful note awaiting the colonel when, after an absence of a fortnight, he returned to Frayne, but the Farrars were gone. The doctor had said they could not too soon move Ellis, once she could be moved at all, to southern California, and with a month's leave in his pocket, thither had Will escorted them, Kitty going too, as a matter of course. Jack Ormsby came West once more to meet Malcolm Leale, and to tenderly conduct him, sightless and suffering, to New York, and Fenton felt that vengeance indeed had been wrought by Thorpe and that the Lord had been with the Philistines across the stream, for the light had gone out of his life, and smiles and sunshine seemed to have vanished from Fort Frayne. Will came back in February and threw himself enthusiastically into his duties with his troop, and Wayne went mooning night after night to the colonel's fireside, and Terry Rorke, crippled with a rheumatic twinge about an old bullet hole, was limping and growling about the post, and Fenton prayed for the coming of spring and sunshine and June and roses, for Kitty had still another freak—she would be married only from under the shadow of the flag and Uncle Fenton's roof. With Ellis better, but still not well, the Farrars and Kitty had taken the "Sunset Route" from Monterey to New Orleans the end of March and reached Gotham just as the buds were opening in the park; and Wayne, East on leave on some mysterious mission, called to welcome them home and to say that Ormsby was to sail at once with Malcolm Leale, who was to go to Germany to consult an eminent oculist, and Ellis lost the color which was fluttering in her cheeks when they hove in sight of the familiar landmarks of the beautiful harbor, and Helen Daunton strove to conquer her own disappointment that she might comfort the poor girl, who, since the tragic night of her brother's death, had neither seen nor heard from the lover she had rebuffed and wronged, even though here and now she had written, admitting her sin against him and humbly yet confidently asking his forgiveness. That was Thursday night, and there was ample time, but he sailed on Saturday with never a word.

## CHAPTER XX.

JUNE had come, a radiant June, and all at Frayne was joyous anticipation, despite the momentous fact that the Platte had overleaped its bounds and was raging like some mad mountain torrent far as the eye could see. The flats to the west of the post were one broad, muddy lake. The grassy bench beneath the bluffs to the east was partially torn away. Part of Bunco Jim's frontier stronghold still clung to the opposite bank, but some of it was distributed in driftwood long leagues down stream. Across the river, at a point half a mile above the ruin of the ferry house, a troop of cavalry, caught on return from scout, had pitched its tents and picketed its horses, and was waiting for the falling of the waters to enable it to return to its station, and with that troop, the maddest man in all Wyoming, was Lieutenant Will Farrar.

Six or seven weeks previously an order had come to Fenton to send two troops to scout the western slopes of the Big Horn and keep the peace between the settlers and the Shoshones. Time was when these latter rarely ventured across the Big Horn River, partly through fear of the Sioux, who claimed sovereignty over all the lands east of the Shoshone preserves in the Wind River Valley, partly through regard for the orders of their loyal old chief, Washakie, who for long, long years of his life, had kept faith with the Great White Father, held his people in check and suffered the inevitable consequences of poverty and neglect; the policy of the Indian Bureau being to load with favors only those of its wards who defy it and deal death to the whites. Settlers seldom encroach upon the Sioux, those gentry being abundantly able and more than willing to take care of themselves, but the Shoshones had known long years of enervating peace, and, being held in subjection by their chief, became the natural prey of the whites, who mistook subordination for subservience,—as is natural to free-born Americans and as easily adopted by fellow-citizens of foreign birth—and who soon began to encroach on their own account, stealing Shoshone crops and cattle and promptly accusing the army officer, on duty as agent, of cattle stealing and all-round rascality when he reseized the captured stock. Then, while this badgered official was defending himself in court, the Shoshones had to defend themselves in the field, and that peripatetic buffer between the oppressor and the oppressed, the corporations and the cranks, the law and the lawless —the much-bedeviled army—was sent out as usual to receive the slings and arrows of outrageous fortune and of both parties. Finding it difficult to swindle the Shoshones so long as their new agent—the army agent—remained in power, the obvious thing was to down him by misrepresentation at Washington, and, if that didn't work, by deft manipulation of the local law. Of course they didn't expect to prove him guilty of anything, but there was no law against lying, and they could compel him to come into court and prove himself innocent, and leave his unarmed wards to the mercy of the settler in the meantime, and so it happened that there were high jinks up the Wind River Valley and along those wonderful ranges in the wild valleys of the Gray Bull, the Meeyero, the Meeteetsee, north of the Owl Creek Mountains, and, the cavalry having long since been withdrawn from that section, that was how the detail fell on old Fort Frayne.

"You can straighten matters out in a month," said the commanding officer to Major Wayne, who had hastened back from the East to take command, and when it came to selecting the troops to go, even though it lacked less than two months to his wedding day, Will Farrar gloried in the fact that his was one of them. It is hard to conceive of a lot in which a spirited, soldierly fellow of twenty-one could possibly be happier than commanding a troop of cavalry on an expedition through so glorious a country. Amory's troop and Leale's were designated, and, the latter captain being still in Berlin and the senior subaltern on staff duty in the East, Farrar was his own captain and troop commander, and, despite the troubles of the Christmas season, long since buried so far as he was concerned, just about the happiest fellow that wore the army blue.

The expedition had proved even longer than was planned, but at last, while Wayne with Amory and the recaptured cattle and rounded-up Shoshones went over the Owl Creek Mountains to render account of his stewardship at Fort Washakie, Will was told to make the best of his way homeward with his own command, and, marching leisurely along in the radiant spring mornings, through a country unmatched for wild beauty in all America; shooting, fishing, plunging in mountain streams, sleeping dreamlessly in the open air by night, they reached the valley of the Platte toward mid June. The blessed landmark of the Eagle Buttes came in sight one peerless morning. The blue summits of the Medicine Bow loomed up across the horizon to the southeast. The flag-tipped bluffs of old Fort Frayne would greet their eyes before the close of to-morrow's march, and so they did —but with a raging torrent tearing at their base, and this was Monday, and less than forty-eight hours to Will's wedding day.

Meanwhile, there had been a partial reunion within the walls of the fort, and already a joyous bevy of army folk had gathered in anticipation of the June wedding with Kitty Ormsby as the center of attraction, since she was the colonel's niece, and he was to give her away, and Wayne was to be best man, by order of the bride, provided he didn't get things mixed in his own inimitable way and turn up unexpectedly at some one else's affair, as he did the night of the Willett's dinner to Captain and Mrs. "Billy" Ray of the —th, where, with army bonhomie, a seat was squeezed in close beside that of the winsome guest of the evening, and where he was charmingly welcomed and made at home despite the fact, which dawned upon him only with the champagne, that he was due at the Amorys', where a similar function was being held in honor of the Truscotts of the same regiment, then on the march from Kansas to Montana. "You'll rue it, Kitty, that ever you insisted on my having Wayne for best man," wrote poor Will, with prophetic but unavailing protest. "Wayne saved my Willy," was the positive rejoinder, and no one but Wayne would do. "All right," said Will, "if you find, years later, that there's been some fatal flaw in the proceedings, don't blame me."

But here, on this glad June morning, all sunshine and serenity aloft, all perturbation at the post, all raging river about it, it looked as though the proceedings themselves would be delayed, and that instead of a military wedding in the post chapel at high noon, with everybody *en grande tenue*, there would be no wedding at all, even though Will, like a modern Leander, swam this wild Western Hellespont in search of his bride. Far away to the east the floods had swept their battering ram of logs and trees and dashed it against the bridge abutments at the railway, and though the Farrars were safely here, and had been for several days, Kitty's train, that which bore her and Jack on their westward way, had been brought up standing long miles toward Cheyenne, and there was no telling when the passengers could be transferred to the waiting cars upon the hither shore. And so, each believing the other in waiting at the post, bride and groom elect woke to their wedding morn to rail at fate. It would have been some comfort could they have known that, though miles apart, they were at least on the same side of the stream that swept between them and the altar of their hopes.

And there was deep anxiety under the roof where once again the Farrars were installed, for the mother was possessed with the fear that Willy would be mad enough to try to swim the stream, and though Fentor. had had his signal men out forbidding any such attempt, no acknowledgment had been received to the effect that the repeated message was understood. An Indian, who thought he could cross at Casper Rocks, several miles up stream, was swept from his pony and only saved by the strength of his horsehair lariat. A scow that was launched at the bend was battered to flinders, and bottle after bottle, corked and slung long yards out into the steam, went bobbing derisively away, carrying its penciled contents with them. Arrows, with silken strings attached, dropped helplessly in the stream. Bullets, similarly tethered, snapped their frail attachments and whistled over the opposite shore and told no tale other than that of anxiety. Every fieldglass at the post, when brought to bear, revealed Farrar at nine o'clock of his bridal morning striding and probably swearing up and down the bank, tugging at his tiny moustache and sprouting beard, and possibly threatening self-destruction. It was a thrilling scene.

Then many other people seemed burdened with troubles of their own. Ellis had never recovered either strength or spirits since the events of that Christmas week, and her lovely face was thin, and the bright, brave eyes of old were shadowed with a pathetic sorrow, but, though this shadow had come into her life, another one, much harder to bear, had been swept aside. Ever since her lover's words had revealed to Ellis that it was her own brother to save whom Malcolm Leale had periled life and lost his sight, the girl's eyes seemed gradually to open to the utter cruelty of her suspicions, the injustice of her treatment of Helen Daunton, the woman whose life that very brother had well-nigh wrecked forever. In the long hours of her convalescence she had turned to Helen in humility that was sweet to see, and now the love and trust between them was something inexpressible. But there was something even Helen could neither explain nor justify, and that was Jack Ormsby's conduct since her convalescence.

True, Ellis had told him in their last interview that all was at an end between them, that he had forfeited trust, faith, and even respect, and placed a barrier between himself and her forever. She had refused him further audience, and her last words to him had been full of scorn, even of insult. But no word of anger or resentment had escaped him, and surely no man who deeply loved would harbor anger now. Sobbing her heart out, the girl had thrown herself on Helen's breast just before their return to Frayne, and told a part of her story until then concealed, how, in their last interview, Ormsby had gently said that he would vex her no more with his pleadings, but if a time should ever come when her eyes were opened and when she could believe him honest and worthy, he would come at her call, and she had humbled herself and called, but all in vain. To Helen she had told the whole story of that humble letter, and that neither by word or sign had he acknowledged it.

But Helen saw a ray of hope. The little note had been intrusted to Wayne late that Thursday night, and he had promised to deliver it early Friday morning, and all that day had Ellis waited eagerly, and nightfall came without the looked-for visit. Wayne came on Saturday to convey some conventional words of farewell from both officers—"so surprised to hear of the sudden return from California, so sorry not to have seen them, but time was very short," and—would she never hear the last of the Seventh?—Ormsby had had to attend the review at the armory Friday night, and then there was just time to rejoin Leale and get him aboard, for their good ship sailed at 7 A. M. to catch the early tide at Sandy Hook. Falteringly Ellis had asked if he were sure he had given Ormsby her note—if—if Mr. Ormsby had read it. Wayne was quite positive.

But Helen would not believe, and, with unabated hope, she awaited Wayne's return to the post. They arrived a week before him, for on leaving his charge at Washakie the previous month he had hurried straight to Washington in response to a summons from the Secretary of War, had made his report, and then gone to New York. Not until the Monday before the wedding did he reappear, and then only by determined effort did Helen corner him long enough for cross-examination. "Certainly," said Wayne. "I remember the note perfectly well. I put it with one from the club that I found there and handed both to him together. He'll be here to the wedding. He's coming right along with Kitty. I'll ask him again, if you like."

"Don't dare ever mention it, major; or that I asked any questions concerning it. How long has he been back?" asked Helen, with vivid interest, another question uppermost in her mind.

"Not a week. Just back, you know. I only saw him a minute. I was just starting for the train. He looked astonishingly well, and—you know—I forgot to ask was Leale better. He was full of his wedding preparations."

"*Her* wedding preparations—Kitty's—you mean, do you not, major?"

"No, his; I give you my word. He said so, you know. He told me the lady's name—part of it, at least—Effie something. I can't recall it just now. He'll tell you. Oh, it was all on that account, you know, Kitty couldn't start sooner. She had to wait for him."

Helen was astounded. It was news she declared she would never believe, and yet she remembered having heard mention of an attractive cousin, a Miss Effie Leale, and might it not have been possible that, in his wanderings—with the blinded invalid—with his own sore heart, Jack Ormsby had met and found consolation in this fair relative of his stricken friend

—that she in turn had quickly learned to admire the manly fellow who was so devoted to their particular hero? At all events, it was something not to be mentioned to Ellis, said Helen.

But what was the use! Wayne told it to Lucretia; Lucretia to a dozen during the day. It was all over the post before night, and despite Helen's effort, Ellis heard it among the first. One more among the many mishaps with which to usher in Will's wedding day!

At ten that beautiful June morning there was something more than pathetic about poor Lucretia's sorrows. While Fenton, Mrs. Farrar, Helen, silent, brave-faced Ellis, and a dozen sympathetic souls from all over the post were gathered on the north piazza overhanging the bluff and the roaring waters of the Platte, signaling to Will and watching eagerly his vigorous movements, the lady of the house remained within doors, wept unceasingly, and refused to be comforted.

"It is dreadful to think of the condition that chicken salad will be in," she moaned. "It is preposterous to talk to me of patience! I've said all along it was to be an unlucky day, because you all know perfectly well—at least if you don't, you ought to— that it is just thirteen years ago this day we were all gathered at Fort Crook for the funeral of Captain Crocus, which was to take place the moment the ambulance got in from the front, and the band was all ready—and the escort and the hearse—and—and after all the whole thing had to be abandoned, for when the ambulance got in there were no remains at all—at least there were, but they weren't ready for burial because they'd revived and were sitting up and saying shocking things. Why, I think a wedding without a bride is ten times worse than a funeral without a—without a—"

But here, it must be admitted, the burst of laughter in which Rorke indulged was too much for her determination to weep and, blazing through her tears, the maiden demanded explanation of his unseemly conduct. Rorke was a permanent member of the colonel's establishment now, but he could not risk Miss Lucretia's displeasure, and was wise and knew his danger, and fled to the kitchen, there to tell cook and Chinaman the lady's plaintive monologue, while Amory, equally conscienceless, ran out to convulse with it the party on the porch. And then, in the midst of all the laughter, came delirious news from the "best man" sent to meet the bride and Ormsby at the Station and break to them the direful news that "the bridegroom was late." The train had passed Fetterman Bend. The bride would be there in twenty minutes.

And she came—and what a scene there was! And how she was hugged and kissed and mauled and pulled about, and how she strove to tell of her tribulations and could not for the volume of welcome, exclamation and interrogation; and, not until trunks, boxes, and what alls had been whisked away to her room aloft and somebody said it was almost eleven o'clock, did she find breath and opportunity to say, "Gracious Heavens! And I'm to be married at noon! And not a thing done yet! Why! Wh—where's Willy?"

Aghast, they looked at one another. Was not all this to have been explained by Wayne? Hadn't Wayne told her? Told her? Told her what? All Major Wayne said to her about Willy was that he was almost frantic with impatience to meet her, but he'd—he'd have to take his bath first. What did he mean by sending such riduculous stuff? What were they all laughing—crying at? Isn't *here*? Couldn't *cross*? Can't he swim? Why! the man she thought he was would swim *Niagara* rather than miss his wedding day! And then—oh day of days!—perhaps her words annihilated space and reached the ears of the maddened lover, for at the very moment came an Irish howl from the porch without. "Oh, fur the luv of God! shtop him! Don't let him! Oh, Mother of Moses, it's drownin' he is!" And then, all shrieks and terror, did most of the party scatter for the balconies, while, all shrieks and terror and protestations that she'd never speak to him again if he dared to, Kitty collapsed upon a sofa.

Was ever there a wedding day to match it? Soaked to the skin, dripping but triumphant, Will Farrar rode out of the floods and up the heights, amid the frenzied acclamations of the garrison, and, throwing himself from saddle at the colonel's gate demanded to see—if not to squeeze—his bride. There were they gathered—the *elite* of Fort Frayne—some in wedding garb, some in traveling dress, and what a cheer went up as he sprang to the porch, and his mother wanted to clasp him, dripping though he was, to her heart of hearts. Not so Kitty. "Don't you come near me, you dreadful thing!" she cried. And, laughing and protesting, he was led away, to be caparisoned for the ceremony. Lucretia's spirits were once more in ebullition. Wayne was back; the remains had come, so why longer delay—proceedings?

They were not. There was as blithe and bright and joyous a soldier wedding that perfect noon day as ever was seen within the walls of old Fort Frayne, and Kitty made a bewitching bride and there was a wonderful unloading of sorrow from heart after heart onto the shoulders of one luckless, sorely-tried man—Major Percival Wayne. Oh, Mad Anthony! but here was one of thy descendents ten times worthy thy name! In that one day there came crushing in upon him the consequences of a generation of misdoing.

It was enough that he should have failed to explain matters to Kitty. It was worse when he took the first opportunity to explain matters to Jack. His way of doing it was somewhat as follows, and they were dressing for the ceremony, and Jack—gorgeous in his full-dress uniform as a lieutenant of the Seventh, was sick at heart over the cold, constrained greeting accorded him by Ellis.

"Why, of course, old fellow, you didn't impose

silence on me, and I s'pose I let out about your engagement—"

"My what?" says poor Jack, aghast.

"Your engagement. You said, even to attend Kitty's wedding, you couldn't get away until yours was fulfilled—on the 10th, wasn't it?"

"Certainly—our annual inspection. No man in the Seventh would miss that for love or money."

"But, Jack, don't you know? I'm sure you told me a lady was in the case. You told me her name, and—indeed, you did—that Effie and you were to be tied—"

"You transcendental idiot! I told you 'F' and 'I'—Company 'F' and Company 'I'—were tied for place, and neither dare lose a point."

And then, instead of smashing Wayne, as was his first thought, Jack fled down stairs in search of Ellis and found her, and told her Wayne's story, and then his own, breathlessly, eagerly, imploringly, and there were blushes and tears and soft laughter, and soft, happy murmurs, and—and how horribly those big epaulets get in the way, and service medals and sautache braid scratch at such times! And at last did Jack uplift his voice again to say: "Ellis, I'm in heaven!" and then did she uplift a blushing, tear-stained, kiss-rumpled face to archly inquire, "A *Seventh* heaven, Jack?" and then did old Fenton come blustering in to take a veteran's share in the engagement. It was known all over the house before the wedding party started.

Then came the next scene in Mad Anthony's play.

Amory and the chaplain declare to this day that when the party was duly marshaled at the altar the major clicked his heels together and raised his hand in salute, and began: "Sir, the parade is—" when Ormsby caught the hand and brought it down, but when it came to the ring there was consternation. To the horror of the groom, the despair of the bride, but to the marked and tremulous emotion of Aunt Lucretia, the circlet produced for the occasion by the dazed best man was an old-fashioned, but beautiful, cluster of flashing gems. Only by a miracle did it happen that the other ring was in his possession. How the mixture occurred there was no time to tell, until later, when all were gathered, for there were two whose fortunes we have followed through these long, long chapters, who were absent from the ceremony—who, in fact, were having one of their own, and to these two, while the band without is softly playing in front of the chapel, and in eager hundreds the men are gathered to cheer the bride and groom on their reappearance, let us turn—and listen.

"No, dear Mrs. Farrar," were Helen Daunton's words as the eager guests were pouring forth to the wedding. "They are bringing him here—even now —so that he may welcome Will and Kitty on their return from the wedding he cannot see."

And no sooner was the party fairly at the chapel than there drove to the colonel's door the old Concord, and two soldiers assisted to alight and led to the doorway the soldierly form of Captain Leale—his eyes still covered by the deep green shade. It was Helen

Daunton's hand that guided him into the lately crowded parlor, and he knew the touch and thrilled with the joy of it.

"Helen!" he cried. "They told me all were gone. What a blessed welcome! I've been so long in exile! With your voice, the old home feeling I've been groping for comes to me through the dark."

"Then—it is still dark with you?" she faltered.

There was a moment's pause. The band had just ceased the joyous march with which it had "trooped" the wedding party into the chapel, and then, as though in accompaniment to the ceremony just beginning and to the sweet romance already throbbing here, the exquisite strains of the "Traeumerei" softly thrilled upon the fragrant air.

"Helen!" he spoke, his deep voice trembling as did the hand that still clung to hers. "You know that for me the lights went out before ever that powder-flash crossed my eyes." She strove, hardly knowing why, to release her hand. "No, dear," he went on gently. "Don't be afraid I have come back to vex you with my sorrows; but listen, they will all be here in a moment. I went away hoping to teach my heart a friendship for you that should give me the right to come again and serve you as your friend. When I found that it was almost sure that I should walk in darkness all my life, I said: 'Now at least I can accept the blessing of her friendship—even as she offered it to me.' A man maimed and set apart from his fellows can learn thankfulness for a great good, though it is not his heart's desire." And here her graceful head was bowed and silently her tears came gushing forth. "But time has taught me the falsity of that," he went on, firmly now. "You shall never misunderstand me. Even in the dark my pulse-beat gave the lie to friendship. I loved you! I love you, and so—have come to say a long good-by. I've made my fight to be your friend—and failed. At least I have been a soldier. I will not be a coward."

She could control herself no longer. Though she had freed her hands, she seemed involuntarily stretching them forth. Then, leaning upon the table for support, one hand found the glove that he had removed and laid there. He had withdrawn a pace and lifted his head as though the blighted eyes were striving to peer from under their shade for one look at the face they had gazed upon in such passionate farewell so many months before. The strains of the "Traeumerei" were still thrilling softly through the open casements, and, overcome with emotion, tenderness, and passion, Helen bent and laid her soft lips in fervent pressure on the senseless glove.

Then the room rang with a sudden, startling joyous cry. The shade went whizzing into space, and the next instant Leale had sprung to and seized her in his arms.

"Helen, darling—not that! Don't waste those kisses," and she sank sobbing in his arms just as, grand, joyous, triumphant, the strains of the wedding march burst forth, re-echoing among the walls of Fort Frayne.

Rorke was the first man to come tearing in to announce the return of the wedding party and the guests, but Fenton was close on his heels "on hospitable cares intent," and exploding over Wayne's performances. There was no time for a formal reception. "Proceedings" had been delayed well-nigh an hour as it was, and the east-bound train was reported unaccountably on time. Bride and bridegroom, bridesmaids, ushers, bachelors and benedicks, maids and matrons, Fort Frayne seemed surging tumultuously up the Colonel's step, surrounding and bedeviling poor Wayne to the verge of distraction. He laid the blame on his spring overcoat, a venerable garment of the fashion of twenty years agone, but that he had so seldom worn as to cause it to seem to him ever new and available, and for this garment he darted into the adjoining quarters while the laughing guests came tripping up the steps in the wake of the bride, who, totally ignoring Helen and Leale now, who were gazing into each other's eyes in the deep bow window, rushed at her uncle with characteristic and explosive abuse.

"I'll never be married at Fort Frayne again as long as I live! What on earth did Major—" but she could go no further, for the shout of laughter that greeted her sally, and the exclamations which resulted from the discovery of Leale and Helen, silenced her completely. And then the bride was rushed away to doff her finery and reappear in traveling garb, and then Will was hustled to his quarters to change his full-dress uniform for the conventional garb of civil life, just as Wayne came in, dazed, half-demented, overcoat in one hand and a package in the other, that he now half-dreamily held forth to Ormsby, who took it, as wonderingly opened, and began slowly counting over a number of "greenbacks," sole contents of the wrapper, but he dropped them as of little consequence, when the bewildered major produced a moment later another—a little note from the depths of an inner pocket. They were all crowding around him now, but at sight of this missive Ellis made a spring and captured it, only just in time, and was seized in turn by Ormsby, who pleaded for possession of what was plainly addressed to him, and then came renewed uproar, for Will reappeared in uniform trousers and unfastened blouse, and a towering rage.

"Of all things that could have happened to a man, think of this," he cried. "Major Wayne, didn't you promise me from the field to send that dispatch to Hatfield the moment you got to the post?"

"I did, and I pledge my solemn word that I kept it. I sent it the very first post I struck."

"You did, for a fact, you moonstruck—Oh, but just listen, all of you! Instead of my traveling suit here's what I find—a letter from Hatfield, forwarded from Fort Washakie. 'Dear Sir: In accordance with your telegraphic instructions, we have this day forwarded to you a cutaway tweed traveling suit by American Express, and trust the same is,' etc., 'also statement of'—um, never mind that—'We are'—now, mark this, all of you, good people—'we are somewhat at a loss to understand your sudden change of address, but are compelled to act on your telegram, a copy of which is inclosed. "Fort Washakie, May 25. Have tweed cutaway traveling suit here by 13th prox. without fail. W. Farrar."' Fort Washakie! Gracious powers! Think of my traveling suit at Washakie and I here and the train coming!"

"But Willy, dear," said his mother, soothingly, "surely you can wear for just a day or two last year's suit."

"That? Now? Why, heavens ablaze! Rorke couldn't squeeze me into it with a shoehorn. I'll have to travel in my pajamas. Oh, couldn't I murder you, Major Percival Wayne!"

Poor Wayne's cup was indeed full to overflowing. Martin and some of the youngsters lugged Will off to squeeze him into his last year's garments, made on cadet measure, and then down came Kitty, the bonniest of brides, in the daintiest and most coquettish of costumes, and while Rorke and his satellites were passing the champagne, and everybody—no, almost everybody—was crowding about the bride, there stood poor Wayne still diving into those long forgotten placer mines of his pockets and fetching up bills and billets and odds and ends, while Lucretia tremulously, and Fenton, Farwell and Amory delightedly, watched him, and then came a new excitement. Enter Will, squeezed at last into the light gray tweeds he had so complacently donned a year before, and that now fitted him like the skin of a sausage. A sudden move of one arm carried away the breast button.

"It's no use!" he cried, "I'm worse off than Peggoty. Every jump's a button!" and then Kitty caught sight of him, and then there came a scene.

"What's that?" she exclaimed. "That isn't the man I married! I won't stir a step with him in those things."

"But I haven't any other," pleaded Will, in despair.

"Who wants you to wear such things?" she fairly screamed, in almost hysterical laughter. "I married a soldier. Your uniform, sir, your best blouse and trousers and forage cap, and don't you dare wear cits till I tell you."

And, as it was manifest that he couldn't wear those now encasing him, the groom a third time hastened away to the upper regions, and, while dozens clustered as before about Kittie, an absorbed group still hung upon the movements of the major. The light, as of other days, was dawning on his face. He was searching still, and at last he found and drew forth a tiny box, at sight of which Lucretia's maiden heart fluttered almost out of her throat.

"And now what have you unearthed, old Rip Van Winkle?" boomed Fenton. "A ring, by all that's gorgeous—a ring, and a beauty, and an inscription on it. P. W. to L. F., 1874. Who's P. W? Who's —but a glance at his sister's transfigured face as she tottered there at his side warned the old warrior to desist.

Wme was panting with excitement. "I know," he crid. "Of course it wasn't my class ring; it was this. I got it for—" and here he turned and drew her to his rm, and the others considerately moved away, as at last that ring was fitted to the finger that had been waiting for it twenty long years.

Five minutes more, and with Rorke leading off in the cheers, with music and sunshine, mirth and gladness, smiles and tears, and prayers and blessings, the young couple were whirled away to the station, bound for the bliss of the honeymoon.

But what made that wedding day so remarkable was that it seemed to lead to so many more. There came a letter from Martin to Jack Ormsby only the other day. The latter, being a New York guardsman, was sweltering in his tent at Peekskill, while Mrs. Jack consoled herself by a brief visit to the Leales at West Point. The former, being a West Pointer, fell back naturally into the vernacular of his cadet days and this was somewhat as he wrote: "Your blessed brother-in-law continues to be the joy of the Twelfth, and the dovecote is every whit as hospitable as Amory's. But of course Will and Mrs. Will haven't outlived their salad days, and their tiffs and make-ups are too funny for anything. Will is just as true a soldier as ever, but we always know when the 'wind's in the east' at the cote by his becoming even more aggressively, austerely, self-denyingly military. Just now all is bliss, for dear Lady Farrar, 'Queen Mother,' as we learned to call her from your sweet wife—my salutations to her ladyship—is, as you know, in the third week of her first visit to 'the children,' and this, Jack, old boy, brings me to a prediction. In our cadet days we used to say 'extras breed extras,' and I'm thinking what that wedding day of Will's is responsible for. First there's you and Miss Ellis—God bless 'em!—there's Leale and Mrs. Royle Farrar—God reward 'em! There's Old-Man-Heap-Mashed-in-the-Moon and Miss Lucretia—God help 'em! But, do you know, we believe our bully old colonel has the promise now of being made at last just the happiest man in old **Fort Frayne.**"

**THE END.**

# URANIA.

## By CAMILLE FLAMMARION.

**Profusely Illustrated with Half-tone Engravings.**

Cloth, $1.25; paper, 50c.

The celebrated French astronomer is seen at his best in this work of science and fiction, and his admirers, who number legion in this country, may well be satisfied to sound his praises anew. The work is certainly pleasing to a degree bordering on the marvelous. No writer of the present day wields such a wizard pen as Camille Flammarion, when dealing with scenes that touch upon the possibilities of science in relation to our world and its manifest destiny. The touch of a master is apparent in almost every line. Nor has the mechanical part of the book been slighted in the least degree. The paper, the letter-press, the beautiful half-tone engravings scattered lavishly all through the volume unite to form a most pleasing result. There can rarely be found a more handsome book from a New York press, and "Urania" adds another link to that pleasant chain with which Mr. Neely is fast binding the reading public to his triumphant chariot.

---

For sale everywhere, or sent post-paid on receipt of price.

**F. TENNYSON NEELY, Publisher,**

96 Queen Street, London.    114 Fifth Avenue, New York.

# Two Strange Adventures.

## By KINAHAN CORNWALLIS.

Neely's Popular Library.

### Paper, 25c.

This book is well calculated to please readers of adventure, since there is not a dry chapter from cover to cover. In many ways it is impossible enough for Jules Verne, and yet through the whole runs a delicate yet charming thread of love seldom to be found in the works of that French master of adventurous fiction. Those who pick up the volume will hardly be satisfied until they reach the end. Mr. Cornwallis has written many charming stories in verse, the most popular being his "Conquest of Mexico and Peru" and the patriotic "Song of America and Columbus," which latter fitly graced the period of our World's Fair. "Two Strange Adventures" met with such a hearty welcome that the first edition was immediately exhausted.

---

# A Conspiracy of the Carbonari.

## By MISS MUHLBACH.

Translated by MARY J. SAFFORD.

### Cloth, gilt top, 50c.

This is one of the most charming tales from the pen of the celebrated German novelist. It gives many side lights to the story of Napoleon in the height of his power, and would prove interesting even to those who have never admired the genius of the great Bonaparte. The translation by Miss Safford leaves nothing to be desired, since it could not be improved. For years she has stood in the leading rank of translators, with a charm of expression wholly her own. "A Conspiracy of the Carbonari" has proven very popular in this neat form so well adapted to the pocket and satchel, and eagerly sought after by the traveling public.

---

For sale everywhere, or sent post-paid on receipt of price.

**F. TENNYSON NEELY, Publisher,**

96 Queen Street, London.   114 Fifth Avenue, New York.

# THE DAUGHTER OF A HUNDRED MILLIONS.

By VIRGINIA NILES LEEDS.

✣✣

Neely's International Library.

Cloth, 12mo, $1.25.

✣✣

A cynical public has long since decided the status of the usual Anglo-American marriage. *She* weds for position and an honorable name that can be traced far back to the days of chivalry; while milord seeks a colossal fortune, it does not matter how acquired, with which to free his noble chateau from debt and the moldy hand of decay. This state of affairs has gone on from year to year, until the American public wearies of the story, and raises its sceptical hands in disdain at the mere mention of love ever entering into the calculations of these high-contracting parties. And yet there have been frequent cases of romantic attachments between even the rulers of Europe and those they espoused. While improbable, such a love-match is far from impossible. Virginia Niles Leeds has seized upon an occurrence of this sort to weave among the stern facts a most subtle and fascinating thread of love. The beautiful and proud heiress to millions is betrothed to an English lord. She has reasons for believing his estates to be in a bad way, and that he has come to America for the sole purpose of buying a wealthy bride with his title. On his part, he has been so long angled after by designing British maids and matrons that he quite despairs of having anyone love the man who bears this illustrious name. When the fact is disclosed that each of them is, in reality, madly in love with the other, it is easy for the reader to realize the strong possibilities for dramatic scenes. Miss Leeds rises to the occasion heroically, nor does she allow the deep interest to flag for a moment up to the very closing chapter. Through the book there runs a quaint vein of comedy that relieves some of its more sombre situations.

"The Daughter of a Hundred Millions" gives evidence of proving the most popular novel of the season, and will without doubt create a decided sensation among those upper circles in which the fair authoress, as a New York society girl, is evidently at home.

---

For sale everywhere, or sent post-paid on receipt of price.

**F. TENNYSON NEELY, Publisher,**

96 Queen Street, London.     114 Fifth Avenue, New York.

# AT MARKET VALUE.
### By GRANT ALLEN,
Author of "The Woman Who Did," "The Duchess of Powysland," "This Mortal Coil," "Blood Royal," etc.

### Cloth, $1.25; paper, 25c.

**Harrisburg Telegram** "Interesting and well told."
**Indianapolis Sentinel** "The story is an entertaining one. An American gentleman plays an important part, and gives the author occasion to pay us a compliment by saying that 'Where women are concerned there is no person so delicately chivalrous than your American gentlemen.'"
**Post Intelligencer** "The mere announcement of a story from Grant Allen's pen is sufficient for those who enjoy the work of a masterhand."
**New York Independent** "A right charming style of story-telling, and everything he writes enforces attention."
**Chicago Mail** "Excellently planned, and entertainingly carried out"
**Boston Ideas** "The depth and sincerity of its suggestiveness forms a valuable novel. Its manner is very frank and clear."
**Commercial Appeal** "Mr. Allen's English is vigorous, and his characters are very strongly drawn in the main. We find a charm in the book we did not expect to find."
**Daily Register** "Mr. Allen has constructed a remarkably clever story. Its characters are interesting, and there is action throughout to keep up the interest."
**Penny Press** "The book contains both bits of modern philosophy and love episodes of decidedly romantic nature."

---

# In Strange Company.
### By GUY BOOTHBY,
Author of "On the Wallaby." Six Full Page Illustrations by Stanley L. Wood.

### Cloth, $1.25; paper, 25c.

**Cincinnati Tribune** "It is a novel with a purpose—that is, to entertain and interest, and it certainly succeeds."
**The World** "A capital novel of its kind—the sensational adventurous. It has the quality of life and stir, and will carry the reader with curiosity unabated to the end."
**The Pall Mall Budget** "The best of them is 'In Strange Company.' . . . The book is a good tale of adventure; it has plenty of astonishing incidents which yet have an air of versimilitude."
**The Yorkshire Post** "One of the most successful novels of its order we have recently seen. Its general resemblance is to what may be called the buried treasure class. . . . The story hangs well together; its villains are picturesque and almost engaging people; its dialogue singularly free from the melodramatic element."
**The Glasgow Herald** "Mr. Boothby gives the reader no chance of skipping. 'In Strange Company' is full of strange adventures to the end. . . . A thoroughly exciting story told with considerable ability."
**The Morning Post** "Will prove far more interesting to him who is past his first youth than the majority of tales of adventure. Its incidents are as exciting as is the rule in books of this kind, but they remain fairly within the bounds of the possible, and there is a picturesque vigor in the author's description of Chili and the southern seas."

---

For sale everywhere, or sent post-paid on receipt of price.

## F. TENNYSON NEELY, Publisher,
96 Queen Street, London.　　114 Fifth Avenue, New York.

# NIL.
## A NOVEL.
### BY FREDERICK A. RANDLE.

**NEELY'S CONTINENTAL LIBRARY.** Cloth, $1.25; paper, 50 cents.

Competent critics have pronounced this book the most elaborate and interesting work of the author. Mr. Randle comes honestly by his literary ability, his mother being a Powers, and closely connected with that family so famous for its sculptors and artists. His present work, *Nil*, abounds in quick action, and may be classified with that delightful and humorous line of fiction so eagerly sought by the lover of travel and adventure.

Nesta Storovski, a young Polish lady and belle of Kazan, Russia, Vala, a noble Aleut maiden of the Island of Unalaska, Laila, a beautiful Ayan girl whose home is on picturesque Upper Yukon, Imla Van Xen, an Imperial Guard of the Winter Palace, St. Petersburg, are characters in the story commanding highest admiration; so also Michael O'Finerty, a verdant son of Erin, and Jacob Schmidt, an unsophisticated young man from Holland, both so unaffected in their ways that they fairly dispel seriousness, take a leading part in the thrilling scenes that mark the progress of the romance.

The renowned city of Amsterdam on the Zuyder-Zee, Utrecht, a city of the Netherlands where lived the old Dutch aristocracy, Lake Wener and the River Klar, Sweden, the Aleutian Islands, and Alaska are places of importance in the story, made fascinatingly interesting by a wizard pen.

One feature of this novel may cause reviewers to classify it an extravaganza, since to an excessive degree the author amusingly portrays the officiousness of the police world to arrest people on the merest resemblance to fugitives; ridiculous blunders of mistaken identity filling the history of such official activity. In this portrayal, Nil is almost as "far fetched" as "A Comedy of Errors" and as amusing as "The Merry Wives of Windsor."

The story in a unique manner concludes at Nokomis, Illinois, a little city noted for romance and chivalry.

---

For sale everywhere, or sent post-paid on receipt of price.

### F. TENNYSON NEELY, Publisher,
96 Queen Street, London.   114 Fifth Avenue, New York.

# AN ALTRUIST
## By "OUIDA."

**Neely's Prismatic Library.**

Gilt Top, 50c.

. A new story by "OUIDA" is an event to be eagerly anticipated by a large class of readers. Few modern writers have a more devoted *clientèle* than this graceful and charming author, and the mere announcement of a romance from her magic pen is enough to arouse enthusiasm. In the **Altruist,** as the title would indicate, the author of "Under Two Flags" enters a new field, and breaks a lance in a worthy cause. As might be expected, the action is spirited and the dialogue crisp and to the point. The story is written in the light vein so taking with the general reader, and once begun arouses a keen desire to continue on to the end.

**An Altruist** will be found one of the best things "OUIDA" has written for a long time and in many ways revives keen recollections of the days when her *nom-de-plume* was one with which to conjure, and readers of many countries were content to count themselves under her magic spell.

---

For sale everywhere, or sent post-paid on receipt of price,

**F. TENNYSON NEELY, Publisher,**

96 Queen Street, London.    114 Fifth Avenue, New York.

# TRUE TO THEMSELVES.

A Psychological Study by

## ALEXANDER J. C. SKENE, M.D., LL.D.

Cloth, $1.25.    Paper, 50c.

THOSE of our readers who are familiar with Dr. Skene's medical works, "Diseases of Women," "Medical Gynæcology," etc., will welcome with considerable interest his venture in the domain of romance. Perhaps no profession offers such splendid opportunities for studying human nature as that of medicine and surgery; and Dr. Skene has always been recognized as a close student. Of course, the novel is only used as a vehicle to convey certain positive principles of the author. His argument is plausible and worthy of the closest inspection. "True to Themselves" is certainly a story that is bound to arouse considerable interest and criticism among thinking readers, on account of the bold stand taken by the well-known physician regarding what constitutes the enduring elements of domestic life. There are other features in the volume that will prove of intense interest to members of the medical profession, always ready to investigate those wonderful mysteries with which humanity is surrounded. Besides this expression of his views, the Doctor has given us quite a charming little love story, with enough of the prevailing Scotch dialect to please those who follow the fad of the hour.

### PRESS NOTICES.

*ROCHESTER HERALD.*

In "True to Themselves" the matter of marriage is discussed according to the laws of nature, and according to the laws of church and man; and in which a good-sized church squabble is sufficiently aired.

*BOSTON COURIER.*

"True to Themselves" is certainly a story that is bound to arouse considerable interest and criticism among thinking readers, on account of the bold stand taken by the well-known physician with regard to what constitutes the enduring element of domestic life. Besides this expression of his well-known views, the Doctor has given us quite a charming little love story.

*KANSAS CITY TIMES.*

"True to Themselves" is a psychological study which will doubtless be welcomed with interest by those who are familiar with the author's medical works, "Diseases of Women," "Medical Gynæcology," etc.

This venture into the domain of romance is, of course, only to allow the author the use of a vehicle to convey certain of his positive principles.

Perhaps no profession offers such splendid opportunities for the study of human nature as does that of medicine and surgery. Dr. Skene is a close student. His argument is plausible and worthy of consideration. There is much in the volume that will prove of interest both to the average reader and to members of the medical profession.

For sale everywhere, or sent post-paid on receipt of price.

## F. TENNYSON NEELY, Publisher,

96 Queen Street, London.        114 Fifth Avenue, New York.

# IN THE QUARTER.

## By ROBERT W. CHAMBERS,

Author of "The King in Yellow."

---

### Neely's Prismatic Library.

Gilt Top, 50 cents.

A new novel by the author of that wonderful book, "The King in Yellow," is an event of considerable importance to the reading public; nor will a perusal of "In the Quarter" disappoint those critics who have predicted such a glorious future for Robert W. Chambers. As the title would indicate, the story deals with life in the Quartier Latin, in Paris, where the merry art students live and move and have their being, and over which the halo of romance ever hangs; a peculiar people with whom we have spent many an entrancing hour in company with such volumes as "Trilby" and "A King in Yellow."

### PRESS NOTICES:

BOOK BUYER, New York:—"It is a story of a man who tried to reconcile irreconcilable facts. . . . Mr. Chambers tells it with a happy choice of words, thus putting 'to proof the art alien to the artists.' . . It is not a book for the unsophisticated, yet its morality is high and unmistakable."

BROOKLYN CITIZEN :—" Full of romantic incidents."

BOSTON COURIER :—" Interesting novel of French life."

BOSTON TRAVELER :—" A story of student life written with dash and surety of handling."

BOSTON TIMES :—"Well written, bright, vivid; the ending is highly dramatic."

NEW YORK SUNDAY WORLD :—"Charming story of Bohemian life, with its bouyancy, its romance, and its wild joy of youth . . vividly depicted in this graceful tale by one who, like Daudet, knows his Paris. Some pages are exquisitely beautiful."

PHILADELPHIA BULLETIN :—"Idyllic—charming. Mr. Chambers' story is delicately told."

NEW YORK EVENING TELEGRAM :—" It is a good story in its way. It is good in several ways. There are glimpses of the model and of the grisette—all dainty enough. The most of it might have come from so severe a moralist as George Eliot or even Bayard Taylor."

NEW YORK COMMERCIAL ADVERTISER :—" A very vivid and touchingly told story. The tale is interesting because it reflects with fidelity the life led by certain sets of art students. A genuine romance, charmingly told."

CONGREGATIONALIST, Boston :—" Vivid, realistic. There is much of nobility in it. A decided and excellent moral influence. It is charmingly written from cover to cover."

---

For sale everywhere, or sent post-paid on receipt of price.

### F. TENNYSON NEELY, Publisher,

96 Queen Street, London.    114 Fifth Avenue, New York.

# Remarks by Bill Nye.

## THE FUNNIEST OF BOOKS.

"It will cure the blues quicker than the doctor and at half the price."—*New York Herald.*

**Over 500 Pages.
Fully Illustrated.**

Cloth, $1.50 ; Paper, 50c.

## LAUGH AND GROW FAT.

A collection of the best writings of this great author, most profusely illustrated, with over 500 pages. It is the funniest of books. Bill Nye needs no introduction. The mention of the book is enough.

"I have passed through an earthquake and an Indian outbreak, but I would rather ride an earthquake without saddle or bridle, than to bestride a successful broncho eruption."—*Bill Nye.*

"Age brings caution and a lot of shop-worn experience, purchased at the highest market price. Time brings vain regrets and wisdom teeth that can be left in a glass of water over night."—*Bill Nye.*

**SPARKS FROM THE PEN OF BILL NYE. 192 PAGES. PAPER, 25c.
WIT AND HUMOR. BY NYE AND RILEY. PAPER, 25c.**

---

For sale everywhere, or sent post-paid on receipt of price.

### F. TENNYSON NEELY, Publisher,

96 Queen Street, London.       114 Fifth Avenue, New York.

# In the Day of Battle.

## A Romance.

### BY J. A. STEUART.

Author of "Kilgroom; a Story of Ireland," etc.

Neely's Library of Choice Literature.

Cloth, $1.25; paper, 50c.

**London Globe** "There is not a dull page. Narrative and descriptive power of a high order is shown in all, and the tale as a whole will be voted striking and absorbing in the extreme."
**National Observer** "The author has not been afraid to break new ground The story moves. It carries the reader on from page to page under the influence of an excitement which rarely fails, and it leaves him at the end a little breathless perhaps, but in no sense exhausted. To say this is to say that Mr. Steuart has succeeded in his object."
**Daily Telegram** "A good, honest, wholesome novel. In the ranks of our new school of romance the author deserves to find a prominent place."
**World** "A bold and stirring story, full of color incident and strife."
**Sun** "A splendid story. The book must be read in its entirety to be fairly appreciated. It raises its author to a high rank among contemporary novelists."
**Observer** "A book to read and to enjoy."
**Court Journal** "An altogether exceptional book. Full of romance and excitement. Well written and of unflagging interest from the title-page to the end."
**Author** "Has succeeded in giving his tale an almost breathless realism, and if it is success to drive his reader on from page to page until one reaches the last he has certainly succeeded."
**St. James Budget** "It is a strong, stirring, and attractive story, promising well for what Mr. Steuart may give us in the future."
**Liverpool Post** "Mr. Steuart has a lively and flowing style. His invention is never at fault and his book may safely be put in the hands of the juveniles."
**St. Paul's** "A book of this kind cannot be too highly recommended."
**Literary World** "Whether Mr. John Steuart sat down to the task of writing a novel that should, as far as bounty of adventures goes, out-Stevenson Stevenson, out-Weyman Weyman, out-Haggard Haggard, we cannot pretend to say; but whatever his intentions may have been, it is quite certain that the author yields to no individual of this trio in administrating to his readers a dose of events stirring enough to make old blood run with the impetus of youth."
**Guardian** "Exceedingly good."
**Cincinnati Times-Star** "It is not lacking in exciting adventures and picturesque descriptions."
**Denver Times** "The mind reverts to Weyman and Haggard and Stevenson in the reading of this story."
**Cincinnati Tribune** "Told in good style and intensely interesting."

---

For sale everywhere, or sent post-paid on receipt of price.

www.ingramcontent.com/pod-product-compliance
Lightning Source LLC
Chambersburg PA
CBHW030753230426
43667CB00007B/955